Baed

DENMARK

Cover picture: Kronborg Castle, Helsingør

122 colour photographs
30 maps and plans
1 large road map

Text (part): Axel Patitz
Editorial work and completion: Baedeker (Gisela Bockamp, Peter M. Nahm)
Cartography: Gert Oberländer, Munich
Mairs Geographischer Verlag, Ostfildern-Kemnat (road map)
Design and layout: Creative GmbH, Ulrich Kolb, Stuttgart

Conception and general direction: Dr Peter Baumgarten, Baedeker Stuttgart

English translation: Alec Court

US and Canadian edition
Prentice Hall Press

Licensed User
Mairs Geographischer Verlag GmbH & Co., Ostfildern-Kemnat bei Stuttgart

In a time of rapid change it is difficult to ensure that all the information given is entirely accurate and up to date and the possibility of error can never be entirely eliminated. Although the publishers can accept no responsibility for inaccuracies and omissions they are always grateful for corrections and suggestions for improvement.

Printed in Great Britain by Jarrold Printing, Norwich

0–13–058124–0 US and Canada
0 86145 611 4 UK
3–87504–117–8 Germany

Source of illustrations:

Ålborg Turistvorening (4), Århus Turistforening (1), Bendtsen (1), Bilderdienst Süd-deutscher Verlag (2), Danish Tourist Board (76), dpa (3), Elmelunde Church/Møn (1), Esbjerg Turistforening (2), Hanssen (1), Historia-Photo (4), Legoland (2) Musseet på Koldinghus/Kolding (2), Museum Louisiana (1), Odense Domkirke (1), Ribe Turistbureau (2), Sperber (1), Pedersen (1), Uthoff (3), Vordingborg Turistforening (1), Wadmanns Forlag (1), Wüchner (1), Zefa (1).

How to Use this Guide

The principal towns and areas of tourist interest are described in alphabetical order. The names of other places referred to under these general headings can be found in the full index.

Following the tradition established by Karl Baedeker in 1844, sights of particular interest and hotels of particular quality are distinguished by one or two asterisks.

The symbol (i) at the beginning of an entry or on a town plan indicates the local tourist office or other organisation from which further information can be obtained. The post-horn symbol on a town plan indicates a post office.

Only a selection of hotels and restaurants can be given: no reflection is implied, therefore, on establishments not included.

In Danish, geographical terms such as "lake" or "street" (see list on page 163) are usually suffixed to the place-name and do not appear as separate words. The suffixes "en" and "et" are the definite article ("rådhuset" = the town hall).

The Danish language has three letters in addition to those in the English alphabet; these are æ (pronounced as the "e" in well), ø (as "ur" in hurt) and å (as "aw" in law). These are normally placed at the end of the alphabet, but in order not to confuse English-speaking users of this guide they are here placed in their normal alphabetical order. Also ø can be written as ö and å can be given as aa.

This guidebook forms part of a completely new series of the world-famous Baedeker Guides to Europe.

Each volume is the result of long and careful preparation and, true to the traditions of Baedeker, is designed in every respect to meet the needs and expectations of the modern traveller.

The name of Baedeker has long been identified in the field of guidebooks with reliable, comprehensive and up-to-date information, prepared by expert writers who work from detailed, first-hand knowledge of the country concerned. Following a tradition that goes back over 150 years to the date when Karl Baedeker published the first of his handbooks for travellers, these guides have been planned to give the tourist all the essential information about the country and its inhabitants: where to go, how to get there and what to see. Baedeker's account of a country was always based on his personal observation and experience during his travels in that country. This tradition of writing a guidebook in the field rather than at an office desk has been maintained by Baedeker ever since.

Lavishly illustrated with superb colour photographs and numerous specially drawn maps and street plans of the major towns, the new Baedeker Guides concentrate on making available to the modern traveller all the information he needs in a format that is both attractive and easy to follow. For every place that appears in the gazetteer, the principal features of architectural, artistic and historic interest are described, as are its main areas of scenic beauty. Selected hotels and restaurants are also included. Features of exceptional merit are indicated by either one or two asterisks.

A special section at the end of each book contains practical information, details of leisure activities and useful addresses. The separate road map will prove an invaluable aid to planning your route and your travel within the country.

Contents

Introduction to Denmark

The Little Mermaid, emblem of Copenhagen

Denmark consists of the peninsula of Jutland and numerous islands and also has external possessions of the Faroe Islands and Greenland. These two are dealt with individually in the A–Z section of this guide.

Denmark (Danish "Danmark") is situated between latitude 54° 34′ and 57° 45′ and longitude 8° 5′ and 12° 35′ (Bornholm Island longitude 15° 12′). The southern part of the country is bordered by the **Federal Republic of Germany**, but the remainder is everywhere surrounded by water. The long border with Germany which runs obliquely across the peninsula of Jutland is about 68 km (42 miles) in length. The coast has a total length of 7400 km (4598 miles). Denmark is bordered in the west by the North Sea but a large part of its territory is in the area of the Baltic. Narrow stretches of water known as the Kattegat and Skagerrak (east and north-west of Jutland respectively) mark the transition from the Baltic, an inland sea, to the North Sea which borders the Atlantic Ocean. Because of its position Denmark forms a bridge between central Europe and the Scandinavian peninsula countries – as the crow flies.

The exact *size* of the country is not easy to designate, since its area is frequently altering as a consequence of the action of the sea and the recovery of new stretches of land. In coastal areas which are subject to the action of tides the line of the coast can change considerably at high tide and low tide. This for example is apparent on the west coast of South Jutland. The *land area* includes lakes and watercourses, fjords and bays with an open connection to the sea. If one adopts this definition then Denmark has an area of 43,075 sq. km (26,767 sq. miles). Of this the largest part consists of the peninsula of Jutland (*Jylland*) which covers 29,766 sq. km (11,496 sq. miles), while the 406 islands, of which 97 are inhabited, together make up 13,309 sq. km (5137 sq. miles). The largest island is Zealand (*Sjælland*) with an area of 7026 sq. km (4366 sq. miles) followed by Funen (*Fyn*) 2984 sq. km (1117 sq. miles) and Lolland 1243 sq. km (480 sq. miles), Bornholm 588 sq. km (227 sq. miles) and Falster, 514 sq. km (198 sq. miles). If one adds the Faroes and Greenland, the largest island in the world, to Denmark the total area amounts to approximately 2.2 million sq. km (840,000 sq. miles).

Denmark is a low-lying country, the highest point being *Yding Skovhjøj* (173 m (568 ft)) in east Jutland south of Skanderborg. The landscape is distinguished by hills, forests, lakes, little rivers and beaches, often excellent for bathing.

Geologically the peninsula of Jutland and the Danish islands consist of layers of chalk. On the Limfjord and on certain of the islands the chalk is revealed as outcrops. The island of Bornholm, however, consists of ancient granites.

Like the whole of northern Europe Denmark was covered by huge expanses of ice for thousands of years. After the Ice Age glaciers melted, about 10,000 years ago, diluvial moraine was left in many places; this consists of a mixture of granite and detritus which has become amalgamated with the rock of the substrata. The most recent period of the Ice Age which was characterised by alternate periods of warm and cold weather, is known in Northern Europe as Vistula icing. The outer edge of the ice bisected the Jutland Peninsula not far from the Limfjord from north to south. The west side of Jutland is, therefore, primarily composed of sandy infertile deposits of the older Ice Age. The east side of the peninsula and the islands were, on the other hand, covered by the fertile terminal and basic moraines of the most recent Ice Age.

In the period after the Ice Ages the level of the sea rose and so did the land. Since the rise of the land was, however, less than that of the sea, parts of the former mainland were flooded. The land connection between Sweden and Denmark as well as that between the Danish islands and the mainland disappeared. Flooding was the origin of the waterways, now called sounds, and the Great and Little Belt.

About one tenth of the entire surface area of Denmark consists of coastal plains mainly in the northern part of Jutland. These are made up of marine deposits of the Late Ice Age known as the Yoldia phase. The coast of Jutland in the west is

Farms and Windmill at Bagenkop on Langeland

enclosed in an almost unbroken girdle of dunes. In Skagen can be found the last shifting dune in Denmark. This is the Råbjerg Mile which moves annually 8–10 m (9–11 yd) eastward. On the west coast of Jutland many of the bays have become enclosed by spits of radiated land and formed into lagoons so there are few harbours apart from the *Limfjord* which has a length of 112 miles (180 km) and is the longest fjord in Denmark. Numerous fjords especially on the coast of East Jutland are glacier channels flooded by the sea. The protection which they afforded gave rise to ports. The majority of the islands have flat coastlines. Only on the east side of Falster and Mon and the south-eastern coasts can chalk cliffs be seen.

In the north of the island of Bornholm a narrow horst of primeval rocks shows above the more recent deposits. By erosion and glacial activity in the Ice Age long deep valleys were formed in the granite.

Since Denmark is situated on the edge of the Central European climatic zone, the *vegetation* found there is primarily also that of Central Europe. Cultivation, however, has had the effect of considerably reducing the area of deciduous forest. Only some 10 per cent of the area is woodland, and this is mostly afforestation. Natural deciduous forests, principally consisting of beech, oak, elm and lime, can be found only in a few places. Beech forests which are typical of the country mainly occur in East Jutland and on the islands. The natural vegetation also includes plants typical of the dunes and heaths. Together with the fenland this vegetation, which is mainly in West Jutland, covers about 8 per cent of the land area.

Heathland is also present on the steep granite slopes of Bornholm, but in addition the vegetation of the island differs considerably from that of the rest of Denmark. There is a whole series of plant species which are more widespread there than in the rest of the country. An example of the Mediterranean character of the vegetation of this island is provided by the so-called Bornholm anemone, the natural home of which is to the south of the Alps.

The natural stock of *mammals* has been heavily reduced by a high density of population and extensive cultivation of

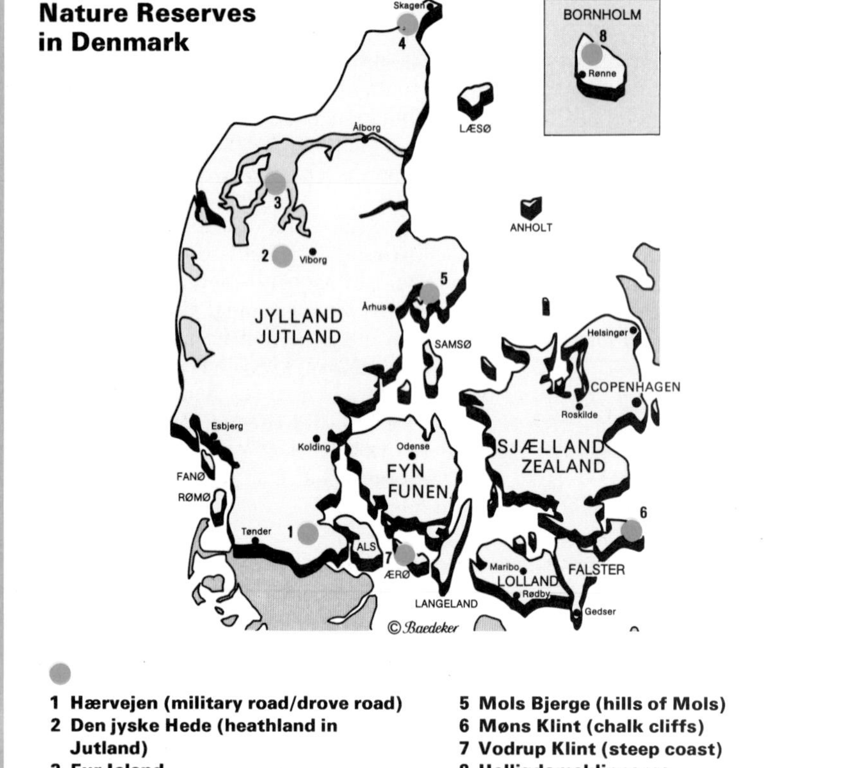

1 Hærvejen (military road/drove road)
2 Den jyske Hede (heathland in Jutland)
3 Fur Island
4 Råbjerg Mile (shifting dunes)
5 Mols Bjerge (hills of Mols)
6 Møns Klint (chalk cliffs)
7 Vodrup Klint (steep coast)
8 Helligdomsklipperne (rocky cliffs)

the land. In the afforested regions of Denmark red deer, hares, wild rabbits and small predators are found. There are more than 300 kinds of *birds* of which about 160 breed here. Especially numerous are the aquatic birds of the coasts.

About 3.5 per cent or 156 ha (385,476 acres) of Denmark's land area is legally protected. In accordance with the protection law each area has definitive regulations of protection. Their aim is to maintain landscapes which are of importance for their own sake, for their situation or for their particular character. These mainly consist of areas of pasture land which are still reserves.

Among the *protected areas* are the various coastal landscapes of the islands, including the chalk cliffs of Møn, the Helligdom cliffs of Bornholm, the steep coasts of Vodrup and the east coast of the island of Ærø. On Jutland a section of the former military road ("Hærvej") with an old bridge is a protected area. A region of the Jutland heath, part of the island of Fur (Limfjord), the hills of Mols (east coast) and the shifting dunes of Råbjerg Mile are also protected areas.

Climate

Denmark, a country on the edge of the Central European climatic zone which, with the exception of the land frontier with the Federal Republic of Germany, is surrounded on all sides by the sea, has a cool *temperate maritime climate* similar to that of the northern half of England and of Scotland. Since Denmark is situated on the west side of the Euro-Asian land mass and borders the Atlantic Ocean, it is influenced by the Gulf Stream which brings warmth from southern latitudes.

Throughout the year the winds are predominantly from a westerly direction and the *Gulf Stream* exercises a moderating influence on the temperature during the winter. The average temperature of the coldest months in Denmark is somewhat higher than the average in other parts of the world lying on the same line of latitude, i.e. 56° N.

In addition the waters of the Baltic, which separate Denmark from the land masses of East Europe, prevent the country from coming under the influence of continental climate conditions in most years. Should the Baltic be iced up, so that the water cannot store warmth, then cold masses of air from the east penetrate into Denmark and are the cause of considerable cold spells. These occur only rarely. In the summer, however, air from the east can influence the effect of the winds from the west coming from the sea and consequently can cause a heat wave.

A further characteristic of the climate is the meeting of heavy cold Arctic air and damp, relatively warm air from the Atlantic. When these meet, the masses of air do not mix but form fronts which mark the boundaries between areas of different types of weather. Since these fronts are moving throughout the year over the territory of Denmark the climate of the country is characterised by frequent changes.

As a consequence of the small area of Denmark, *temperatures* vary very little. The annual average ranges from 7.2 °C (45 °F) at Rugbjerg (north-east of Tøndor) to 7.9 °C (46.2 °F) at Odense. The February temperature ranges from −1.2 °C (29.8 °F) at Copenhagen to 1.4 °C (34.5 °F) at Skagen, the July average from 15.5 °C (59.9 °F) at Tønder and Rugbjerg to 17.2 °C (63 °F) at Copenhagen. The

By Svendborg Sound

average of the coldest month (February) is 0.3 °C (32.5 °F), the average of the warmest month (July) 17 °C (63 °F). The annual range varies from between 14.5 °C (58 °F) at Tønder and 18.4 °C (65.1 °F) at Copenhagen.

On the coast the frost-free period lasts for more than 200 days and in northern Jutland about 150 days.

The average annual *precipitation* (rainfall) in Denmark is 550–650 mm (21.5–25.5 in) – Copenhagen 579 mm (22.8 in), Odense 621 mm (24.4 in), Ålborg 611 mm (24.1 in), Rønne 559 mm (22 in), on some of the eastern islands below 500 mm (20 in); at Christiansø 419 mm (16.5 in) and above this level in West Jutland, particularly in Schleswig at Åbenraa 762 mm (30 in) and Tønder 750 mm (29.5 in). The rainiest month is almost invariably August, at Copenhagen 75 mm (3 in), Tønder 98 mm (3.9 in), Christiansø 52 mm (2 in); the driest February, at Copenhagen 32 mm (1.3 in), Tønder 41 mm (1.6 in), Christiansø 22 mm (0.9 in).

The number of days of precipitation is between 120 and 200 per year; in general there is good weather from April to July; on the other hand from August to October there are periods of rainy weather.

Snow falls during the months of January to March on 6–9 days.

The *westerly winds* predominate, especially when storms are approaching. Storm damage is most frequent in West Jutland. In the months of spring, when precipitation is low, severe damage is caused by winds which erode the humus of the soil.

State and Society

The Kingdom of Denmark ("Kongeriget Danmark") is a parliamentary democratic constitutional monarchy. The territory includes the peninsula of Jutland and the numerous Danish islands as well as the Faroes and Greenland. The Faroes form an autonomous country under the Danish Crown; Greenland also has internal autonomy.

The Danish national flag is known as the "Dannebrog" (Danish *brog* = colourful cloth). It consists of a white cross on a red ground. According to legend The Dannebrog fell from heaven in the year 1219 during the Battle of Lyndanisse in Estland.

Parliament consists of a single chamber, the *Folketing*. Its members come from the various parties and two representatives each from Greenland and the Faroes. All women and men over 18 years of age are able to vote for the Folketing which is the law-making body. The power of government, which is formally with the Crown, is carried out by a Cabinet, the members of which are elected by parliament. The Head of Government is the Prime Minister and the Head of State is the Monarch (since 1972 Queen Margrethe II) whose principal role is to represent the kingdom in dealings with other countries.

For the purpose of administration Denmark is divided into 14 districts (*amts*) and two parishes (*kommune*). The latter are København and Frederiksberg which are the two central parishes of Copenhagen.

Denmark, which because of its history and culture is one of the five Scandinavian countries, has 5.1 million inhabitants. The *density of population* is about 119 per sq. km (308 per sq. mile). The annual increase of population amounts to less than 1 per cent.

Jutland and the smaller islands reveal a relatively low population density. The more heavily settled parts of the country are Funen and Zealand with the conurbation of Copenhagen, where about a quarter of the total population lives. There is a German minority (1.7 per cent) in northern Schleswig and there is also a Swedish element (0.4 per cent).

The most important church is the Evangelical Lutheran Church to which some 98 per cent of the population belong. There are 27,000 Catholics and 6500 Jews.

Denmark's most important contribution to education is the introduction of the *adult education centre*. This form of educational establishment has spread from Denmark into other European countries and, in a modified form, into countries outside Europe.

The idea of founding a new kind of educational institution was originated by the poet and theologian Bishop *Nikolai Friedrich Severin Grundtvig* (1783–1872). When the democratic form of government was beginning to take hold in Denmark Grundtvig sought to counter the lack of knowledge in great parts of the population. The first ever education centre was built in Rødding in South Jutland in 1844 and others followed. After the centres had served to further the education of the rural population in the 19th c. they received an impetus after the Second World War from all classes of society. In Denmark the average age of participants lies between 18 and 35.

It is difficult to establish the *character* of the Danish people. In many ways one can find parallels with the Dutch, as Denmark and the Netherlands have a great deal in common from the point of view of trade, but there are many more towns in the Netherlands than in Denmark. In many respects the Dane has remained more rural. He is more inclined to brood over and to philosophise over things than the Swede; Hans Christian Andersen and Søren Kierkegaard, even though they are very different in character, can stand as typical Danes.

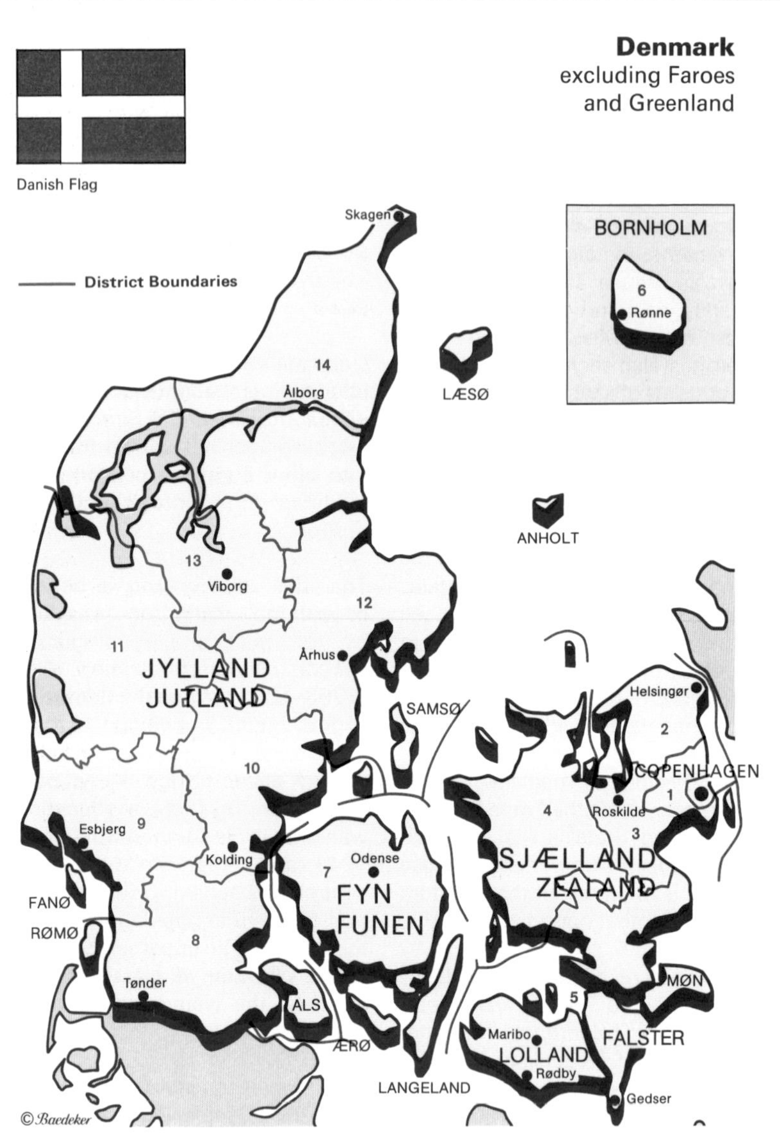

District (amt)/ Commune	Area sq. km	Area sq. miles	Population
1 **Københavns amt**	619	239	1,185,000
2 **Frederiksborg amt**	1347	520	331,000
3 **Roskilde amt**	891	344	205,000
4 **Vestsjællands amt**	2984	1152	278,000
5 **Storstrøms amt**	3398	1311	259,000
6 **Bornholms amt**	588	227	47,000
7 **Fyns amt**	3486	1346	454,000
8 **Sønderjyllands amt**	3930	1517	250,000
9 **Ribe amt**	3131	1210	215,000
10 **Vejle amt**	2997	1157	215,000
11 **Ringkøbing amt**	4853	1873	264,000
12 **Århus amt**	4561	1761	578,000
13 **Viborg amt**	4122	1591	232,000
14 **Nordjyllands amt**	6173	2383	482,000
Denmark (excluding Faroes and Greenland)	43,080	16,629	5,106,000

Economy and Transport

On the basis of moraine soil and marl East Jutland and the Danish Islands are a region of intensive *agriculture*. About 70 per cent of the entire area of the country is used for agriculture. Although livestock-breeding – cattle, pigs, poultry – plays a dominant role, wheat and sugarbeet as well as barley, oats and other cereals are cultivated. The growing of flowers and vegetables has also increased considerably. In addition there are some 2500 mink farms which are mostly associated with agricultural concerns. In order to be able to deliver products of a high quality, Denmark established at an early date finishing works on a co-operative basis. Heavy rationalisation and mechanisation of agriculture has resulted in the fact that today only 8 per cent of employees are engaged in this branch of the economy.

Fishing is also of considerable importance for the economy of the country. Because the waters along the Danish coast became over-fished, an increasing number of vessels seek their catches in the North Sea and the Baltic. The most important fish are herring, cod, plaice, mackerel, eel and flat fish. The largest fishing port is Esbjerg on the west coast of Jutland.

In recent years Denmark completed the conversion from a typical agrarian country to a modern industrial State, not least because of changed export conditions and demand in world markets. Today *industry*, with more than 400,000 employees, is Denmark's second largest branch of the economy after the service sector.

Since Denmark has few minerals almost all industrial raw materials must be imported from abroad. The most important industry is metal-working. At the beginning of the 1940s a steel and rolling mill, working principally with scrap metal, was established at Frederiksværk on Roskilde Fjord in Zealand. This provides the necessary building material for the shipyards in Copenhagen, Helsingør, Odense, Ålborg and other places. The ships are built not only for Danish firms but also for foreign orders. Also of importance is the production of agricultural and electrical machines and apparatus of all kinds. The second largest branch of industry in the country is the processing of agricultural products. A leading role is played in the

Wind energy converter

Carlsberg Brewery

preparation and canning of meat products. Milk is primarily converted into butter and cheese. Alcoholic drinks, including aquavit and beer, are also produced in Denmark. The two largest Danish breweries, Carlsberg and Tuborg in Copenhagen, are visited every year by more than 250,000 people. The textile industry in Jutland, which was formally based on the rearing of sheep, stamps its mark on a few of the smaller towns. In addition furniture, carpets and ceramic objects are made. The chemical industry produces chemicals of all kinds as well as fertilisers.

A prerequisite for the upswing of industry is the extension of the provision of *energy*, a field which is heavily dependent on imports. In this connection the division of the eastern part of the North Sea gas- and oilfield between the Nordic states is of importance. An example of a modern plant for the provision of energy is the Stigsnæs works on the coast of Zealand, near which a refinery is also to be found.

In recent years plants for the production of alternative forms of energy have become important in Denmark, including solar collectors and heating installations which can use straw or wind as fuel. The Danes have been especially successful in harnessing wind power for the production of electrical energy. The wind energy converters (windmills) are generally not used on their own but are connected together in windmill parks; at present the largest of these parks is in Ebeltoft (Jutland). Small and moderate-sized factories have produced wind machines for the commercial market as well as for export (for example there are many such "windmills" in California, USA).

The most important *export markets* of Denmark are Federal Germany, Great Britain, Sweden, Norway and Finland. Products of the highly developed milk industry, such as cheese and butter, as well as meat, eggs and poultry are exported principally to Great Britain and Germany. The chief markets for the export of fish are also Great Britain and Germany as well as other European countries such as Sweden, Italy, Belgium, France and Switzerland and also the United States. The continuous debit balance of trade, however, cannot be compensated for by the export of agricultural products. After the export of industrial goods about the middle of the 1960s had reached the same level as that of food products, at the beginning of the 1980s industrial products accounted for approximately two-thirds of the exports which include machines, vehicles, textiles and medical preparations. The chemical industry produces pharmaceutical products, artificial materials, pesticides and dyes for export.

For the economy of Denmark, which in addition to Jutland consists of a multitude of islands, reliable *transport* facilities are an important prerequisite. Every part of the country is provided with a dense network of railways and well-engineered roads. There is generous provision of main traffic arteries – highways, motorways and main roads of motorway standard. The numerous ferries between the islands are also of great importance. In places huge bridges span the waterways so that an uninterrupted route from Central Europe to Denmark and even to other parts of Scandinavia is possible.

Tourism forms an important part of the Danish economy and is an increasing source of income. A leading factor is the renting of holiday homes, whereas hotel bookings are of less consequence. Tourist traffic used to be principally concentrated in the area of Copenhagen and the resorts but, in recent years, has been much more widely spread. Among the most favoured of the resorts are those on the north coast of Zealand near Copenhagen. Less frequented on the other hand are the resorts on the west coast of Jutland as far as Skagen, on the north coast of Jutland. While every year the Farm Holidays, mainly in Funen and Jutland, are becoming extremely popular, particularly for those with children, and Odense, the birthplace of H.C. Andersen, attracts hundreds of thousands from all over the world annually. A favourite place for vacations is the charming island of Bornholm with its beautiful beaches. Denmark also has a number of sanatoriums which have the climatic advantage of being situated on the coast.

Those interested in sport have the opportunity of making use of leisure arrangements offered by the Danish Tourist Bureau as well as by local tourist offices. Arrangements can be made for vacations for anglers, horse-riders, for tours by cycle and for golfers.

Noted Danish Figures

Hans Christian Andersen or, as he is always called in Denmark, H. C. Andersen was the son of a poor cobbler living in Odense, the "capital" of the island of Funen. He was born there on 2 April, 1805. His father was always poor, but was gifted with great imagination, love of music and art. He adored his son and would spend hours making paper cut-outs or toy theatres for him. His mother, 15 years older than her husband, illegitimate and completely illiterate was loving, good natured and full of the joy of life. Between them they gave their son an enquiring mind, a knowledge of folk-tales, a sense of theatre and a ready tongue. His father died when H.C. was 11; his mother married again to another younger man, also a cobbler. She being cared for, Andersen left for Copenhagen in 1819 as he said himself "to become famous".

In Copenhagen, he took singing lessons, haunted the Royal Theatre, acted as a kind of odd-job man, was given the occasional small part in the chorus or as an extra in a play, but, all the time, often on the verge of starvation, he was observing, learning, making friends; above all, he was trying to write. As soon as he could raise the money he started travelling, first to Germany and then to Italy, always writing, his diaries, letters to his friends embellished with pen and ink sketches and pieces which he hoped would be published. His first published work was a historical novel, "The Improvisor" followed by a number of articles about his travels and other short pieces and, as a result, in 1838 he was given a grant by the King to help him with his work, quite a regular practice in those days. He worked hard, but he was an indefatigable traveller and he made use of the things he saw and did in his work.

From 1831 to 1871 he travelled continuously; to England where he was twice the guest of Dickens, Scotland where he wrote a work in the manner of Scott whom, with Dickens, he thought the greatest "English" writers, to France, Italy Switzerland, Austria, Hungary, Greece, Turkey and many other places which he portrayed in words and sketches. When he was in Germany (1845–46) the "Story of my Life" was written and published ten years before it was published in Denmark. Though he wanted to succeed as a playwright and poet, he won international fame for his "Eventyr" (Fairy-tales) which he started to write in 1835 and continued to write until 1872, only three years before he died. In these tales, first written for children in an apparently naïve style he created a world of fantasy, but one peopled with recognisable types; tales full of humour and, often, ironic wit and tempered by a calm resignation.

Among the 168 fairy-tales he wrote were "The Emperor's New Clothes", "The Ugly Duckling", "The Steadfast Tin Soldier", "The Little Mermaid" and "The Red Shoes". His later ones began to have a deeper significance because he was not writing them for children, but for adults.

Because he had lived in deep poverty and had to struggle Andersen was able to view the most insignificant things from unexpected angles. His novels, which were not so well known outside Denmark, laid the foundations of modern realistic prose-writing in Scandinavia. He also wrote plays, poems and delightful letters and diaries which he decorated with sketches.

Not content with this vast amount of work, he delighted in and mastered the then fashionable art of "paper-cutting" and several books of Andersen Paper Cuts have been printed.

He started life as an uneducated and very poor boy, but through his own efforts became an illustrious man of letters whose works were praised and plagiarised throughout the world. He was a hypochondriac who could make fun of his own despair. He delighted in the company of women and adored children, but never married. His greatest love was Jenny Lind, "the Swedish Nightingale" and she loved him, but only "as a brother". He had a gift for friendship and became friends with Princes and the Great so that, in many ways, he became an aristocrat, but he never lost the common touch and loved his fellow men. Above all, he never lost his enquiring mind and when he died of cancer at the age of 70 he was in the process of planning other voyages and explorations. It is for all these reasons that he is thought of and remains Denmark's greatest Dane. He died in Copenhagen in 1875 and was buried in Assiens Churchyard, the largest in the city.

Karen Blixen was born at Rungstedland, north of Copenhagen, in 1885, and grew up in an atmosphere which was aristocratic and heroic. From her father, Wilhelm Dinesen, soldier, sportsman and writer, she inherited both a thirst for adventure and a literary flair. When she was 20 she wrote her first stories which were quite well received, but at that time she had no thought of becoming a writer and the next year she married her cousin, the Swedish Baron Bror Blixen-Finecke and they started a coffee farm in Kenya. It was not a happy marriage and in 1921 they divorced and Karen Blixen, as she now called herself, ran the farm alone until compelled by the Depression of 1931 to give it up and return to Denmark. Back home with her Mother she started writing again. She had already written two stories while in Africa; to these she added a further five and, as they were all written in English she had them published as "Seven Gothic Tales" in England and then, as they were successful, she had them published a year later, in 1935, in Danish under the pseudonym of *Isak Dinesen*. In 1937 she wrote what many consider her finest work "Out of Africa", which, in 1985, was made into the Award-winning film. The book is, in effect, an autobiography telling the story of the 17 years she spent on the coffee plantation at the foot of Mount Ngong; she talks of the events of those years, the good things and the unhappy ones; of the pleasure she found in flying and the admiration she felt for her neighbours, the Masai – "the Warrior Tribe" with whom she spent days hunting and her trust in her Somali servant Farah.

In 1944, during the German occupation, she had published a book in Danish under the name of Pierre Andrezel. She called it a "thriller" and set the scene 200 years ago. It was called "The Paths of Retribution". It was very topical in its theme of the nature of evil and just retribution. Many people guessed the book was written by Karen Blixen, but, understandably she kept silent and did not acknowledge it for many years.

After 1945 she began a whole new career in broadcasting, telling the tales of her African farm, her youth and her varied experiences many of which she turned into books. She became a celebrity and was invited to many countries, but her last years were trouble by much illness. She retreated to Rungstedlund and died in 1962.

Niels Bohr (full name Niels Hendrik David Bohr), who was born on 7 October 1885 in Copenhagen, is the greatest Danish physicist. In 1916 he became Professor of Theoretical Physics. In 1913 he developed Ernest Rutherford's atomic model into the Bohr atomic model and discovered the principle of correspondence between classical physics and quantum physics. For his research he was awarded the Nobel Prize for Physics in 1922. In 1943, when Denmark was occupied by German troops, Bohr was smuggled out of the country disguised as a fisherman and, via Sweden and Britain, he found his way to the United States where he worked on the development of the atomic bomb, although he was apprehensive of its possible consequences. After the Second World War he returned to Copenhagen and continued his work at the Institute of Theoretical Physics. In 1947 he received the Order of the Elephant, Denmark's highest honour.

Tycho Brahe was born at Knudstrup in southern Sweden on 14 December 1546. He first studied law and later turned to astronomy. In 1572 he discovered a new star in the constellation of Cassiopeia in the Northern Hemisphere which he called the Nova Cassiopeia. After a journey in Europe Brahe gave lectures in Copenhagen and in 1576 he received from King Frederik II an endowment and the offer of the island of Ven in the Sound where he built the observatory of Uranienborg and continued his researches. After the death of Frederik II in 1588 difficulties arose for the astronomer and in 1599 he left Denmark and went to Prague. There he became the Royal Astronomer to the Emperor Rudolf II. He died on 24 October 1601. Brahe was the most important astronomical observer before the discovery of the telescope. By his observations of the position of the planets, especially his observation of Mars, he

Niels Bohr

Tycho Brahe

King Christian IV

created the conditions for Kepler's work on the paths of the planets. Brahe developed the "Tychonic System" named after him. According to this theory the sun and moon circle the earth which remains in the centre of the universe, while the other planets circle the sun. In addition he proved that comets can not be manifestations in the atmosphere of the earth, as Aristotle had accepted.

King Christian IV was born on 12 December 1577; he lost his father some years before he ascended the throne in 1588. He became the most popular Danish king. While still a child Christian IV had given evidence of artistic gifts; he later had many Renaissance buildings erected, including *Rosenborg Castle* in Copenhagen and *Frederiksborg Castle* near Helsingør. On his initiative houses for his seafarers were built at Nyboder as was the district of Christianshavn (both in Copenhagen). However, in the political field the King was less successful. From 1625 the Danish Army was embroiled in the Thirty Years War, suffering heavy defeats, and Christian was unable to force Sweden to join a league of northern states under Danish leadership. He died in Copenhagen, unhappy and disillusioned, on 28 February 1648.

Born on 15 December 1860 at Torshavn in the Faroes, the physician **Niels Ryberg Finsen** founded in 1896 in Copenhagen an institute for light-theraphy. He invented the method of treating tuberculosis of the skin with the *"Finsen Lamp"*, a carbon-arc lamp with cooled light which is rich in ultra-violet rays. Treatment of smallpox with infra-red light was another field of research. Finsen received the Nobel Prize for Medicine in 1903; he died a year later.

Søren Kierkegaard was born on 5 May 1813 in Copenhagen, the seventh child of a prosperous wool merchant. He studied theology and philosophy at Copenhagen University. In 1840 he became engaged to the 17-year-old Regine Olsen, but the engagement was broken off a year later. Thereafter he lived as a freelance writer on money which he had inherited. Kierkegaard published most of his books under pseudonyms. In imitation of Socrates he often chose dialogue form. In his writing the terms *"angst"* and *"existence"* play a significant part; freedom and decision are subordinate to them. His thinking leads to the conclusion that only the grace of God can overcome doubt and despair. Since Kierkegaard as a religious theorist took an emphatically subjective standpoint, he came into conflict with the Danish Lutheran Church of his time and finally completely renounced a Church which professes to have a closed system of objective truth. His works of religious philosophy had great influence on many thinkers of the 20th c.; to a considerable degree the ideas expressed in them formed the basis of dialectic theology and Existentialism. Among his important works are: "Either-Or" (1843), "Fear and Trembling" (1843), "The Concept of Fear" (1844), "Sickness unto Death" (1849), "Practice in Christianity" (1850). Kierkegaard died on 11 November 1855 in Copenhagen, where he was interred in the Assistens Kirkegard (cemetery).

The Danish actress **Asta Nielsen**, born 11 September 1885, gained her first success in films under the direction of Urban Gad, who was her second husband. From 1911 until 1914 and again from 1919 she worked in Berlin, playing tragic roles in silent films. Among her

Søren Kierkegaard

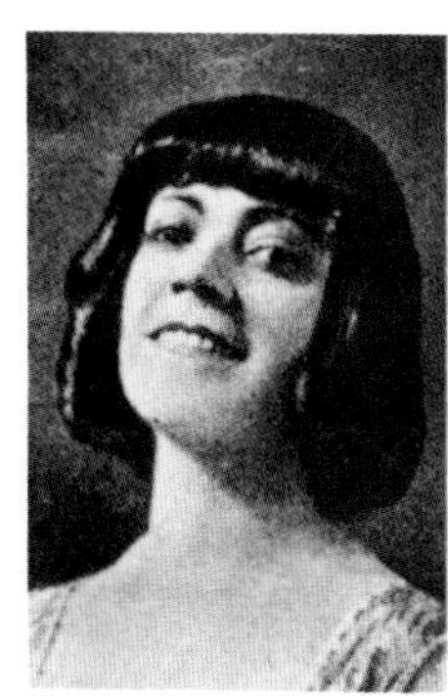

Asta Nielsen

Bertel Thorvaldsen

best-known films are: "Afgrunden" (Precipices; 1910), "Little Angel" (1913), "Ecstasy" (1919), "Hamlet" (1920), "Miss Julie" (1921), "Vanina Vanini" (1922), "The Cheerless Street" (1925) and "Impossible Love" (1932). Asta Nielsen is the authoress of "Den Tiende Muse" (The Silent Muse; 1945).

While still a pupil at the Academy of Art in Copenhagen, **Bertel Thorvaldsen**, born 19 November 1770, showed great promise and he won the Great Gold Medal in 1793. He became Denmark's greatest sculptor. With the aid of a Travelling Scholarship from the Academy he was enabled to go to Rome, where he settled and began to create sculptures in marble. In Rome he discovered the classical style which is so typical of his work. He sculpted youthful figures, busts, reliefs, monuments and memorials, including the "Christ" in the Church of Our Lady in Copenhagen. The sculptor acquired a European reputation and returned to Copenhagen in 1838, where between 1839 and 1848 a museum was erected for the works which Thorvaldsen had given to his native city before his death on 24 March 1844.

Bjorn Wiinblad was born on 20 September 1919 in Copenhagen, where he studied painting and illustration at the Academy of Art. As well as book illustrations he designed posters, stage sets and costumes for the theatre. However, he soon became interested in other materials and techniques, designing wallpaper, tapestries and ceramic articles. Ceramic work brought him his first real success at exhibitions in Copenhagen, Sweden and Norway. In 1954 he exhibited in New York. Of his various creations his work with ceramics remained the dominant factor. His shapes and decoration have an attractive and satisfying effect. Wiinblad made designs for dinner-services, glassware, vases and decorative wall-plates. In some cases he was responsible for both shape and decoration, in others for only one or the other. The surfaces are covered with ornamentation, with painted figures or with scenes from fictional tales ("Thousand and One Nights"). As well as black and white articles he also produced some in colour. Bjorn Wiinblad has worked for many years for the firm of Rosenthal, which is noted for its procelain and ceramic ware and which has its headquarters in Bavaria.

History

10,000–8000 **End of the Ice Age; forests and animals increase.**

7000–1800 **Stone Age;** through the raising and sinking of various areas the country of Denmark as we known it today is formed.

In the **New Stone Age** the transition to agriculture and stock-breeding is complete; settlements appear.

1800–500 **Bronze Age;** the people use coffins of oak which add to their durability; there are important grave finds including clothing made of wool – clothes of the "Egtved girl"; today in the National Museum in Copenhagen.

500 B.C. **Iron Age;** Villages of this time can be detected and traces of the so-called prehistoric fields (fields in the form of a depression surrounded by an earth rampart). Indications of human life are provided by the bog corpses, among them the corpse of the Tollund man of about 50 B.C.

A.D. 1–800 The period of Danish history from A.D. 1 to A.D. 800 is wrapped in mystery and historians are still arguing about it. At school children learn that the first King of Denmark was called Gorm and that he reigned from about 900 to 940. There were, in fact, a number of petty kings in various areas of what we now call Denmark, but Gorm den Gamle (Gorm the Old) is important for he is the subject of the first known piece of recorded Danish history – not that it was recorded in Danish; it was written in runic script on a stone which can be seen today in the small town of Jelling in Jutland. It says, in runic, "Gorm, King, made this monument to Thyra his wife". Beside it stands another and much bigger stone, also inscribed in runic, with the words, "This stone is erected to the memory of his father, King Gorm den Gamle and his mother, Queen Thyra by Harald Bluetooth, that Harald who won all Denmark and Norway and made the Danes Christians". It is a beautifully engraved stone with the figure of Christ on one side and the runes emblazoned on the other. What the King was actually stating was that all the parts of Denmark were in process of being Christianised under the rule of *one* King. In other words, Christianity was joining the people in one common belief which, in turn, led to a greater feeling of unity which made it easier for the King to appoint himself the sole ruler.

We do, however, know increasingly more about the history of Denmark between 400 and 800. For example, from the Latin we learn that Ansgar was sent to Jutland to bring Christianity to the Norsemen; that he baptised "King Klak" in 826, soon after he arrived and spent nearly 40 years as a missionary in the Northern countries.

It is, however, Denmark's geographical position which decided her destiny; Jutland, standing as it does as a cross-road or frontier post through which passed goods and fighting men. Hedeby in southern Jutland became a great transit port and, as such, attracted the notice and envy of the Angles, Jutes and Saxons from the south and the Swedes from the east, all anxious to own this profitable entrance to the Baltic. According to continental records this struggle began well before 350 and we know that it was still continuing in 800. It is more than probable that the petty kings in Jutland also fought each other with the same end in view; the stronger ones would swallow the weaker so that, gradually, the little kingdoms became bigger and more powerful and, as their rulers grew stronger and built more ships, they turned their eyes to the richer lands of the south and west. So were born the first Vikings.

About 449 Vortigern, the British King, harassed by the Saxons and Angles which were a constant threat, asked for help from one of the petty kings of Jutland whose name we do not know. This King sent Hengist and Horsa, two of his generals to help. If reports can be believed, Hengist and his brother Horsa, collected a motley crowd of fighting men, Danes, Jutes, Angles, Franks and Saxons and landed on Thanet. At first Vortigern's plan paid off, but, with success and the booty they garnered, this mixed crew grew rich and quarrelsome. The Angles, named from Angel in South Jutland, and the Saxons from Holstein the most northerly branch of the *Later German* stock went home to plan and enrol men for further attacks on this "green and pleasant land" of Britain, so much richer than their own harsh acres. Hengist, too, had his own plans and, by now, a well-drilled army. In 455 they quarrelled with the Britons and, according to the Britons' reports, "they revolted over a matter of food supplies and overran the land". Hengist led his troops into battle against the Britons at Aylesford and scored a convincing victory, but his brother, Horsa was killed and buried in a village near by which still bears his name; the village of "Horsted".

In the following year Hengist conquered the whole of Kent and proclaimed himself "King of Kent". He went on to conquer the Isle of Wight and the Hampshire coast opposite, where Hengist himself was killed in battle and, if rumour or hearsay are true, was buried on Hengistbury Head. In the meantime, the Saxons from Holstein arrived in ever-increasing numbers – hence the Saxon names of Essex, Sussex and Middlesex. More important from the point of view of English-speaking nations, was the onslaught of the Jutes' neighbours, the most southerly Danish kingdom, the Angles. They landed on the more northerly shores of Briton and conquered almost the whole of the north-eastern part of Britain including East Anglia, Mercia and Northumberland by the end of the 5th c. Certainly, they were a more organised crowd, more efficient and strong, perhaps because they came from a kingdom ruled by a strong King. As a result, they gave their name to the country as a whole for Angelland and England are the same. It is a curious coincidence of history that from 1945 to 1950 the Headquarters of the British Army were placed in Angel in South Slesvig; the only area in Europe which could rightfully be called England!

Emergence of the Danish State

800–1060 By 800 we can safely say that the Danes were on their way to becoming a united nation. Up to that time they had been called Norsemen as were those from Norway, Sweden and their various dependences. We cannot even say with any real certainty where the name "Dane" and hence "Danmark" (Denmark) came from. In all probability it arose from the name of one petty kingdom, but no one really knows. What is even more important is the fact that they were beginning to produce their own language. By the first centuries of the Christian era there had arisen a great change in the language of the Norseman, i.e. those who lived north of the River Eider as opposed to the language of the Germanic and Teutonic inhabitants to the south. For hundreds of years the Norsemen spoke a common language, Norse. Gradually, however, subdivisions began to occur and by approximately 1000 Danish, Norwegian and Swedish began to emerge as separate, but closely related languages.

In 812 comes the first authenticated date in Danish history for on that date a treaty was signed between Charlemagne and King Godfred fixing the frontier of what was becoming the Kingdom of Denmark at the *River Eider*. Charlemagne had come to northern Germany to fight the Saxons and, somehow or other, had ended up fighting Godfred as well. The Franks must have considered him to be a pretty good fighting man, head of a well-organised kingdom, small though it might be, to have put pressure on him to agree to a definite boundary line. It is probable that Godfred was a very astute man and that he agreed and realised that a formal agreement with the Franks would be a very good insurance against the inroads of the Saxons and other Germanic tribes. Strangely enough a vast number of Danes have never heard of King Godfred and he is mentioned in very few histories. When the North German historians and the Frankish chronicles are mentioned the reply is that these referred to a King Gottfried, which is a German name. That, of course, is true, but, as the Danes had no written language for another 200 years, it is natural that the account should be written in German and reasonable for the writer to use the German equivalent to "Godfred".

Another moot and interesting question refers to the "Danevirke", the defensive ramparts erected between this time and 900. Many historians still say that the Danevirke was erected by Gorm den Gamle; some even state that they were built by Queen Thyra because it is known that part of them was called, several hundred years later, "Queen Thyra's

Dyke", but it does seem most likely that the first defensive rampart would be put up to keep the Saxons out and, presumably, on Godfred's or his successors' orders. They would, necessarily, need repairing in the course of a century and, perhaps King Gorm did have them repaired and strengthened and dedicated one stretch to his Queen.

King Gorm died in 940 and his son Harald Bluetooth persuaded the "Ting" to elect him King. It is interesting to note that the Danish Kings were elected for many centuries after this. They did not succeed as of right. This was the Harald who had the great runic stone erected in Jelling where his capital was at first. He did, indeed, manage to unite Denmark and enlarge it after some very fierce fighting. Denmark in his time and for some hundreds of years was very much bigger than it is today. He fought the King of the Sveas (Swedes), whose kingdom covered the whole of Central Sweden, for the area roughly covering what is now called Skåne and won it. At that time it was mainly covered by marshes and thick forest and it is possible that, to the Sveas, with their long Baltic coastline and outlook to the east, did not really think it was very important.

The Western Vikings

Danes and Norwegians though still called Norsemen began their second Viking campaign in the 800s. Their targets were the north-west and north and also the south-west. The Swedes, on the other hand, turned their attentions to the east and battled their way through what is now called Russia, the Baltic States to Constantinople. Though the largest tribe was the Svea which later gave its name to the whole country, they were, as a body, called the "Rus or Russ" and it is from this name that we owe the word "Russia" today.

The Norwegians, on the other hand, attacked westward and north. They began the settlement of Iceland in 874 and of Greenland in 983 and there is now little doubt that Leif Eriksson, sailing from Greenland, made the first settlement of America. The Norwegians also conquered the Faroes, the north of Scotland, the Isle of Man, a large part of Ireland and landed in the north of France, thence called "Normandy". The Viking Chief, Rollo, was created Duke of Normandy in 911 and it was his descendant, William of Normandy, who conquered England for the last time in 1066.

By the time of Harald Bluetooth's death in about 985, Scandinavia, particularly Denmark, was becoming over-populated and her primitive agriculture could not feed its growing population. Accordingly, there was a great increase in Viking invasion and conquest. Harald's son, *"Swein Forkbeard"*, was a doughty and enthusiastic Viking; he based his power on war expeditions and conquest. He made acquisitions in Norway and Scania, but his main object was the conquest of England. He did succeed, but not until 1013, when he was crowned "King of England". He did not reign long, for, the following year, 1014, he died leaving his realms to his young son, *"Knud"* (Canute) who was, at that time between 16 and 19. King Canute, though young and bred as a fighter, rightly earned the name of *"Canute the Great"* for he was a young man of great character, very patient and surprisingly tolerant for that age. He succeeded in holding his heterogenous realm together and even increasing it by conquest in southern Norway. He made peace with the English, ruled wisely, brought law and order to the country and was held in high esteem, not only in England, but throughout Europe. He was considered one of the great Princes of Christendom, entering into relations with the German Emperor and the Pope. In Denmark, however, though he was admired and revered, his direct influence was probably slight. Had he lived until he was 60, things would probably have changed and, perhaps, the history of western Europe been different. Unfortunately for both Denmark and England, Canute died in 1035 leaving only young sons to follow. *"Hardicanute"* went to Norway to claim the throne, but was soon beaten and the Norwegians seceded from the Union. *"Harald Harefoot"* was crowned King of England, but only succeeded in holding it for a few years and by 1042 all trace of Danish authority had gone.

Period of transition

1060–1157 After the break-up of the great kingdom of the North Sea, Zealand under *"Svend II"* became the heart of the kingdom of Denmark and *Roskilde* the ecclesiastical centre. One of Canute's descendants, *"Swein Estrithson"* united with the Church, which was largely Anglo-Saxon, but under the archbishopric of Bremen, and the Church's influence grew to massive proportions. Bishoprics were established up and down the country and churches were built in every conceivable place and, naturally, they had to be built by the peasants. Not only that, the clergy, especially the bishops, began to press for "tithes". Time after time, the peasants, who had always before been "free men", revolted and the revolts were put down bloodily. To make matters worse, the kings and bishops did not always agree and, in addition, fierce dynastic struggles raged.

The Age of the Valdemars

1157–1375 After a period of civil war, *Valdemar I* (1157–81), with the help of his friend Archbishop Absolon, successfully opposed the Wends who had occupied the island of Rügen from which they had made many attacks on the Danish coast. Valdemar, later called "the Great", with the help of Absolon, re-established the unit of the country. Not only was he recognised as a powerful monarch by the rest of Europe, but he also made important administrative and legislative progress in internal affairs. Valdemar's son, *Knud VI*, supported by Absolon, continued his father's policy, and began a series of conquests on the German side of the Baltic clearly aimed at seizing a position of real power in that area and internal German dissension facilitated his project. Under *Valdemar II* (1202–41) Holstein was subjugated, the important town of Lübeck became a Danish possession and large parts of Mecklenburg came under Danish rule. In 1214 the German Emperor ceded the lands north of the Elbe and Elde rivers to Denmark and in 1219 a large Danish fleet conquered and Christianised pagan Esthonia. With remarkable suddenness "Valdemar the Victorious", as he was called, was defeated. He and his son were captured by one of his enemies, the German Count Heinrich of Schwerin and his Baltic realm, based on his own strength, but not consolidated by any Danish colonisation, fell to pieces.

Valdemar II failed to recover his lost lands in the Baltic. All he retained was Rügen and Esthonia, but the dream of regaining the domination of the Baltic was part of the main policy of Danish Kings for more than 400 years. It had a weakening effect on the country because the task far exceeded its economic powers. Nevertheless, Valdemar II's is a great success story. The influence of the monarchy grew in strength; his revenues swelled and he really was responsible for the first public officials. He also made the King the fountain of law and justice. Up to his time the people had been responsible for their own affairs and through the "Ting" had administered justice. The King, however, felt the need for a uniform administration and a judicature common to the country as a whole and so, shortly before he died, Valdemar the Victorious issued the first Royal Statute Book – *"The Jutland Law"*, perhaps the finest monument he could have left behind.

After his death there was a period of internal strife. Both the Church and nobility trying to seize power; this was aggravated by the various Kings' attempts to regain the Baltic and compounded by the fact that Valdemar II, had, as was the custom, handed over large tracts of the country to his young sons on his death. One son was given the Dukedom of Slesvig. The Ducal family began, in time, to assert its independence and married into the family of its ancient rivals, the Counts of Holstein. With the aid of the Holsteiners the Slesvig Duke Valdemar in 1326 actually managed to become King. The influence of the Holsteiners grew rapidly because, owing to the constant strife, the royal coffers were empty and the King was obliged to mortgage province after province to his creditors the Dukes of Holstein. By 1332 practically the whole of the country was mortgaged, the King was deposed and for eight years the country had no ruler. In 1340 the Jutlanders revolted against the foreign Holsteiners who decided sensibly to recognise the late King's son, another Valdemar as monarch, probably in the hope of recovering some of their money.

Valdemar IV was faced with a terrifying task, but bit by bit he stubbornly strove to make his kingdom viable once more. He sold Esthonia; he pressed creditors to wait a bit longer for repayment and it took him 20 years. It did not, of course, make him popular, but his people began, first in ridicule and then in admiration to call him "Valdemar Atterdag" (Another day). By 1360 Valdemar had made such progress that he began to turn his gaze abroad. The Swedish King had occupied the Danish provinces in Seanla, but partly by strategy and partly on promise of payment, Valdemar regained them. Then, in 1361, for the first time he was rash and made a fatal mistake. He mounted an expedition against Gotland in the Baltic which though nominally Swedish was controlled by the Hanseatic League. He conquered the island, but this led to an all-out war with the Hansa towns. He lost and at the Peace of Stralsund in 1370 Valdemar was forced to give up, not only Gotland, but all hopes of ever being a Baltic Power again.

The Union

Valdemar Atterdag had in furtherance of his plans married his daughter Margarethe to the Swedish King's son Håkon who had become King of Norway. On his death in 1375, Valdemar was succeeded to the Danish throne by Håkon and Margarethe's son, Oluf, who, a few years later, on the death of his father, also ascended the throne of his father. Thus was established a Union between Denmark and Norway which lasted for over 400 years. When Oluf died, still very young, in 1387, both Denmark and Norway did a remarkable thing. Margarethe had acted as Regent for her son and both countries took the heretofore unheard of step and elected Margarethe as their Ruler. So, for the first time until the present day, Denmark was ruled by a Queen.

Margarethe was a wise and capable woman. She continued her father's work of improving the administration of the Crown lands; she restricted the influence of the aristocracy and the Church and forbade them to buy up more farmland for, by now, only 10 to 15 per cent of Danish land was held by the farmers. The German Albrecht of Mecklenburg had been elected to the Crown of Sweden after the death of Håkon, but he was hated by the Swedish nobles who asked Margarethe to help them get rid of him. This gave Margarethe the chance of real statesmanship; in 1389 she beat Albrecht in battle and broke his power. Then, in 1397 she persuaded the nobles of all three nations to join in a meeting at Kalmar in Sweden where the Union of Denmark, Norway and Sweden was proclaimed. This *"Union of Kalmar"* is one of the most important events recorded in the North's history. Margarethe refused the Crown for herself, but proposed that her nephew, Erik of Pomerania should be King as she had already chosen him for her successor. In the event, she retained control and was called "Queen of all Scandinavia". In addition, she engaged strongly in trying to restore Denmark itself to its former size and possessions. In 1386 she persuaded the Counts of Holstein, who had, by that time, gained all of it to recognise South Jutland (Slesvig) as a fiefdom of Denmark; she began, slowly, to regain the castles one by one. The Holsteiners tried to retain their influence by fighting, but she wore them down and had almost accomplished her aim when she died in 1412.

Queen Margarethe has, rightly, been recognised as one of the greatest of Denmark's "Kings". She was regarded in her own time in Denmark with the same reverence and mystique with which the first Elizabeth was later regarded in England. Indeed, in many ways they were very alike and it is a curious thing and rather attractive to remember that when Frederik IX died leaving no son, his eldest daughter whose name, happily, was also Margarethe, was raised to the throne as "Queen Margarethe II" in much the same fashion as the crowning of Queen Elizabeth was cheered as the second Elizabeth.

Queen Margarethe's ascendency can best be gauged by the events which followed her death. King Erik was a weak man. He suffered defeat after defeat at the hands of the Holsteiners aided by the Hanseatic League and ruled Sweden with the help of Danish and German bailiffs so, in 1439, the Danes and the Swedes joined together and deposed him, and it was only through the continuing disputes among the Swedish nobility that successive Danish Kings were able to claim that they were King of all three countries. It was not until 1448 when the nephew of the Holstein

Count Adolf was elected King of Denmark as *"King Christian I"* that things began to improve for Denmark. Christian was from the House of Oldenburg and, therefore, acceptable to the Danish people and he founded the dynasty which still reigns in Denmark.
The Estates of Slesvig and Holstein elected Christian as their Duke. This personal union of the two Duchies, which was confirmed by Christian, with Denmark led to later conflict, for example in 1848–64. In 1479 King Christian gained Papal dispensation to build a University in Copenhagen. The nobles still held all the high offices of State and Church, but the new University and the effect of the Reformation helped to bring about a decline in the power of the nobility. Christian I died in 1481.

1481–1513 *King Hans* – under whose rule Danish trade grew steadily and the foundation of a national Navy was made to support it. He also held a meeting of the first Danish Diet where the presence, not only of the nobles, but also burghers and peasants showed that the middle classes of Denmark were becoming a part, if only still a small part, in the power game.

1513–1523 *King Christian II* openly demonstrated his powers and directed central administration. This led to open hostility between the classes. Christian spurned the nobles and clergy and appointed commoners as his advisers. As a result, his enemies united against him; the Lübeckers launched a war to uphold their commercial interests, the Swedes revolted once more and the bishops and nobles withdrew their allegiance and called in his paternal uncle Frederik of the Duchy of Slesvig to be the Pretender. The burghers and peasants rallied to the side of Christian, but so powerful was the opposition that he was forced to flee. He sought help from his brother-in-law Charles V. Failing to get a great deal of support, he was still determined to maintain Danish rule in Sweden. He gathered his forces together and made for Stockholm. There he surprised a Court gathering and had 82 of the nobility executed, the famous "Blood Bath", an event which united all of Sweden against Denmark. Under the leadership of Gustavus Vasa, Christian was decisively beaten and, when he returned to Denmark the power and hatred of the nobles was such that he fled again to the protection of his brother-in-law, the Emperor. In Holland he made plans to return via Norway, but his forces were not strong enough to beat the nobles; he was caught in Copenhagen and forced to cede the throne.
Christian II was, in some ways, a remarkably gifted man with a fierce desire for "reform", but he lacked balanced judgement and tried to push his reforms through so impetuously that he alienated the few nobles who might have helped him. The common people loved him, but the Church and nobility hated him; though he was often impetuous and bad tempered, he was admired by his adherent and his little Queen, Elizabeth (Isabella), the daughter of the Emperor Charles, whom he married when she was only 13, loved him deeply and admired him greatly until she died in 1526 at the age of 25. There is a charming and very good portrait of her carved by Klaus Berg on the altar-piece of St Knud's Church in Odense.

The struggle for supremacy in the Baltic

1523–1533 *Frederik I* – during the whole of his brief reign there was a continual and bitter struggle between the King and nobles and with the other powers in the Baltic. Frederik was unable to prevent the aristocracy from consolidating its influence and repressing the people. The nobles began to act as minor kings; they began to intimidate, fine and imprison as they wished. The result was ceaseless peasant unrest throughout the country. In addition, the reformist ideas of Luther had for years been spreading among the lesser clergy many of whom left the monasteries and got married. The King saw the advantage which might be gained from this and supported *Hans Tavson*, a brilliant Lutheran preacher who won over large numbers of the middle classes who were tired of the greed and scheming of the nobility and higher Churchmen.
In 1533 Frederik I died, but his son, Christian, had adopted the Lutheran faith, and the Bishops and the Council of

the Realm refused to elect him to succeed his father. So, once again, Christian II returned to Denmark and raised a rebellion of the burghers and peasants against the ruling aristocracy. They were joined in this revolt by forces from Lübeck who were afraid of the increasing power of the Netherlands. As a result, the nobles were forced to climb down and elect Christian III (1536–59) as King. There then ensued a period of bitter fighting which ended with the power firmly in Christian's hands. Immediately, he set about reforming the Church which was created a Lutheran State Church with the King as its Head. The Church lands went to the Crown whose power was thus strengthened enormously.

1534–1536 At the beginning of the reign of *Christian III* (1534–1559) Denmark and Sweden combine in the "Counts' War" against Lübeck's commercial domination in the Baltic. Lübeck suffers a defeat.

1536 The **Reformation** is established in Denmark and the property of the church secularised.

1563–1570 The so-called War of the Three Kings against Sweden in the time of *Frederik II* (1559–88) brings bitter fighting but no territorial changes. However, Sweden is compelled to recognise the customs dues levied in the Øresund.

1576–1597 Under Frederik's patronage, and later under Christian IV's patronage *Tycho Brahe* (1576–97) considerably increases the accuracy of astronomical observations – observatory on the island of Ven in the Øresund.

1588 *Christian IV* succeeds to the throne (until 1648); he is the most popular of Danish kings.
He is commemorated in the popular song "King Christian stood at the Topmost Mast", composed in 1778.

1611–1613 Successful campaign against Sweden and North Swedish Lapland (Kalmar War).

1625–1629 Christian IV intervenes in Germany during the **Thirty Years War.** His defeat by Tilly at Lutter seriously weakens Denmark.

1643–1645 The Swedish-Danish War leads to a change in the balance of power in the Baltic. By the Peace of Brömsebro (1645) Denmark has to cede to Sweden the Norwegian provinces of Jämtland and Harjedalen, the islands of Gotland and Ösel and, for 30 years, Halland.

1657–1660 Under *Frederik III* (1648–70) Denmark fights two more wars against Sweden.
Charles X of Sweden suddenly invades Denmark. After an heroic defence of Copenhagen and a victory at Nyborg, Denmark is defeated and has to hand back to Sweden its territory in the south of that country – Schonen, Halland, Blekinge, Bohuslän – and the Norwegian town of Trondheim and the island of Bornholm (signing of the treaty in Roskilde on 2 February 1658).
At the Peace of Copenhagen (1660) Denmark receives back Trondheim and Bornholm.

The Age of Absolutism

1660–1848 Denmark becomes an **hereditary monarchy** and experiences a period of relative calm; in the 19th c. it loses Norway.

1660 Under King Frederik III Denmark is converted from an electoral kingdom into a hereditary monarchy by decree of the Rigsdag in which the clergy and the bourgeoisie are the decisive factor and the nobility acquiesces.

1661 The King proclaims an *"Act of Hereditary Absolution"* and the Royal Act which, in spite of the opposition of the nobles, becomes final, laying down the unrestricted powers of the monarchy. These Acts are confirmed by Norway, Iceland and the Faroes under the name of "The King's Royal Law". At the same time the "Augsberg Confession" (Lutheranism) is declared the State religion.

1671 *Christian V* (1670–99) establishes a Court and "administrative nobility".

1675–1720 Under Christian V and

Frederik IV (1699–1730) who attempt to recover the territory lost to Sweden, the Danish fleet wins several naval battles: 1677 in Køge Bay under Neils Juel, in 1715 at Rügen and in 1719 at Marstrand under Tordenskjold.
With the end of the Nordic War (1700–20) a lengthy period of peace begins for Denmark in which the country experiences an economic and intellectual revival.

1751 Under *Frederik V* (1746–66) *Count Johann Hartwig Ernst Bernstorff* becomes Prime Minister. He supports scholars including the German poet Fredrich Gottlieb Klopstock who lives in Copenhagen from 1751 to 1770 and receives an annual salary.

1788 Minister *Count Andreas Peter Bernstorff*, a nephew of Count Johann Hartwig Ernst Bernstorff, introduces measures leading to the emancipation of the peasantry in Denmark.

1806 Napoleon compels Denmark to join the Continental Blockade – the prohibition of the import of English goods into continental ports.

1807 In order to prevent the closing of the Baltic the British bombard Copenhagen and destroy the Danish fleet.

1808 Under *Frederik VI* (1808–39), who has acted as Regent for his mentally ill father, *Christian VII*, Denmark allies itself with France after the British attack of 1807 and thus becomes involved in the Napoleonic Wars.

1814 Under the Treaty of Kiel Denmark loses Norway to Sweden and Heligoland to Great Britain but receives in turn the Duchy of Lauenburg.

Denmark as a Modern State

Under *Frederik VII* (1848–63) a new constitution comes into being. Denmark becomes a constitutional monarchy.

1849 The country gets a two-chamber parliament, the Landsting, the majority of the members of which are large landowners, and the Folketing, the organ of the people's parties.

1850 The Schleswig-Holsteiners are defeated at Idstedt; the Danes occupy Schleswig. However, Denmark has to make a solemn declaration to Prussia and Austria that it will never annex Schleswig.

1857 Denmark renounces contractually the right to raise customs duties at the Øresund which have been levied for centuries.

1863 *Christian IX* (1863–1906) confirms the constitution which, in contradiction to the arrangement made, forsees the incorporation of Schleswig in Denmark.

1864 When Denmark persists in its position Prussian and Austrian troops march into Schleswig. After decisive victories by the German troops Denmark has to cede the dukedoms of Schleswig, Holstein and Lauenburg to Prussia and Austria – the Treaty of Vienna.

1866 Reform of the constitution which is altered in a conservative direction.
In the following decades struggles between the Conservative government and the Liberal-Radical majority in the Folketing characterise Danish internal politics. Under the Conservative Cabinet of *Estrup* (1875–94) the bickering reaches its climax.

1901 Under *Johann Heinrich Deuntzer* a Liberal Government comes into power.

1903 Iceland obtains an autonomous constitution.

1912 *Christian X* becomes King.

1914 Beginning of the First World War in which Denmark remains neutral.

1915 The country receives a new democratic constitution with women getting the vote.

1917 Denmark has to sell its West Indian possessions (islands) to the United States of America.

1918 End of the First World War. Iceland becomes an independent kingdom in personal union with Denmark.

1920 In accordance with the provisions of the Treaty of Versailles a plebiscite is held in the Danish-speaking northern part of Schleswig, the result of which is a vote of 75 per cent for Denmark. Denmark acquires an area of some 4000 sq. km (1534 sq. miles) with more than 160,000 inhabitants (about 25 per cent of them German).

1924 Under *Thorvald Stauning* a Social Democrat Government comes to power for the first time in Denmark.
In the following decades the government is carried on either by the Social Democrats, the Liberals or by coalitions in which Conservatives are also included.

1939 Outbreak of the Second World War; Germany and Denmark conclude a non-aggression pact on 31 May.

1940 Occupation of the country by German troops in April; a national movement is formed within the population.

1944 Iceland separates itself from Denmark and becomes a republic.

1945 End of the Second World War.

1947 Christian X dies; *Frederik IX* becomes King.

1948 The Faroe Islands receive independence in all internal matters; the Danish Parliament, in which the Faroes are represented by two members, is responsible for foreign policy and defence (23 March).

1949 Denmark joins the North Atlantic Treaty Organisation (**NATO**).

1952 Denmark beomes a member of the Nordic Council, an inter-parliamentary advisory body to which Finland, Iceland, Norway and Sweden also belong.

1953 By a constitutional reform of 5 June the single-chamber system (Folketing) is introduced and the necessary measure to permit female succession to the throne is passed.
Greenland becomes a part of the kingdom with equal rights and two members in the Folketing.

1958 Formation of a passport and customs union between Norway, Sweden, Finland, Denmark and Iceland.

1960 Denmark becomes a founder-member of the European Free Trade Association (EFTA) until 1972. This is an association for the protection of commercial interests of States which do not belong to the European Economic Community.

1972 Death of *King Frederik IX*; Crown Princess Margarethe is proclaimed Queen as *Margarethe II.*

1973 Denmark joins the EEC on 1 January; membership of EFTA is therefore cancelled.
Establishment of diplomatic relations with the German Democratic Republic on 12 January.

1976 Abolition of the death penalty.

1979 Greenland is given internal autonomy and its own administration (government and parliament for internal matters), but remains under Danish sovereignty (1 February).
Elections to the Folketing strengthen the Social Democrats and Conservatives. The Prime Minister in office, *Anker Jørgensen*, forms a Social Democrat minority government.

1980 Second UN World Conference of Women meets in Copenhagen. In the Faroes, an autonomous country under the Danish Crown, the Social Democrats suffer an electoral defeat (November).

1981 Dispute between Germany and Denmark over the quota of cod permitted to be caught by West German fishermen off Greenland.
Fresh elections to the Folketing in December result in loss of votes for the Social Democrats. Jørgensen forms another Social Democrat minority government.

1982 In a referendum the people of Greenland vote to withdraw from the EEC on 23 February.
Jørgensen's government, which is unable to overcome economic problems, resigns on 2 September.

Poul Schlüter, the leader of the Conservatives, forms on 7 September a four-party minority government, in which women take part for the first time; The head of government is sworn in on 10 September.
On 16 October a drastic programme of economies is passed by the Folketing.

1983 On 22 June Mogens Glistrup, lawyer and Chairman of the Progressive Party, is sentenced to prison and fined for tax evasion.
A border dispute with Sweden concerning Danish test borings in the island of Hesselø in the Kattegat is settled by the signing of an agreement on 29 October of maritime boundaries in the Skagerrak, Kattegat, Øresund and the waters round Bornholm.
By a vote of 87 to 75 the Folketing opposes the stationing of new US middle-range rockets in Denmark on 1 December.
Prime Minister Poul Schlüter resigns on 16 December.

1984 In the parliamentary elections on 10 January Schlüter's KFP (Det konservative folkeparti) improves its position. In the newly elected Folketing the civil government can count on the support of 90 of the 179 members.
The strongest party is the SPD (Det socialdemokratiske parti).
The Faroes on 23 February declare the islands a zone free of nuclear weapons.
By the abstention of the governing coalition on 5 March the Folketing approves an SPD proposal to create a zone banning nuclear weapons in northern Europe.
The parliament of Greenland declares the island a zone free of atomic weapons (18 November).
In the parliamentary elections in the Faroes the Social Democrats, who have hitherto been in opposition, achieve gains. In November a coalition of Social Democrats, Republicans and the People's Party forms the new government, the Prime Minister of which is the Social Democrat *Atli Dam.*

1985 Greenland leaves the EEC on 1 February and receives the special status of an "overseas country or territory".
It undertakes to achieve a balance of fishing rights off its coasts; in return the country will receive an annual financial recompense from the EEC budget.
In Denmark on 24 March thousands of people go on strike; they demand increased pay and a shorter working week; lockouts occur; after more than a week the strike is settled; the result is increased pay of 2 per cent for 1985 and 1·5 per cent for 1986 and from 1986 a reduction in the working week from 40 to 39 hours with no loss of pay.
The parliamentary opposition which has a majority compels the government on 14 May to refuse to take any part in the US SDI programme.
Denmark claims a sea area in the Atlantic south of the Faroes where oilfields are believed to exist; other countries (Great Britain, Ireland) have already asserted their interests in this region (end May).
The Danish Government in December takes measures to reduce internal demand and therefore imports, in order to lessen the deficit in foreign trade.

1986 After first refusing to sign the agreement to extend the European Economic Community, in February a proposal which has the aim of broadening the internal market in Europe, a referendum produces a vote of 56 per cent of Danes in favour of the agreement.

Art

In Denmark there is a great deal of evidence of important creative art; from the finds of prehistoric times, the cathedral-building of the Romanesque period, the work of the Renaissance and Classicism up to the present time with its modern buildings and sculpture.

The Stone Age. Among the relics of prehistory the numerous Megalithic graves of the New Stone Age, about 3000–1800 B.C., are of particular interest. Dolmens of unhewn granite blocks and funeral mounds which conceal chambers of stone chests are in many places features of the landscape. Implements of flint and earthenware vessels have also been found. Creative decoration can also be recognised on many vessels in the form of scratches but nothing has remained of the houses where people lived.

The Bronze Age, 1800–500 B.C., provided new possibilities by the introduction of the new material, bronze, in technical and artistic development. There arose especially metal vessels and implements, for example swords with bronze blades, and female ornaments. These were provided with severe lineal ornamentation which had the form of concentric circles and wavy lines. Characteristic of this period are the trumpets known as lurs. The sun-cult of this period can be seen in very many representations of the disc of the sun, for instance in the "sun chariot" of Trundholm, a cult object in the form of a cart which is about 60 cm (2 ft) long and today is in the National Museum of Copenhagen.

The Iron Age. In the Iron Age, which began about the middle of the first century (500 B.C.–A.D. 800), instead of bronze the far harder iron was used in the making of various objects, including the blades of swords. At the same time knowledge of writing made its appearance – *runic script*. During the Iron Age few ornamental objects were made. The magnificent silver cauldron of Gundestrup, discovered in a bog near Ålborg in North Jutland, has been identified as a cult object of Celtic origin. The half-length figures of gods on the outside and scenes of sacrifice on the inside testify to this origin. The cauldron can be seen today in the National Museum of Copenhagen.

Dolmen near Dyreborg on Fune (Fyn)

The Viking era. There are very many finds from the Viking era (A.D. 800–1060). The upsurge of the Vikings was made possible by their keeled boats, with strengthened bottoms to take the mast and keel, instead of rowing boats. In the Viking Ship Hall at Roskilde there are displayed several reconstructed boats which had been sunk between 100 and 1050 in Roskilde fjord in order to form a dam. An idea of the building method of the Vikings is provided in the Viking camp of Trelleborg near Slagelse, the remains of the Viking fortress at Fyrkat near Hobro and the excavated settlement on the Lindholm Høje (Lindholm Hill) north of Ålborg. There can be seen a large number of graves marked by stones. These *standing stones* in the form of ships date from the Viking period.

Important evidence of this period is provided by the runic stones of Jelling which have on them pictures and characters. The runic stone of *Harald Bluetooth* (*c.* 985) is considered the most important Viking sculpture extant, the first written evidence in Danish history. While in the older sculptures the ornament considered primarily of animals this stone shows, as well as a lion devouring a snake, the figure of Christ. The inscriptions and pictures on runic stones were presumably marked out in clay. A copy of the Harald Bluetooth stone which has been painted with colours of the Viking era, can be seen in Copenhagen National Museum.

The Romanesque period. Danish *farmhouses,* which emerged in the early Middle Ages, were made principally of wood. In the period 1060–1265 stone, and later also brick was used as building material. Most *cathedrals* appeared during the reign of *Valdemar the Great* (1157–82), among them the stately cathedrals of Ribe and Viborg which were influenced by the cathedrals of the Lower Rhine; they are three-aisled basilicas with two west towers. Also should be mentioned the west part of Århus Cathedral, the Benedictine Church of Ringsted, the Church of Sorø, which belonged to a Cistercian monastery and the five-towered Church of Our Lady at Kalundborg.

This period also saw the building of *round churches*, with a circular plan; these were conceived to serve both as churches and also as fortresses. Their sturdy form made them similar to rural fortresses. Four of the seven round churches in Denmark are situated on Bornholm. As a rule they have several storeys joined by a staircase.

Among the principal works of Romanesque sculpture in stone are the arched windows in the Cathedral of Ribe, with an impressive *"Descent from the Cross"*. Denmark has an unequalled store of altar-pieces of beaten and gilded copper of the 12th and 13th c. The museums in Copenhagen possess very many treasures of this kind.

Gothic. Gothic (1265–1525/50) which had its origins in France about 1140 and the characteristics of which include pointed arches, influenced architecture in Denmark from the 13th c. The Cathedral of Roskilde (begun *c.* 1170), where most of the Danish kings have been buried, was completed in the Gothic style. Many churches came into being in the 12th c., but there are not many examples in the following centuries and few Gothic monuments have survived.

The churches of St Mary and St Olaf in Helsingør and St Knud in Odense with their elegant interiors, the Cathedral of Århus and St Peter's Church in Næstved owe allegiance to the German Gothic style.

Gothic sculptures are principally done in wood or ivory. Late Gothic sculpture was certainly heavily influenced by Germany and reached its zenith in the work of *Bernt Notke* (*c.* 1440–1509), the master of the winged altar in the Cathedral of Århus, and *Claus Berg* (*c.* 1470–1532), the creator of the great altar-screen in Odense at St Knud's Church. Note the portrait of Christian II's little Queen, Elizabeth, on the altar-piece.

In the Middle Ages many country churches were embellished with *frescoes*. The themes are taken from Biblical history or from Christian motifs. Of particular interest is the wall-painting of the *Elmelunde Master* whose work can be seen in several churches, including the Fanefjord Church on the Island of Møn (*c.* 1500).

Tombs in Roskilde Cathedral

Egeskov Mansion on Funen

Renaissance. The Renaissance movement, originally an Italian style, came to Denmark from the Netherlands in 1550–1650/60. The Reformation was successful here in 1536, an event which also influenced architecture. The window arches now became flatter and later squared openings became the norm. In this period secular buildings arose in great numbers, especially mansions and manor houses.

The architecture of the Dutch Renaissance was the preferred style of *Frederik II* (1559–88) and *Christian IV* (1588–1648). Its exponents were *Anthonis van Opbergen* of Mechelen and *Hans Steenwinkel the Elder* from Antwerp to whom should be added their sons Laurence and Hans. Under Frederick II Kronborg Castle at Helsingør (1574–84) was erected. Christian IV had the Castle of Frederiksborg built by *Hans van Steenwinkel the Younger* between 1602 and 1620; in Copenhagen the little Rosenborg Castle (1610–26), erected under Christian IV, reveals particularly Danish Renaissance features.

Among the manor houses are Rosenholm and Gammel Estrup in East Jutland, Holckenhavn on Funen and Holsteinborg in South Zealand. In addition there are picturesque moated mansions at Egeskov and Rygård on Funen.

In the time of the Renaissance and particularly concerning sculpture, impressive funeral monuments were created. Among the most striking is the funeral monument of *Christian III* (1575) in the Chapel of the Three Kings on Roskilde Cathedral; this is designed in the form of a temple made of marble and alabaster with rich decoration and statues.

Baroque and Rococo. Although originating in Italy Baroque came to Denmark from Holland (1660–1750/60). In addition French and South German influences were present in Danish architecture in this period. Symmetry in the use of space became an important feature. A feature of intensive building began in Copenhagen. One of the first baroque buildings is Charlottenburg Palace which has been the seat of the Royal Academy of Art since 1754. In the 18th c. on the site of an old fortress there arose Christiansborg Palace in the Viennese Baroque style, which was burned down in 1794 and rebuilt by the architect *Christian Frederik Hansen.*

About 1750 a beginning was made to redesign "Frederiksstad", the quarter situated round the present Amalienborg Palace; the area covered about 2 sq. km (0.75 sq. mile). Closely associated with this project of town-planning was the architect *Niels Nikolai Eigtved* (1701–54) who also built the Rococo Amalienborg Palace, one of the principal works of the 18th c. Since the destruction of Christiansborg Palace (see above) Amalienborg Palace has been the royal residence. Eigtved was also responsible for the Prince's Palace in Rococo style built on the model of the Hôtel de Ville in Paris and which now belongs to the National Museum.

In the field of sculpture during the Baroque period equestrian statues were the most important works. Of these a statue of *Christian V* in Kongens Nytorv in Copenhagen, designed in 1688 by *Abraham César L'Amoureux* of Lyons and the statue of *Frederik V* by *Jacques François Saly* from Valenciennes, which was set up in 1768 on Amalienborg Square, are two good examples.

Classicism. As a continuation of Rococo, Louis XVI style another French development, appeared in Denmark. This period, which lasted for only a few decades, is known as Classicism (1760–1825/35). The most important architect of Classicism was *Christian Fredrik Hansen* (1756–1845). He was responsible for the Church of Our Lady in Copenhagen and the Law Courts on Nytorv. Together with his teacher, *Kaspar Fredrik Harsdorff* (1735–99), Hansen created the linking range between the Amalienborg Palaces after 1794.

Bertel Thorvaldsen (1770–1844), the most important Danish sculptor realised the classic ideal in the field of sculpture in its purest form; however, he became addicted to the weaknesses of the style which have been attributed to him. From 1819 he worked on the interior of the Church of Our Lady in Copenhagen creating large statues of the Apostles with relief friezes on the life of Christ and as his *pièce de résistance* the great statue of the Blessed Redeemer. He bequeathed his collection of his own and foreign works to Copenhagen where he was born and today these can be seen in the Thorvaldsen Museum. Also of note are the sculptors *Wilhelm Bissen* (1798–1868) and *Jens Adolf Jerichau* (1816–83).

From 1815 painting, especially of landscapes, gained in importance. Classic works were created by *Jens Juel* (1745–1802), *Nikolai A. Abildgaard* (1743–1809) and *Christopher Wilhelm Eckersberg* (1783–1853), who, in particular, influenced the next generation of painters. The Copenhagen Academy attracted many Germans in about 1800, among them the Romantic artist Caspar David Friedrich.

Historicism. Influences of romanticism on architecture led to the imitation of medieval styles. Several important buildings, especially in Copenhagen, date from the period of Historicism (1835–1915). *Martin Nyrop* (1849–1921) built the City Hall. *Michael Gottlieb Bindesbøll* (1800–65) designed the Thorvaldsen Museum. The Grundvig Church in west Copenhagen was planned by *Peter Wilhelm Jensen Klint* (1853–1930); although it has features of Historicism it already forms a transition to modern architecture.

In painting, *Christian Købke* (1810–48) continued the legacy of *Ch. W. Eckersberg*, Professor in the Copenhagen Academy of Art. Købke and other pupils of the landscape- and portrait-painter form the focus of artistic creation during the "Golden Age" of Danish painting which is characterised by balance of composition and colour.

In the second half of the 19th c. a group of painters, who distanced themselves from academic conditions, painted in Skagen (North Jutland) in the open air; among them were *Peter Severin Krøyer* (1851–1909) and *Anna Ancher* (1859–1935). Their example was followed by painters on the island of Funen, including *Johannes Larsen* (1867–1961). For both groups light formed the central element in painting.

20th Century. Scandinavia is extremely important for 20th c. architecture. In the 1920s and 1930s the "down-to-earth" style was very popular, one example of this being the *"Bakkehuse"* (= hill houses) of the Dane *Ivar Bentsen* (1876–1943). Creators of the new architectural style include in particular *Erik Møller* and *Arne Jacobsen*, to whose prize-winning plans the new City Hall in Århus was built between 1938 and 1942 in reinforced concrete. Arne Jacobsen (1902–71), whose buildings have a clarity of design and are technically well executed, is probably internationally the best-known Danish architect.

Among the notable sculptors of the 20th c. should be mentioned *Robert Jacobsen* (b. 1912), who worked in metal, and *Kai Nielsen* (1882–1924), the creator of a new monumental style. Others include *Bengt Sørensen* (b. 1923), *Gunnar Westmann* (b. 1915) and *Svend H. Hansen* (b. 1922). They all work in the current modern styles.

Well-known painters of the 20th c. are *Richard Mortensen* (b. 1910), *Ejler Bille* (b. 1910), *Else Alfelt* (1910–74), *Carl-Henning Pedersen* (b. 1913) and *Asger Jorn* (1914–73). Under the influence of the increasing danger of war. *Egill Jacobsen* (b. 1910) painted in 1937–38 the picture *"Ophobning"* (Accumulation), which is considered the first Abstract-Expressionist Danish work of art. In 1948 Asger Jorn founded the COBRA group which also included Dutch and Belgian artists; it was disbanded in 1951.

Among the Danish artists who came into prominence in the 1960s *Per Kirkeby* (b. 1938), *Richard Winter* (b. 1926), *Paul Gernes* (b. 1925) and *Bjørn Norgård* (b. 1947) were associated in the Experimental School of Art (Den *Eksperimenterende Kunstskole*), a private institution which was founded as a protest against the instruction in the Academy of Art.

A considerable proportion of the work of the members of this circle and of other important Danish artists did not find its way into museums or other private collections.

The National Art Fund, an establishment for the encouragement of Danish art provides money for the embellishment of public buildings. The work is commissioned from artists. Asgar Jorn carried out in 1959 one of the first projects, a ceramic relief for the State Grammar School in Århus. Thanks to the National Art Fund young artists are given the opportunity of expressing themselves in a monumental format.

In addition to art in its narrower sense, Danish design has also found international acclaim. This is true of furniture, procelain and ceramics. As far as form and decoration are concerned, the tendency in the most recent times has been in the direction of functional work.

Historic Military and Drove Roads

In the period of pre- and early history and in the Middle Ages so-called military roads (*Hærvejen*) led through Jutland and continued into Schleswig-Holstein which is now part of the Federal Republic of Germany. The military roads not only provided passage for armies in times of war but were also used as trade routes and pilgrims' paths. Together with the regional network of tracks they formed the only north–south link on the Danish Peninsular. An important medieval military road led from Viborg southwards towards North Germany. Along the earlier military roads can be seen burial sites, memorial tablets and old resting-places.

From the late Middle Ages everywhere in Europe *drove roads* were made. From areas where the population was mainly concerned with cattle-raising, the farmers used these roads to drive their cattle to towns where the inhabitants needed meat. From Jutland the animals were driven as far as Hamburg and Lübeck. As well as the cattle, sheep and pigs were also sold to the inhabitants of the most heavily populated parts of the country. The eastern drove road led from Hobro via Vejle to Haderslev, the central one began in Skive and, following an old military road, went first via Parup and the Kongeå near Foldingbro to Tønder. Then it joined the western drove road which led from Holstebro via Varde and Tønder southwards to Husum.

In the 15th and 16th c. trade in cattle increased in volume and at this time along the drove roads arose the inns called "jugs" (*kroer*) to provide accommodation and food for the drovers. The animals, too, received fodder there. With the coming of the railway in the 19th c. the drove roads lost their importance for the transport of cattle. When modern roads began to be built, these were originally laid on stretches of the old tracks. Various sections of the military and drove roads, however, remain in their original condition and some of them are nationally protected.

Particularly beautiful stretches of the old military roads can be found between Nørre Snede and Kollemorten and in South Jutland near Haderslev. This road which follows the high ridge of Jutland and for considerable distances lies alongside the main road, is today very much used by walkers.

Near the German–Danish frontier there are many *boundary posts and waymarks*; these bear the names of the families and communities who were responsible for the maintenance of the roads. The arms of Bov, a little place west of Kruså, include as a souvenir of the former age two oxen and a boundary post. Near the frontier town of Padborg in the area of the old roads are a number of interesting places, among them the Bov Museum "*Oldemorstoft*", a former farm in which relics of the military road are exhibited and others from more recent times. Among these are the *Frøsleviejrens Museum* which was set up in the Frøslev prisoner-of-war camp of the Second World War; there among other exhibits can be seen white buses with red crosses which were used in 1945 to fetch back surviving Scandinavian prisoners from the concentration camps in Germany.

Denmark A to Z

Bird's eye view of Nyhavn, Copenhagen

Åbenrå

Jutland
District: Sønderjyllands amt
Population: 21,000
Postal code: DK–6200
Telephone code: 04
Turistbureau
H.P. Hanssens Gade 5
Tel. 62 35 00
Turistbureau
DK–6310 Broager
Tel. (04) 44 11 00
Turistbureau
Ahlefeldvej 4
DK–6300 Gråston
Tel. (04) 65 09 55
(open only in summer)

HOTELS. – *Grand Hotel*, H.P. Hanssens Gade 10, 75 b.; *Hvide Hus*, Flensborgvej 50, 100 b.; *Missionshotel*, Klinkbjerg 20, 20b.; *Sølyst Kro*, Flensborgvej 164, 40 b.; *Sønder Hostrup Kro*, Ostergade 21, in Sønder Hostrup, 44 b.

RESTAURANTS. – *Landbohjem*, Søndertorv 3; *Sølyst Kro*, Flensborgvej 164; *Viking*, H.P. Hanssens Gade 43.

EVENT. – *Kliplev Mærken* (fair and festival; June).

The Baltic resort of Åbenrå lies in the south-east of Jutland on the west of the fjord of the same name. In addition to shipping and fishing, trade in cereals, cattle and timber is of importance and industries include engineering and the production of animal foodstuffs. Organs are built in Åbenrå.

HISTORY. – In the year 1335 Åbenrå, the town with the largest harbour in South Jutland, received trading rights. In the 17th and 18th c. ships sailed from here to South America and to the Far East. Many fine residences date from this period when the inhabitants were prosperous.

SIGHTS. – In the centre of the town rises the **Church of St Nicholas**, originally a Late Romanesque single-aisled brick building it was restored in 1949–56. The interior is notable for a magnificent Baroque reredos of 1642. Near the church stands the **Town Hall** on the main Market Square; it is a two-storeyed building of yellow brick with a hipped roof; it was built between 1828 and 1830 by Christian Frederik Hansen who was then the leading Danish architect. In the hall can be seen a collection of portraits of Danish kings and queens. Some 18th c. residences, several with beautiful gables, survive in *Slotsgade* (Castle Street). Of these the most beautiful are No. 14 (1767), No. 15 (1713), No. 28 (1797) and No. 29 (1770). Dominating the Vægterpladsen is a statue depicting a watchman.

The town's seafaring tradition is documented in the **Åbenrå Museum** (H.P. Hanssens Gade 33; open Tues.–Sun. 2–4 p.m. summer 10 a.m.–noon, 2–5 p.m.). Owners and captains often had pictures of their ships and the shipping section of the museum exhibits a collection of about 200 paintings and ships in bottles. Other departments of the museum are concerned with pre- and early history, ethnology (especially objects from China) and Danish painting of the 19th and 20th c. To the S of the town is *Brundlund Castle* (12th c.) which was rebuilt in 1411 under Queen Margarethe I, and considerably restored between 1805 and 1807.

SURROUNDINGS. – SE of Åbenrå on the Firth of Flensburg is the pleasant town of *Gråsten* (pop. 3000; hotel: Axelhus, Bargergade 16, 10 b.; restaurant: Den Gamle Kro, Slotsgade 6; 3 camp sites) with a lively harbour. In the middle of the town stands the 16th c. Ghåster Castle which was rebuilt after a fire in 1759. Today it is the summer home of Queen Ingrid, the widow of Frederik IX and can be visited when she is not in residence.

Broager, a little town on the Broagerland Peninsula in South Jutland, between the Bay of Sønderborg and the Firth of Flensburg, has a 12th c. church with twin towers. The interior contains wall-paintings of the 14th and 16th c. and beautiful 16th c. wood-carving. In the cemetery stands Denmark's largest bell-tower (1650). War graves of 1848 and 1864 are reminders of the struggles for Schleswig. The pretty north coast of the Åbenrå Fjord is reached along by-roads. Among the hills of Løjtland stands the *Løjt Church* with a notable Gothic winged altar and frescoes of about 1530.

Æro

District: Fyns amt
Area: 88 sq. km (34 sq. miles)
Population: 9000
Telephone code 09
Turistbureau
Torvet
DK–5970 Æroskøbing
Tel. 52 13 00
Turistbureau
Kirkestraede 25
DK–5960 Marstal
Tel. 53 19 60

The island of Æro is situated S of Funen at the entrance to the Little Belt. The coast is generally steep especially in the SW part. Inland among green hills nestle pretty little villages and good bathing is to be had, especially on the N and E coasts.

Car ferries ply between Æroskøbing (Eroskøbing) and Svendborg (Funen), Marstal and Rudkøbing (Langeland), Søby and Fåborg; (Funen) and between Søby and Monmark (Als).

Although the coast of the island in the W runs in a straight line, the northern part has more spits of land and bays, and it is here that the larger places are situated.

Æroskøbing (pop. 490; hotels: Ærohus, 66 b.; Phønix, 19 b.; restaurants: Landbogården; Mumm; Pilebækken; camp site), an attractive market town, stretches over a promontory of the N coast. The town received its trading rights in 1398 and looks a well-preserved merchants' township of the 17th and 18th c. There are 36 houses which are protected monuments including Denmark's oldest post office (1749) and the Kjøbinghus (1645). Hammerich's House (*c.* 1700), the former building of the sculptor Hammerich, and Hans Billedhugger's House are furnished as museums. Objects of local history are exhibited in the Æro Museum (Brogade). There is also a *shipping museum* (Smedegade) with several hundred examples of ships in bottles.

At the end of the island lies *Marstal* (pop. 4000; hotels: Danmark, 35 b.; Marstal, 10 b.; restaurant: Den Gamle Vingård; youth hostel; camp site), which was one of the most important ports in Denmark in former centuries. There is a naval school in this old fishing and shipping town. In the ***Municipal Museum** of Marstal (Prinsensgade) are 42 model ships on show as well as objects which were brought home by sailors from their voyages – jewellery, weapons, stuffed animals, etc. Model ships can also be found hanging from the roof of the church.

In the NW of the island several windmills have been preserved including the *Vitsø Mølle* and the *Vester Mølle*.

Alborg/Aalborg

Jutland
District: Nordjyllands amt
Altitude: 15 m (50 ft)
Population: 155,000
Postal code: DK–9000
Telephone code: 08

Turistbureau
Osterågade 8
Tel. 12 60 22

Turistbureau
DK–9700 Brønderslev
Tel. (08) 82 55 11

HOTELS. – *Central*, Vesterbro 38, 120 b.; *Hafnia*, J. F. Kennedy Plads 2, 72 b.; *Hvide Huse*, Vesterbro 2, 400 b., golf; *Limfjordshotel*, Ved Stranden 14–16, 360 b.; *Park*, Boulevarden 41, 101 b.; *Pheonix*, Verterbro 77, 300 b.; *Scheelsminde*, Scheelsmidnevej 35, 120 b.; *Schlosshotel*, Rendsborggade, 300 b. (1.6–31.12); *Turist-Hotel*, Prinsensgade 36, 75 b.; *Ålborg Sømandshjem*, Østerbro 27, 80 b. – YOUTH HOSTEL.

CAMP SITES. – Mølleparken, Strandparken, Østervangen, Lindholm (Nørresundby).

RESTAURANTS. – *Bondestuen*, Vingårdgade 5; *Brigaderen*, Vesterbro 77; *Brix's Gård*, C. W. Obels Plads; *Duus Vinkælder*, Østerågade 9 (in Jens Bangs Stenhus); *Ellen Marsvin* (wine bar), Østergade 25; *Faklen*, Jomfru Anegade 21; *Fyrtøjet*, Jomfru Anegade 17; *Kniv og Gaffel*, Maren Tureis Gade 10; *Rio Bravo*, Østerågade 27; *Restaurant Zoo*, in the Zoological Gardens.

EVENTS. – *Amateur Music Festival* (Feb.), *Ålborg Festival* (concerts, etc.; Aug.).

Ålborg or Aalborg (this spelling is preferred by the inhabitants), the fourth largest town in Denmark, is situated on the S bank of the Limfjord which links the North Sea with the Kattegat. A road and rail bridge (1933) and the 553 m (604 yard) long Limfjord Tunnel (1970) lead to Nørresundby on the north of the fjord which is part of Greater Ålborg. Today trade and industry have put their stamp on the economic life of the town. Among the most important branches of industry are shipbuilding and cement-manufacture, tobacco and the production of Ålborg aquavit, a Danish version of schnapps. The modern port is the place from which Danish trade with Greenland is conducted. Ålborg is also a centre of education and training and has been a university town since 1973. The visitor can gain a good impression of the region by

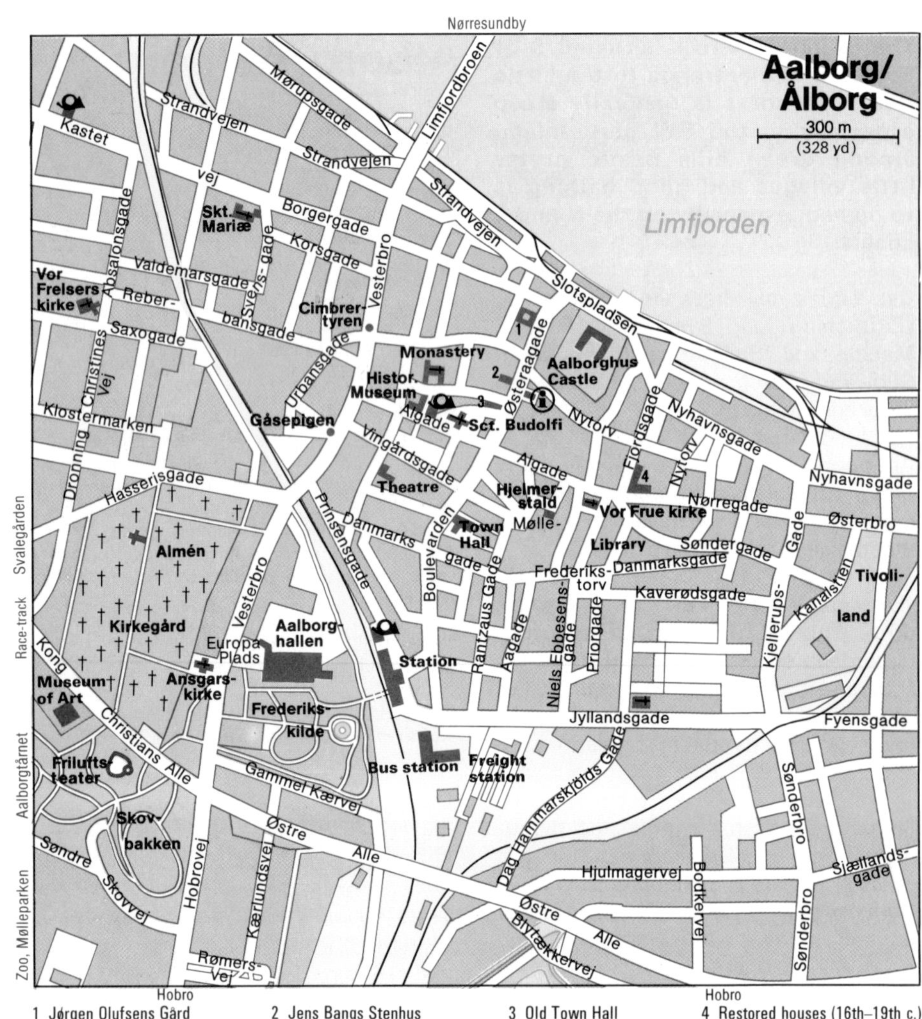

visiting the Art Museum, the Historical Museum, and concerts and theatrical performances. In August the Ålborg Festival takes place. It is also possibly the most international and interesting Danish city apart from Copenhagen.

HISTORY. – Ålborg is mentioned about 1070 by Adam of Bremen as a "well-known shipping town". In 1342 the existing Viking settlement was granted the status of a town. During the Middle Ages there was close connection with Norway. The town had commercial importance; in 1534 Ålborg became the seat of an Evangelical bishop. Until the beginning of the 17th c. Ålborg was a prosperous trading centre but from 1625, because of the quartering of foreign troops (Thirty Years War, wars against Sweden), it entered a period of decline. Only towards the end of the 18th c. did it recover; from 1850 various industries became established. The deepening of the Limfjord was of benefit to the town, because it could now be reached by larger ships. During the Second World War enemy troops caused great damage by aerial attacks.

SIGHTS. – To the S of the place where the *Limfjord Bridge* (Limfjordsbroen) crosses to Nørresundby is the old part of Ålborg with a beautiful townscape and fine buildings and restored houses. In the newer parts, which adjoin on the W and E, can be found well-tended parks, such as *Møllepark*, from the highest point of which the greater part of the town can be seen.

The centre of the Old town is *Budolfi Square* (Budolfi Plads) to the N of which in Algade stands ***St Botolph's Church** (open Mon.–Fri. 9 a.m.–3 p.m., Sat. 9 a.m.–noon) named after an English seafaring saint. The Gothic building, which has been altered on several occasions, was erected about 1430 when the remains of an old Romanesque church were incorporated into the new building. The

St Budolfi Church

Gravensgade pedestrian zone

helm of the tower (1778–80) of this whitewashed brick church is still in Baroque style. In the first half of the 20th c. the church was rebuilt. Between 9 a.m. and 10 p.m. the carillon (1970; 18 bells) plays at every hour. In the vestibule of the church (formerly a Catholic chapel) can be seen some excellent frescoes. In the interior itself are an impressive reredos and a carved pulpit (1689–92, by Laurids Jensen), a marble tablet and – in the northern aisle – a Renaissance gallery with illustrations of the Ten Commandments. In the S aisle are representations of the Way of the Cross and inscriptions with the names of men who were considered important in Ålborg in 1650.

Not far NW of St Botolph's Church in Algade (house No. 48) stands the *Historical Museum* (open daily 10 a.m.–5 p.m.). Its collection includes objects of prehistoric times, an illustrated history of the town as well as a beautiful collection of North Jutland glasses. The Ålborg room of 1602 should on no account be missed because of its Renaissance interior. N of here lies C. W. Obels Plads where, until 1896, the C. W. Obel tobacco factory stood. At the NE corner of the square one finds the former **Monastery of the Holy Ghost**, founded in 1431 as the House of the Holy Spirit and renamed as a monastery. The purpose of the monastery was and is to look after old and sick people. It is Denmark's oldest social foundation (today it is a care centre; inspection on application to the Tourist Office). In the excellently preserved buildings are frescoes of about 1500 and beautiful stepped gables. On the square in front of the building stands a fountain (Dragon Fountain). W of the Ålborg Monastery extends the *Gravensgade*, part of the pedestrian zone with stores, banks and boutiques.

N of St Botolph's Church is the Gammel Torv, a square in which the *Old Town Hall* (1762) stands. If you go northwards from this you will come to the Østerågade. In this street the most impressive building is ***Jens Bangs Stenhus** (1623–24), a beautiful mansion built by the prosperous merchant Jens Bang. With its five storeys it is the largest Renaissance mansion in the north. The house, which in about 1920 was restored to its exact original exterior, is built of brick, has a roof with curved gables. The whole building is covered with sandstone ornament which shows the influence of the Dutch Renaissance. On the W side of the Østerågade

Nordic Renaissance: Jens Bangs Stenhus

is *Jørgen Olufsens Gård*, a merchant's half-timbered property with a stone gateway of 1616. Opposite stands the former *Ålborghus Castle* of 1539 now occupied by the authorities. The ramparts and casemates can be inspected.

SE of Budolfi Plads and reached by Algade can be found the *Church of Our Lady* (Vor Frue Kirke; open Mon.–Fri. 9 a.m.–2 p.m., Sat. 9 a.m.–noon), built about 1100 and altered in 1878; it is one of the oldest churches in the town. When rebuilding was taking place the original N gateway with its granite relief was placed at the main W door. In the typanum can be seen two scenes from the Childhood of Christ surrounding a Majestas Domini (Christ in Majesty). In the interior are tombs and epitaphs (tombs with representations of the dead) of the 17th and 18th c. There are a number of old houses near the church. In Hjelmerstald Lane one finds an historic pottery. In Geviert, which is bordered by Nørregade and Fjordgade, nine houses 150–400 years old, from various parts of the town, have been re-erected and restored. Near the Church of Our Lady (Peder Barkesgade 5) is the *Danish Emigrant Archive* where documents about Danish emigrants can be seen (books, letters, photographs, etc.; open Tues.–Fri. 10 a.m.–3 p.m.). A town house at the Nytorv (No. 26) is the headquarters of the *Regional Library of North Jutland*. It has a large collection of Danish and foreign books and a children's library.

SE on the periphery of the Old Town extends the *Tivoliland* pleasure park with beautiful gardens, fountains and flowers. On the open-air stage musical shows with international artists take place from April to September (admission fee). Vesterbro running N–S forms the western boundary of the Old Town. In this street can be seen two notable sculptures: at the end of Bispegade is the *"Cimbrian Bull"* (Cimbrertyren, 1937) by A. J. Bundgård. On the plinth is a poem by the Nobel Prize-winner Johannes V. Jensen (1873–1950). Further S stands the statue of the *"Goose Girl"* (Gåsepigen) by Gerhard Henning (1937). Vesterbro runs S of *St Ansgar's Church* on the W side of the street. Opposite lies Kilde Park, Ålborg's oldest open space (1802) with a number of sculptures including "The Three Graces" by Thorvaldsen and "The Bacchus Child" by Anne Marie Carl Nielsen. Here also is the **Ålborg Hall**

Standing stones at Lindholm Høje Viking site

(*Ålborghallen* one of the most attractive Civic Halls in Europe; dedicated 1953), a large building for congresses, exhibitions concerts and theatrical performances (3400 seats).

Not far W of the place where Vesterbro joins Kong Christians Allé S of St Ansgar's Church stands the impressive building of the ****North Jutland Museum of Art** (*Nordjyllands Kunstmuseet*; Kong Christians Allé 50; open Tues.–Sun. 10 a.m.–5 p.m., also Mon. in July and Aug.; entrance fee), which was built between 1968 and 1972 to plans of the Finnish architects Elissa and Alva Aalto and the Dane Jean Jacques Baruël. The museum consists of a complex of various shapes and includes an amphitheatre, a sculpture park and space for other events (including a concert hall). The principal exhibits comprise Danish paintings from 1890 and foreign art of the 20th c. The main emphasis is on the works of the COBRA group, founded in 1948 and named after the initial letter of the towns Copenhagen, Brussels and Amsterdam. The group was comprised of Danish, Dutch and Belgian painters (including Asgar Jorn, b. 1914; Karel Appel, b. 1921; Constant, b. 1920; Corneille, b. 1921). To the S of the museum rises a wooded hill known as *Skovbakken*, with an open-air theatre and an observation tower *Ålborgtarnet* (55 m (180 ft)) high.

In the *Møllepark*, 1.5 km (1 mile) W is the *Zoological Garden* with 1600 animals from every country. The newest attraction is a sea-lion and penguin layout in which the animals can be observed under water through a panoramic window (entrance fee from Mar.–Nov.). W of the great park area in the suburb of Hasseris is the *Svalegården*, a residence which has been lived in since 1600. During the modernisation of the old part of the town it was moved here in 1952. In the east of the town is situated the new residential quarter of ÅLBORG ØST (Ålborg East) together with industrial plants. To the S is the University area.

SURROUNDINGS. – On the far side of the Limfjord lies *Nørresundby*. In the market-place, the Nørresund Torv, stands the "Stone Dog" sculpture by Henrik Starcke. In the pedestrian zone can be seen other works of art including those by Edgar Funch, Jørgen Brynjolf and Kaj Nielsen. To the W of Nørresundby is Ålborg Airport from which sightseeing trips can be made.

Near Nørresundby lies ***Lindholm Høje**, with 682 graves dating from the Iron Age and the Viking Age.

Most of the graves which have been excavated contained ashes; the dead were burned, together with burial objects, and afterwards interred in a grave which was marked by a bright stone. Although the old stones are triangular the later ones are round or oval. Upright stones in the form of ships date from the Viking period. The graves originated in the period from A.D. 800 to 1000. To the N of the cemetery is a settlement which has also been investigated. Paths paved with wood, postholes of houses and wells were uncovered. The postholes have in places been filled with cement so that the visitor can gain an impression of the size of the houses. The settlement was abandoned in 1100 as it was often subjected to sandstorms. The best finds of Lindholm Høje are exhibited in the Historical Museum of Ålborg.

20 km (13 miles) S of Ålborg the A14 road leads to the important trade and industrial town of *Brønderslev* (hotel: Atlas, 12b.; restaurant: Borgerstuen Brunderhus). The Romanesque church (*c.* 1150) is used today only as a funerary church. In East Brønderslev, Hallundvej 137, the *Vendelboernes Egnsmuseum* is worth a visit (regional customs). In the vicinity can be found about 60 barrows.

27 km (17 miles) from Ålborg on road A10 in an area of heathland are the charming *Rebild Hills* (Rebild Bakker) declared a ***National Park** on the initiative of Danish Americans (great celebrations on Independence Day, 4th July). At the entrance to the park are a restaurant and a museum (local history; the travelling fiddlers of Jutland). In the park is a replica of *Lincoln's Log Cabin* built in 1934 with logs from America (Museum of Emigration). On a hill to the NE stands the *Cimbrersten*, a rock with the carved figure of a bull and the inscription "Cimbrerne drog ut fra disse egne" ("The Cimbri set out from this area"). Near the park is the village of *Rebild* (youth hostel; two camp sites; holiday homes) and not far W on road A10 the *Tinbæk Limestone Quarry*, in the great subterranean workings of which is a museum with sculpture by Bundgård and Bonnesen (open: May–Oct. 10 a.m.–5 p.m.). To the S of *Rebild* lies the **Rold Skov**, one of the largest and most unspoiled forest areas in Denmark (6400 ha (16,000 acres)) with many rare trees. In the village the rebuilt ring of the Miehe Circus family has been turned into a circus museum. Old equipment, pictures and other objects are souvenirs of the great era of the circus in the first half of the 20th c.

Als

District: Sønderjyllands amt
Area: 315 sq. km (122 sq. miles)
Population: 53,000
Postal code: DK–6400
Telephone code: 04

(i) **Turisbureau**
Rådhustorvet 7
DK–6400 Sønderborg
tel. (04) 42 35 55
Turistbureau
DK–6400 Augustenborg
Tel. (04) 47 17 20

The island of Als, lies at the southern end of the Little Belt, between the Jutland Peninsula and the island of Funen. Although the coastline facing the Belt has a regular course, on the landward side there are many bays. Its beautiful beaches make it a popular place for vacations.

The chief place on the island is the old town of **Sønderborg** (pop. 30,000; hotels: Ansgar, 75 b.; Arnkilhus, 23 b.; Baltic, 28 b.; City, 19 b.; Dybbøl Banke, 28 b.; Scandic, 190 b., Aug–Dec.; restaurants: Bella Italia; Byens Smørrebrød; shooting festival June) which is situated at the S end of the island and which has spread on to the promontory on the opposite side of the Als Sund. The two parts of the town are joined by a bridge over the Sound. The narrow Als Sund extends to the W of the island. In the SE of the town on Sønderborg Bay is a wood of very old trees. The medieval *castle*, a building with four wings, contains a museum with collections of historical material and art; *St Mary's Church* (*c.* 1600; restored in 20th c.) has sculpture of the 17th c. The Town Hall was rebuilt in 1936. S of the centre is the modern College of Sport; the mosaics and sculpture by Danish artists are worth seeing.

The name of the little village of *Dybbøl* to the W of Sønderborg is closely associated with the events of the year 1864. At the Dybbøl Trenches German forces overcame the far less numerous Danes (18 April 1864) and Denmark lost the whole of Schleswig to Prussia. The reconstructed *windmill*, the central point of the defensive battle, and the cannon are today a monument. The mill contains a museum. *Augustenborg* (pop. 6600; hotels: Fjordhotel, 18 b.; Schlosshotel, 15 b.; restaurants: Augustenborghus; Skipperkroen) lies 7 km (4 miles) NE of Sønderborg on the Augustenborg Fjord. In a great park stands the castle, built in 1776 in the Baroque manner, which is today a nursing home for patients suffering from nervous diseases. Road No. 8 leads from the middle of Als to *Fynshav* (restaurant: Færgegarden) on the Little Belt from where a ferry plys to the island of Funen (see entry).

Dybbøl Mill near Sønderborg

Anholt

District: Århus amt
Area: 22 sq. km (8.5 sq. miles)
Population: 160

The island of Anholt lies in the Kattegat about half-way between northern Denmark and Sweden. The island is reached by ferry in about two and a half hours from Grenå.

The area of drifting sand, the *Ørkenen* (the Desert), is unique in Denmark and can be observed from the chain of hills in the west (Sønderbjerg, 48 m (158 ft)). In the NW of the island lies a lagoon with a reserve for wading birds. The lighthouse of 1780 is a protected building. The island has excellent beaches (hotel: Anholt Kro).

Århus

Jutland
District: Århus amt
Population: 249,000
Postal code: DK–8000
Telephone code: 06

ⓘ **Turistbureau**
Rådhuset
Århus C
Tel. 12 16 00
Turistbureau
Torvet 9–11
DK–8400 Ebeltoft
Tel. (06) 34 14 00
Turistbureau
Bibliotekstorvet 2
DK–8660 Skanderborg
Tel. (06) 52 09 33

HOTELS. – *Ansgar Missionhotel*, Bånegardsplads 14, 236 b.; *Årslev Kro og Motel*, Silkeborgvej 900, in Brabrand, 81 b.; *Atlantic*, Europaplads 12–14, 184 b.; *Motel La Tour*, Randersvej 139, 90 b.; *Marselis*, Strandvejen 25, 160 b.; *Mercur*, Viby Torv, in Viby, 220 b.; *Ritz*, Banegårdspladsen 12, 99 b.; *Royal*, Store Torv 4, 208 b.; *Scanticon*, Ny Moesgårdsvej, in Højbjerg, 220 b.; *Windsor*, Skolebakken 17, 54 b.; YOUTH HOSTEL. – Marielundsvej.

CAMP SITES. – Århus Nord, 8.6 km (5 miles) N; Blommerhaven, 5 km (3 miles) S, near beach; Århus Vest, 7 km (4 miles) W.

RESTAURANTS. – Europa, Europaplads 6; "4 Årstider", Vestergade 39; Gammel Åbyhøj, Bakke Allé 1; Greven & Baronen, Åboulevarden 60; Guldhornet, Banegårdsplads 10; Hafnia Bodega, Frederiksgade 75; Kroen-i-Krogen, Banagårdsplads 4; Munkestuen, Klostertorv 5; Musikhusets Restauranter, Thomas Jenens Allé; René, Frue Kirkeplads 1.

EVENT. – Århus Festival Week (concerts, theatre, etc.; September).

Århus, Denmark's second largest city, lies on the E coast of Jutland where the river "Århus Å" flows into the bay of the Kattegat. In the vicinity of the town are parks and woods and along the coast extend beaches for several miles.

The town has various industries; vegetable oils, beer, textiles, machines and engines are produced here and there are shipyards.

Today Århus, which has had a university since 1928, is the cultural and educational centre of mid-Jutland. Periodic exhibitions are mounted in the Art Gallery. The musical scene includes folk, jazz, chamber concerts, operatic perfomances and church concerts. The Århus Festival takes place annually in September and includes events in the open air.

HISTORY. – The settlement is first mentioned in 928 as the see of a bishop and it received its municipal charter in 1441. During the Middle Ages commerce, seafaring and fishing were of considerable importance in Århus. For a time the town played a part in the great herrring markets in Falsterbro on Schonen to which people came from the whole of northern Europe. In the 16th c. and the beginning of the 17th Århus had its heyday, to which agriculture contributed particularly. Trade spread to Germany, Holland and Norway and merchants from other countries even settled here. The prosperity of Århus in this period is shown by a number of well-preserved Renaissance buildings. From 1627 Århus had to suffer occupation by troops in connection with the Thirty Years War and the wars against Sweden. After recovering from the effects of the wars various industries were established here towards the end of the 18th c. In the battles for Schleswig (1848 and 1864) Århus was occupied by German troops. In 1902 the Crown Prince of Denmark, later King Christian X and his Consort were presented by the city with Marselisborg Castle.

"Den Gamle By"

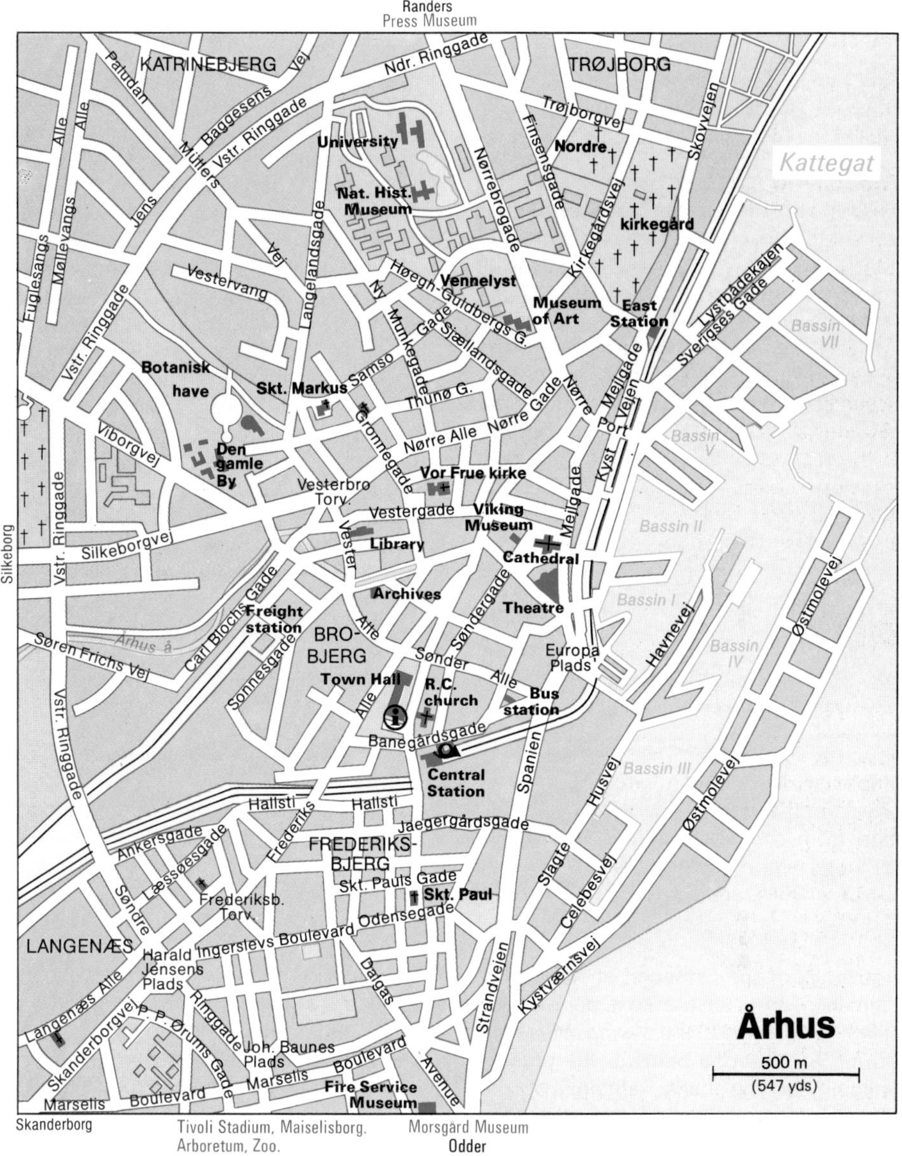

SIGHTS. – The centre of the city is the port, from where there is a ferry service to Kalundborg (Zealand). Some streets in the Inner City – Søndergade, etc. – form a pedestrian zone. In the north of Århus are the educational establishments and in the south a pleasure park.

The Inner City consists of a semicircle enclosed by a ring road (Ringgade) and its heart is the *Great Market* (Store Torv). On the E side stands the ***Cathedral** dedicated to St Clement (open: 1 May–30 Sept. 9.30 a.m.–4 p.m.; 1 Oct.–30 Apr. 10 a.m.–3 p.m.) which, with its 93 m (305 ft) long nave, is the longest church in Denmark. The first church was a Romanesque basilica built between 1200 and 1500. Romanesque elements are still to be found in the external walls of the nave and transepts; the chapels on the E side of the transepts also date from this time. In 1400 the church was converted into a Gothic cathedral and in this work Bishop Jens Iversen Lange (15th c.) was a driving force. The façade was replaced by a front with a single tower which bears the motif of an anchor, the attribute of St Clement. Features of the interior include the winged altar (1479) with a rich array of figures by the Lübeck master Bernt Notke, the beautifully carved 16th c.

Århus Cathedral, exterior

. . . and interior

pulpit by Mikkel van Gröningen, two organs and the font. The vault paintings date from the 15th c. In front of the cathedral stands a *monument to Christian X* (1955) and to the S the *theatre* (1900).

Not far W of the cathedral at No. 6 Skt. Clemens Torv – in the basement of the merchant bank – is the *Viking Museum*. During excavations beneath the present building of the bank remains of the semicircular ramparts, with which the Vikings had surrounded their little settlement a thousand years earlier, were found in the 1960s. In the museum can be seen

Town Hall

a reconstruction of the ramparts, a typical house of the Viking period and tools which the first inhabitants of Århus used. Further SW on the S side of the busy Rådhus Plads, the hub of the city's traffic, stands the **Town Hall** (*Rådhuset*) by Arne Jacobsen and Erki Møller (1938–42). From the tower 16 m (200 ft) high there is a fine view of the city and the bay (ascent of the tower from mid July to mid September daily at noon and 2 p.m.). In summer there are guided tours when the civil hall, the council chamber and the marriage room can be seen. On the W side of the square is the attractive *"Pig Fountain"* (Grise-brønden) by M. Bøggild and at the foot of the City Hall tower the Fountain "Agnes and the Water Carrier". From here it is only a few steps to the concert hall, built in 1982, the headquarters of the Århus Symphony Orchestra and the Opera of Jutland; many events of the Århus Festival also take place in this building.

NW of the cathedral in Vestergade stands the ****Church of Our Lady** (*Vor Frue Kirke*); 13th–15th c.; open: 1 May–31 Aug. Mon.–Fri. 10 a.m.–4 p.m., Sat. 10 a.m.–2 p.m.; 1 Sept.–30 Apr. Mon–Fri. 10 a.m.–2 p.m., Sat. 10 a.m.–noon) originally built by Dominican monks and now a purely Gothic building with frescoes and a magnificent altar-piece from the workshop of Claus Berg (1520). In 1955 beneath the choir of the Church of Our Lady was found a little stone church built of tufa. After careful restoration this vaulted stone church is now a church within a church. The chapter-house which served as an old people's hospital from the Reformation was also dedicated as a church so that the entire complex now contains three churches. The chapter-house has late medieval wall-paintings. Remains of the Gothic cloister of the former Dominican monastery can be seen.

W of the Church of Our Lady, Vesterbrogade borders the *Botanic Garden* where in summer entertainment for children and adults takes place. Here also are hothouses in which subtropical plants from all over the world can be seen (open: Mon.–Sat 1.30–3.30 p.m., Sun. 10.30 a.m.–3.30 p.m.). In the southern part of the Botanic Garden is the interesting open-air museum ***"The Old Town"** (*Den Gamle By*), a collection of more than 60 half-timbered houses from different parts of Denmark. The buildings include old town houses, shops, workshops with their equipment and mills. The central feature is a burgomaster's house of 1597 which contains a collection of furniture (open throughout the year; admission fee).

On the E side of the inner city extends the *port* which is protected by breakwaters; there are five docks (about 9.5 km (6 miles) of quays) and a fishing harbour.

Århus **University** was founded in 1928; its buildings, dating from 1933, are situated in a park in the northern part of the city, with the main building erected in 1936 and the "book tower" by Christian Frederik Møller. In the College of Journalism to the N of the university site is a *Press Museum* which houses a large archive concerning the history of the Press (open: Mon–Fri. 10 a.m.–4 p.m.). In the southern part of the park we find the *Natural History Museum*. The collections are primarily on zoological themes from Denmark and other countries. In addition it includes a geological collection (open: 1 July–31 Aug. daily 10 a.m.–5 p.m.; 1 Oct.–30 Apr. Tues.–Sun. 10 a.m.–4 p.m.; remainder of year daily 10 a.m.–4 p.m.). To the S of the Museum of Natural History in Vennelystpark is the ***Museum of Art** (1967; open: Tues.–Sun. 10 a.m.–5 p.m.)

In the Open-air Museum: "Den Gamle By" (The Old Town)

Head of the "Grauballemann" in the Museum of Pre-history

with Danish work from 1750 to the present day (especially paintings and sculpture). The museum also possesses works by foreign artists.

In the southern part of the city near the shore road (Strandvejen, leading along by the sea) in an old tram depot in Dalgas Avenue is the **Danish Fire Brigade Museum**. It houses about 60 vehicles including some which were pulled by hand or drawn by horses (open: 1 Apr.–31 Oct. daily 10 a.m.–5 p.m.). By following Skovbrynet westwards from the museum one comes to the pleasure park "*Tivoli Friheden*" (Tivoli Freedom) which is surrounded on three sides by the Marselisborg Woods. The park contains a fine floral display; concerts and appearances by artists are included in the entertainment programme. Near by are a sports hall, a stadium, the racecourse of Jutland (horse-racing) and a cycle-track.

Still further S on the far side of Carl Nielsens Vej the little *Marselisborg Palace* stands in a park. It was built in 1902 and is the summer residence of the Danish Royal Family. Near by is the Botanic Garden of Forestry. On the other side of Carl Nielsens Vej a memorial park has been laid out for the Danes from northern Schleswig who fell in the First World War (monument of French euville-limestone). The Marselisborg Woods extend for several kilometres along the coast towards the S. Part of the walk is fenced in and has been furnished as an enclosure for wildlife (fallow deer, wild boar).

SURROUNDINGS. – About 9 km (6 miles) S of the city (leaving on Strandvej) stands the ***Moesgård Prehistoric Museum**, housed in an old manor-house (open: 1 Mar.–20 Oct. daily 10 a.m.–5 p.m.; 21 Oct.–18 Feb. Tues.–Sun. 10 a.m.–5 p.m.). A particularly notable feature of the museum is the "Grauballe Man", a corpse dating back some 1600 years and perfectly preserved in a bog. In the grounds of the museum a "Prehistoric Trail" had been laid out leading past Stone Age and Bronze Age remains and reconstructions of houses of the Iron Age and the Viking period. In the vicinity of the museum there is a new golf-course (18 holes) which is also open to visitors.

If we leave the town centre in a SW direction in 10 km (6 miles) we come to Tranbjerg where the Århus *Aquarium* (No. 3 Tingskov Allé; open daily 10 a.m.–6 p.m.) is well worth a visit. Fish from all parts of the world can be seen here. In the Aqua-Terraria are crocodiles and iguanas and the sea-lion pool attracts very many visitors.

Altar-piece in the Church of Our Lady, Århus

Not far SW of Århus lies the picturesque town of *Skanderborg* (pop: 11,000; hotels: Skanderborghus, 100 b.; Slotskroen, 30 b.; youth hostel; two camp sites) on the lake of the same name (A10). The town had its origins towards the end of the 12th c. in a royal fortress which was pulled down after 1760. There remain part of the south wing with the castle church and a round tower (view). N of the church on the castle hill is a bust of Frederik VI by Bertel Thorvaldsen. A trip from Skanderborg to Hillelbjerg (see entry) is very worth while.

Road A15 leads from Århus into the southern part of the peninsula of *Djursland*, leaving the town in a northerly direction and then following the wide arc of *Kalø Bay*. Near Løgten it branches off to the left to ***Rosenholm Castle** (open: 18 June–7 Aug. daily 10 a.m.–5 p.m.; admission fee). This Renaissance building of the 16th c. has been owned for more than four centuries by the Rosencrantz family, an old Danish aristocratic line. The rooms are decorated with paintings and Gobelin tapestries. There are a lake and a Renaissance pavilion in the park which is open to the public.

About 1 km (1100 yd) from the village of Ronde a little road branches off on the left to *Thorsager* where the only *round church* in Jutland still stands (part dates from 1200). The A15 continues to *Rønde* and from there a road leads SE to Ebeltoft. To the right on a spit of land extending into Kalø Bay can be seen the ruins of *Kalø Castle* (Kalø Slot), destroyed in the 17th c., where Gustav Vasa was held prisoner in 1518. Farther on there is a view of the peninsula of *Mols* ("Posker Stenhus").

Ebeltoft (hotels: Ebeltoft, 14 b.; Ebeltoft Strand, 136 b.; Hvide Huse, 130 b.; restaurants: Gasten; Hvide Kok; Rådhuskroen), on the bay of the same name, is a charming country town with a tiny 16th c. Town Hall little bigger than a cottage and very pretty (now a museum) and the Farvegård, an old dyer's workshop. In the harbour lies the 19th c. frigate "Jylland". Also in Ebeltoft is a remarkable plant for the production of energy. On a pier extending 800 m (875 yd) out into the sea stand 16 "windmills" (wind energy convertors); a larger convertor is also set up on the land. This "windmill park", at present the largest in Denmark, produces enough current in a year to meet the needs of 600 private houses.

Billund

Jutland
District: Ribe amt
Population: 7000
Postal code: DK-190
Telephone code: 05

(i) **Turistbureau**
Ved Legoland
Tel. 33 19 26

HOTELS. – *Antique*, Vejlevej 10, 45 b.; *Hotel vis-à-vis*, Astvej 10, 240 b.

The little town of Billund lies in Central Jutland on the road to Vejle. It is the headquarters of the "Legoland A/S", the factory which produces Lego plastic bricks for children, which are famous the world over.

"Lego" is in Latin "I read" or "I put together". The inventor of the bricks, Ole Kirk Christiansen did not know that. He composed the name from two Danish words "leg godt" (play well). Like many Danes Ole Kirk Christiansen was unemployed in the 1930s at the time of the world economic crisis. The cabinet-maker from the little-known village of Billund had the idea of producing toys of wood which would arouse the imagination of children. The present factory was founded in 1932. In the middle of the 1950s the firm developed plastic bricks which can be locked together, according a building system, into houses, etc.

Designers of the firm had often made large coloured models from Lego bricks for fairs and exhibitions and these were admired by many people. This led to the establishment of a park with miniature buildings made of Lego bricks. On 7 June 1968 ***Legoland Park** was opened near Billund. (Open: 1 May–15 Sept. 10 a.m.–8 p.m.; 16 Sept.–31 Oct. 10 a.m.–5 p.m.; 1 Nov.–30 Apr. Sat. and Sun. 10 a.m.–5 p.m.; closed between Christmas and New Year; admission fee.) From the extensive site which was originally a barren area of heathland, there came into being a large leisure park which included various complexes. Every year about a million people visit this park. The central feature is "Miniland"; here the area has been converted into a landscape with mountains and lakes. Installations and buildings from all over the world – such as a circular canal tour in Amsterdam, Eremitage Castle in "Dyrehaven", near Copenhagen or the starting-ramp of the Columbia space shuttle – are imitated in Lego bricks on a scale 1:20. S of this area we come to "Lego Safari" with elephants, lions, zebras and other animals, and to the N a traffic school for children.

Round this central complex are grouped "Fabuland" (merry-go-rounds, cars for children), the Wild West town of "Legoredo" with an imitation of the Monument

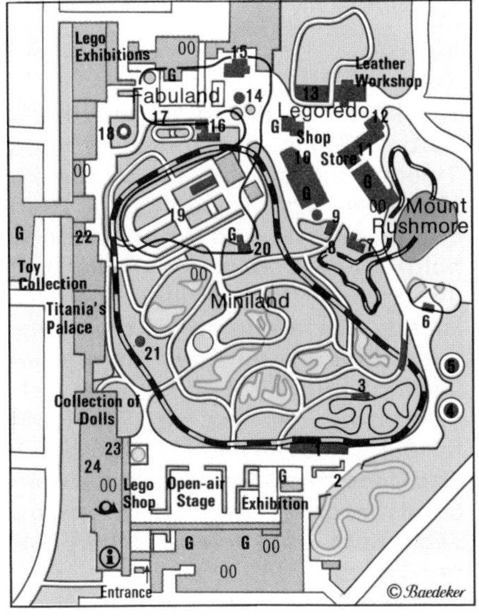

Legoland

1 Lego-train
2 Mini boats
3 Lego Safari
4 Lego-copter
5 Caterpillar (merry-go-round)
6 Timber ride (slide)
7 Gold-mine
8 Mine Train
9 Indian Camp
10 Sheriff's office
11 Legoredo News (press)
12 Photo studio
13 Pony rides
14 Fabuland merry-go-round
15 Lego-games tables
16 Gondola
17 Fabuland cars
18 Legoland planes
19 Traffic school
20 Monorail
21 Lego-top (observation tower)
22 Educational exhibition
23 Puppet theatre
24 Laquerwork pictures collection

G Refreshments
00 Toilets

of the Presidents on Mount Rushmore in the United States (George Washington, Thomas Jefferson, Abraham Lincoln, Theodore Roosevelt), as well as a puppet collection (puppets and puppet rooms) and a toy collection (including mechanical toys).

Of special interest is "Titania's Palace", a palace created by the Englishman Sir Nevile Wilkinson for his little daughter – the girl believed that she had seen elves in the garden. The palace was intended as a dwelling for the fairy queen Titania, her husband Oberon and their seven children. This palace, the rooms of which are furnished with valuable furniture, was auctioned in 1978 by Christie's in London and set up in 1980 in Legoland Park after careful restoration.

Regular exhibitions take place in the park. There are restaurants and shops. The former Esso Motor Hotel, which the Legoland firm continues under the name "vis-à-vis", is linked to the park by a footbridge.

The whole complex is a delight for every age, but for children especially a place of enchantment.

Legoland toys

. . . and animals made from Lego bricks

Bornholm

District: Bornholms amt
Area: 588 sq. km (227 sq. miles)
Population: 47,000

Turistbureau
Ved Havnen
Box No. 60
DK-3700 Rønne
Tel. (03) 95 08 10

Turistbureau
Jernbanegade 1
DK-3720 Akirkeby
Tel. (03) 97 45 20

Turistbureau
Hammershusvej 2
DK-3770 Allinge-Sandvig
Tel. (03) 98 00 01

Turistbureau
Ejnar Mikkelsensvej 28
DK-3760 Gudhjem
Tel. (03) 98 52 10

Turistbureau
Åsen 4
DK-3730 Neksø
Tel. (3) 99 32 00

Turistbureau
Postgade 15
DK-3740 Svaneke
Tel. (03) 99 63 50

EVENT. – *Bornholm Music Festival* (July–Aug.).

RECREATION and SPORTS. – Hire of bicycles; riding; tennis; golf; fishing; scuba-diving; windsurfing; sailing.

The island of Bornholm lies in the Baltic 37 km (23 miles) off the Swedish coast and about 150 km (95 miles) from Copenhagen. There are ferry services to Rønne on Bornholm from Copenhagen and from Sweden. In the Middle Ages the island was an important trading-post. The present-day population lives mainly by fishing and fish-processing (smoked herrings) and farming, but the ceramic industry is also important. The mild climate and good beaches have led to the development of a lively holiday and tourist trade.

The island consists of a great mass of granite, much of it with only a thin coating of soil; on the N it is bounded by fine, steep cliffs and on the S, E and W by dunes. The interior is partly wooded and partly heathland.

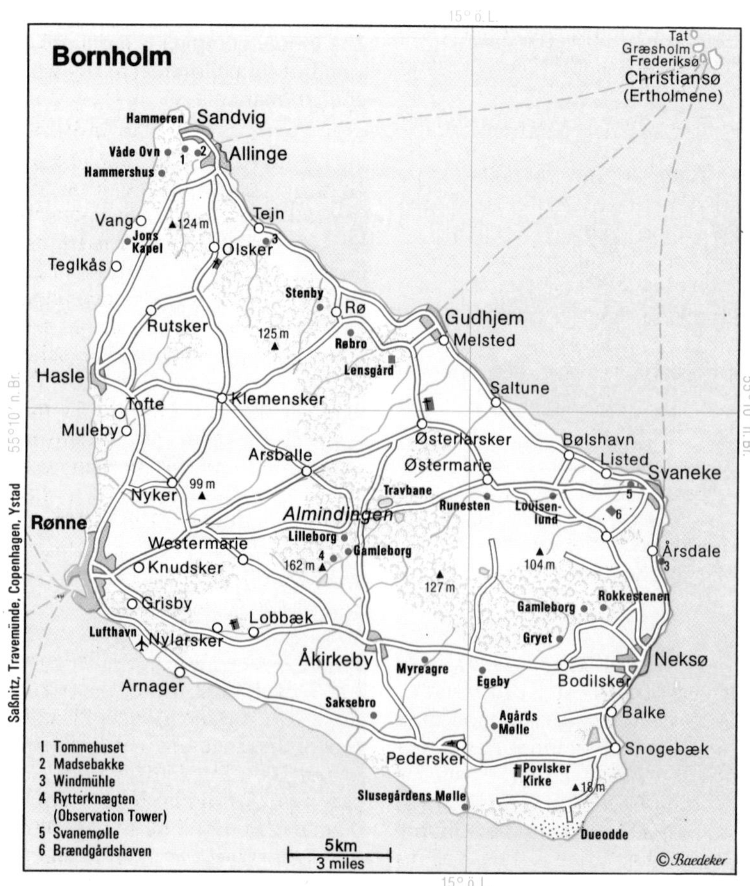

HISTORY. – Until the 2nd c. B.C. Bornholm was inhabited by Burgundians (Burgundarholm). In the 12th c. the island fell to the Archbishopric of Lund (Hammershus Episcopal Castle). The Romanesque round churches (for example Østerlars) were used as fortresses in the war against the piratical Wends. In 1527–75 the island belonged to Lübeck and from 1658 to 1660 to Sweden. Bornholm has been Danish since 1660.

Tour of the island. – The capital and administrative centre of Bornholm is **Rønne** (pop. 15,300; hotels: Fredensborg, 132 b.; Griffen, 284 b.; Ryttergården, 224 b.; May–Oct.; restaurants: Rådhuskroen; Skovly; youth hostel; camp site) which also has the island's airfield and its principal harbour. The harbour is separated into ferry, fishing and yachting basins. There is also a yacht harbour for pleasure-boats farther to the N at the beginning of the northern coastal road (Nordre Kystvej). On a hill in the oldest part of the town stands *St Nicholas's Church* (Music Festival in Aug.), originally 14th c. but largely rebuilt in 1918. Many old houses survive in the roads round the church including the half-timbered house Erichsens Gård (1807) in the Laksegade and the main police station (1745) in the Søndergade. The interesting *Bornholm Museum* (No. 29 Skt.-Mortens-Gade) possesses an art department containing in particular, works by Bornholm painters and natural history collections of the town and island. In the S of Rønne stands the *castle* built about 1650 which has a massive round tower. It was converted into a defence museum where information about the defence of the island can be obtained. In Rønne there are several ceramic factories (guided tours).

8 km (5 miles) NE of Rønne is the *round church of Nyker* (1287) which has two storeys and is the smallest on the island. On the central pillar can be seen paintings representing scenes from the Passion of Christ.

9 km (5½ miles) N of Rønne we come to the *Brogårdsten*, the most important runic stone on Bornholm, which was discovered in 1868 as a coping-stone on a bridge over the Bagå and set up at this spot. The stone which dates from about 1100 bears the following inscription, "Svenger had this stone set up for his father Toste and for his brother Alvaik and for his mother and his sisters".

2 km (1½ miles) farther along the coast is *Hasle* (pop. 6900) a little port with a sturdy 14th c. stone church. In July the Herring Festival is celebrated here. S of the town a sandy beach is bordered by pine woods, and some 7 km (4½ miles) to the N stretches a steep granite coast with a crag known as *Jons Kapel* (John's Chapel; 40 m (31 ft) high).

Following the road to the N one reaches – after a detour to the fishing village of Vang – the twin resorts of **Allinge-Sandvig** (pop. 2100; hotels: Abildgård, in Sandkås, 250 b.; Allinge, 40 b.; Boes-Vang, 68 b.; in Sandvig: Hammersø, 90 b.; Nordland, 43 b.; Pepita, 68 b.; Sandvig, 86 b.; Strandhotel, 76 b.; several holiday apartments; youth hostel; four camp sites), one of the most attractive holiday places on the island ("Sandvig" means "sandy bay"). Tømmehuset (No. 3 Vestergade) in Sandvig houses a little ethnological museum. Outside the cemetery in Allinge stands an obelisk in memory of Russian soldiers who fell in the Second World War and at Borrelyngvej is a little zoo and nature park. There is a rewarding walk to the *Lighthouse of Hammeren* in the N, passing the *Stejleberg* (84 m (276 ft)), the highest cliff on the island. SW of the lighthouse on a rocky plateau lie the ruins of ***Hammershus Castle**. The former castle, built about 1250, was fought for violently on several occasions and then was used as a quarry for building-stone until it was scheduled a protected monument in 1822. There is a magnificent view from the 74 m (240 ft) high cliff. There are interesting boat trips to be made from Hammershus, for example to the *Våde Ovn*, a cave 55 m (180 ft) long and 12 m (40 ft) high. The walk along the footpath to the Slotslyngen woodland is considered one of the most beautiful in Denmark.

Built in the 12th c. and restored in 1950–52 the ***round church of Ols** (*Ols Kirke*) is situated 4 km (2½ miles) S of Allinge. The church, which is dedicated to St Olaf, is 30 m (100 ft) high and is the tallest on Bornholm. Because of the small diameter of the circular nave the church has something of the character of a fortress tower. When the church was restored a ceramic relief by the sculptor Gunnar Hansen ("The Women at the Tomb") was set on the new altar. In the porch are several 16th c. tombstones.

S of Allinge the sea is fringed with cliffs, along which runs a rocky path. Important places are Sandkås, Tejn, Stammershalle, the *Helligdom Cliffs* and the cliffs at Stevelen.

17 km (10 miles) S of Allinge you reach the fishing village of **Gudhjem** (hotels: Feriegården, 62 b.; Gudhjem – apartments; Melstedvej, May–Nov.; restaurants: Bokulhus; Tagskægget; youth hostel; camp site) with a harbour blasted out of the rock. The *Municipal Museum* is housed in the former station building. To the S of the village the open-air *Agricultural Museum* Melstedgård (No. 25 Melstedvej) is recommended.

In the S in **Østerlars**, the village inland from Gudhjem, stands the largest ***round church** of the island; it was built in the 11th c. and dedicated to St Laurence. The central pillar of the round nave is hollow with ribbed vaulting. The space inside, known as the oven, is joined to the rest of the nave by six arcades. On the exterior of the oven can be seen wall-paintings of about 1350 portraying scenes from the Life of Jesus and a picture of the Last Judgment. When the church was restored in 1955 the oven was converted into a baptistery with a granite font.

Round church of St Laurence
in Østerlars on Bornholm

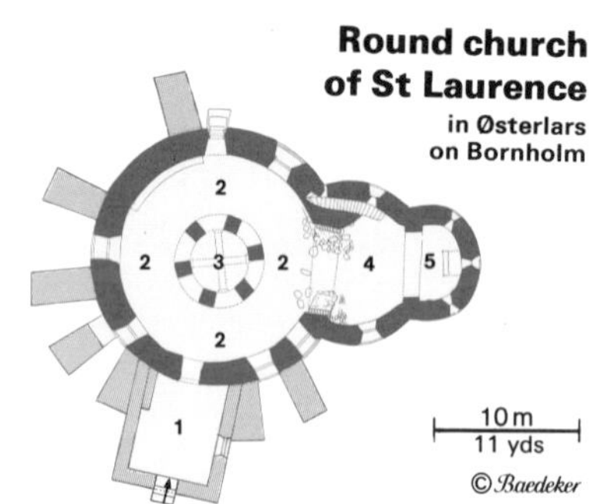

1 Porch
2 Parish room
3 Central pillar
4 Choir
5 Apse

S of Østerlars extends the State Forest of *Almindingen*, planted between 1800 and 1830, with a number of small lakes and the highest hill on the island, the *Rytterknægten* (162 m (530 ft) outlook tower). Twenty minutes to the N are the ruins of *Lilleborg Castle* which ranked with Hammershus as one of the two most important fortresses in Bornholm. 7 km ($4\frac{1}{2}$ miles) E

Ruins of Hammershus Castle

Round church of Ols

Coastal clffs, the "Helligdomsklipper"

of Gudhjem are the *Randkløveskår Cliffs* and 8 km (5 miles) further the picturesque little fishing town of **Svaneke** (pop. 1200; hotel: Siemens Gård, 89 b., Apr.–Oct.; youth hostel; camp sites) with old houses and a post-mill of 1634. 3 km (2 miles) SW lies the *Brændesgårdshaven* amusement park.

The road S passes the beautiful wooded *Paradisbakkerne* (Paradise Hills) to the port of **Neksø** (pop. 8950; hotels: Balka Søbad, 116 b.; Holms Hotel, 100 b.; Neksø Sømandshjem, 30 b.; Harbour Festival at beginning of August), the largest fishing port on the island. The warehouse at the port is now furnished as a museum. Although granite is exposed in the N of Bornholm near Neksø, sandstone forms the subsoil. Many roads are, therefore, paved with sandstone and the garden walls are made of red sandstone. 3 km (2 miles) S is Balke with a beach of fine sand and 7 km ($4\frac{1}{2}$ miles) beyond this the southern tip of the island is reached; here are the *Dueodde Lighthouse*, gently rolling sand-dunes and a beautiful beach.

The only town on Bornholm not on the coast is **Åkirkeby** (pop. 7380; hotels: Pension Breidablik, 28 b.; Dams på Bakken, 44 b.; Rosengården, 46 b.; restaurant: Christianshøy Kroen; holiday apartments; camp site) 15 km (10 miles) inland. It has a handsome 12th c. stave church (font with carved decoration and a runic inscription). The Church of the Rosary (Rosenkranskirken; 1932; R.C.) is one of the most attractive modern churches in Denmark. The road to Rønne (16 km (10 miles)) runs via *Nylars* where stands the latest and best preserved of Bornholm's round churches. In this church can be seen wall-paintings representing in many scenes the Creation and the Fall of Man. In the porch hangs a huge cross dating from the Renaissance.

NE of Bornholm in the Baltic lies the group of islands called *Ertholmene* (Pea Islands); they can be reached by boat from Allinge, Gudhjem and Svaneke. On the main island of **Christiansø** there are extensive fortifications which were set up by Christian V in 1684. When Christiansø lost its importance in the 19th c. as a naval base, poets and painters settled there. The neighbouring island of *Frederiksø* was formerly notorious as a place of exile; on *Græsholm* there is a bird sanctuary.

It should be noted that Bornholm, renowned for its round churches is a wonderful place for all those who want a holiday that is "different", a charmed spot for walkers, historians, bird-watchers and those who love fishing and sailing. The climate is attractive and the inhabitants friendly, but if you want to see it before it becomes "popular" and spoilt, go soon as it is rapidly becoming an "in" place for the continental set.

Copenhagen (København)

Zealand
District: Københavns amt
Population: 620,000 (with suburbs 1,400,000)
Postal code: DK–1000–2900
Telephone code: 01 (02 suburbs)

Danmarks Turistrad
(Danish Tourist Board)
H. C. Andersens Boulevard 22
DK–1553 København V
Tel. 11 13 25

Turistbureau
Nørregade 7A
DK–1165 København K
Tel. 13 70 07

Turistbureau
DK–2800 Lyngby
Tel. (02) 88 66 11

Accommodation Register:
Kiosk P Central Station
Tel. 00451/2 28 80 (Mon.–Fri. 9 a.m.–5 p.m.)

Forenede Danske Motorejers (FDM)
(*Federation of Danish Motorists*)
Blegdamsvej 124
DK–2100 København Ø
Tel. 38 21 12
(Mon.–Fri. 9 a.m.–5 p.m.)

Student Information (DIS)
Skindergade 28,
DK–1159 København K
Tel. 11 00 44

Youth Tourist Information "Use It"
Radhusstræde 13,
Tel. 15 65 18

EMBASSIES. – *United Kingdom*: Kastelsvey 36–40, DK–2100 København Ø, tel. 26 46 00; *United States*: Dag Hammarskjolds Allé 24, tel. 42 31 44; *Canada*: Kr. Bernikowsgade 1, DK–1105 København K, tel. 12 22 99.

HOTELS. – CITY CENTRE: *Absalon*, Helgolandsgade 15, 423 b.; **Hôtel d'Angleterre*, Kongens Nytorv 34, 249 b.; *Missionshotel*, Ansgar, Colbjørnsensgade 29, 150 b.; *Ascot*, Strudiestræde 57, 90 b.; *Astoria*, Banegårdspladsen 4, 153 b.; *Avenue*, Åboulevard 29, 128 b.; *Carlton*, Halmtorvet 14, 100 b.; *Centrum*, Helgolandsgade 14, 125 b.; *City*, Peder Skramsgade 24, 161 b.; *Copenhagen Admiral*, Toldbodgade 24, 815 b.; *Cosmopole*, Colbjørnsensgade 11, 203 b.; *Dania*, Istedgade 3, 100 b.; *Esplanaden*, Bredgade 78, 104 b.; *Excelsior*, Colbjørnsensgade 4, 96 b.; *Globetrotter*, Engvej 171, 305 b.; *Grand Hotel*, Vesterbrogade 9A, 204 b.; *Missionshotel Hebron*, Helgolandsgade 4, 216 b.; *Ibsens Hotel*, Vendersgade 25, 86 b.; *Imperial*, Vester Farimagsgade 9, 301 b.; **Kong Frederik*, Vester Voldgade 23–27, 221 b.; **Ladbroke Palace Hotel*, Rådhuspladsen 57, 293 b.; *Mercur*, Vester Farimagsgade 17, 210 b.; *Missionshotel Nebo*, Istedgade 6, 145 b.; *71 Nyhaven Hotel*, Hyhaven 71, 110 b. (with Lightship Restaurant "Fyrskibet"); *Opera*, Tordenskoldsgade 15, 106 b.; *Østerport*, Oslo Plads 5, 136 b.; **Park Hotel*, Jarmers Plads 3, 107 b.; **Plaza Sheraton*, Bernstorffgade 4, 156 b.; **Richmond*, Vester Farimagsgade 3, 237 b.; **Royal Hotel*, Hammerichsgade 1, 453 b.; *Saga*, Colbjørnsensgade 20, 100 b.; *Savoy*, Vesterbrogade 34, 142 b.; *Scandic Hotel*, Kettevej 4, 450 b.; **Scandinavia*, Amager Boulevard 70, 875 b.; *Selandia*, Helgolandsgade 12, 160 b.; **Sheraton Copenhagen*, Vester Søgade 6, 840 b.; *Sophie Amalie*, Sankt Annae Plads 21, 250 b.; *Tre Falke*, Falkoner Allé 9, 280 b.; *Triton*, Helgolandsgade 7–11, 236 b.; *Union*, Colbjørnsensgade 7, 180 b.; *Viking*, Bredgade 65, 165 b.; *Webers Hotel*, Vesterbrogade 11b, 141 b.; *Westend*, Helgolandsgade 3, 194 b. – TO THE NORTH: *Hellerup Parkhotel*, Hellerup, Strandvejen 203, 128 b.; *Gentofte*, Gentofte, Gentoftegade 29, 127 b. – TO THE WEST **Tre Falke*, Falkoner Allé 9, 295 b.; *Esso Motor Hotel*, Hvidovre, Kettevej 4, 333 b.; *Glostrup Park Hotel*, Glostrup, Hovedvejen 41, 110 b.; *Broadway*, Vesterbrogade 97, 70 b. – TO THE SOUTH: *SAS Globetrotter Hotel*, Engvej 171, 165 b.; *Danhotel*, Kastruplundgade 15, 511 b.; *Bel Air*, Løjtegårdsvej 99, 426 b.; all near Kastrup Airport; *Scandis*, Brydes Allé 21, 216 b.

YOUTH HOSTELS. – Herbergvejen 8, DK-2700 Brønshøj, 336 b., 29 family rooms; Rådvad, DK-2800 Lyngby, 94 b.; *Vesterbro Ungdomsgård*, Absalongade 8, DK-1658 København V, 160 b.; *Sleep In*, Bellahøj.

CAMP SITES. – *Absalon*, Korsdalsvej, DK-2160 Rødovre; *Bellahøj*, Hvidkildevej, DK-2400 København NV; *Nærum*, Ravnebakken, DK-2850 Nærum; *Strandmøllen*, Strandvejen, DK-2930 Klampenborg; *Sundbyvester*, Kongelundsvej 54, DK-2300 Sundbyvester.

RESTAURANTS. – *Bernstorff*, Bernstorffgade 7; *Den Sorte Ravn*, Nyhaven 14; *Det Grønne Køkken* (vegetarian), Larsbjørnstræde 10; *Det Lille Apotek*, Store Kannikestræde 15; *Kong Hans*, Vingådsstræde 6; *Krogs Fiske Restaurant*, Gammel Strand 38; *L'Alsace*, Ny Østergade 9; *Langelinie Pavillionen*, Langelinie; *Lumskebugten*, Esplanaden 21; *Sejlskibet Isefjord* (schooner), Nyhaven near No. 55; *Skt. Gertruds Kloster*, Hauser Plads 32; *Vendersborg*, Nørre Farimagsgade 57; *Viking Carver*, Råhuspladsen 57. – IN KASTRUP: *Allekroen*, Alleen 54; *SAS Royal Restaurant*, at the Airport.

EVENTS. – *New Year Concert* (Jan.); *Queen's Birthday Parade* (16 Apr.); *Jazz Festival* (July/Aug.); *International Rowing Regatta* (July).

The descriptive text on Copenhagen in this Baedeker Guide to Denmark is purposely kept short because in the series of Baedeker City Guides there is a comprehensive guide to Copenhagen.

****Copenhagen, the capital of the Kingdom of Denmark lies on the E side of the island of Zealand and on the island of Amager in the Øresund. The conurbation of Copenhagen (Store København) is a municipal agglomeration which came into being through the incorporation of a number of places including Frederiksberg. With a total area of almost 570 sq. km (220 sq. miles) and a population of about 1.4 million,**

Town Hall Square, Copenhagen

Copenhagen is the largest city in Denmark. The seat of the Government and Parliament (Folketing) and the residence of the Royal Family are in the city.

Copenhagen is the largest commercial and industrial city in Denmark. There are shipyards, motor works, a cable works, textiles and clothing factories, chemicals, foodstuffs and breweries (Carlsberg and Tuborg). The porcelain industry (Royal Porcelain Factory and Bing og Grøndahl) arose from the discovery of large china-clay deposits on the island of Bornholm in 1755. Copenhagen owes its importance as a port of transhipment to its position at the entrance to the Baltic. The quays have a length of 44 km (26 miles). A bridge over the port (Knippelsbro) leads to the island of Amager.

Copenhagen is also the cultural centre of Denmark. Of the many theatres the Royal Theatre is the most versatile; it mounts theatrical, operatic and ballet productions. Although most of the theatrical performances are in Danish, the Mermaid Theatre (NY Vestergade 7) puts on all its plays in English. Every week concerts take place in the concert hall of the Danish Radio (Julius Thomsens Gade); these are given either by the Radio Symphony Orchestra, the Radio Concert Orchestra or the Radio Big Band. The Zealand Symphony Orchestra gives concerts in the concert hall in Tivoli. In Copenhagen there are also many jazz clubs and bars with music; an annual jazz festival takes place in which Danish and foreign jazz musicians take part. There is ample provision in Copenhagen for those interested in art. Besides the two main museums – the Ny Carlsberg Glyptothek and the State Museum of Art – there are a number of private art galleries in the "Latin Quarter" round the university and in Nyhavn there are very many antique shops.

HISTORY. – Copenhagen is first mentioned as *"Havn"* in 1043. In 1167 Valdemar I gave the fishing and trading settlement to Bishop Absalon. He had the fortress of Slotsholmen built as a protection against Wendish pirates (remains can still be seen beneath Christiansborg). Round the fortress arose the place known as *"Kobmanns Havn"* (merchants' port) which soon developed into a thriving trade centre and in 1254 received its municipal charter. In 1416 control of Copenhagen passed to King Eric of Pomerania who made it his capital. From 1397 the town formed the centre of the three united kingdoms – Denmark, Norway and Sweden. The Reformation came to Denmark in 1536 and the Lutheran doctrine was declared the State religion. From this time Copenhagen

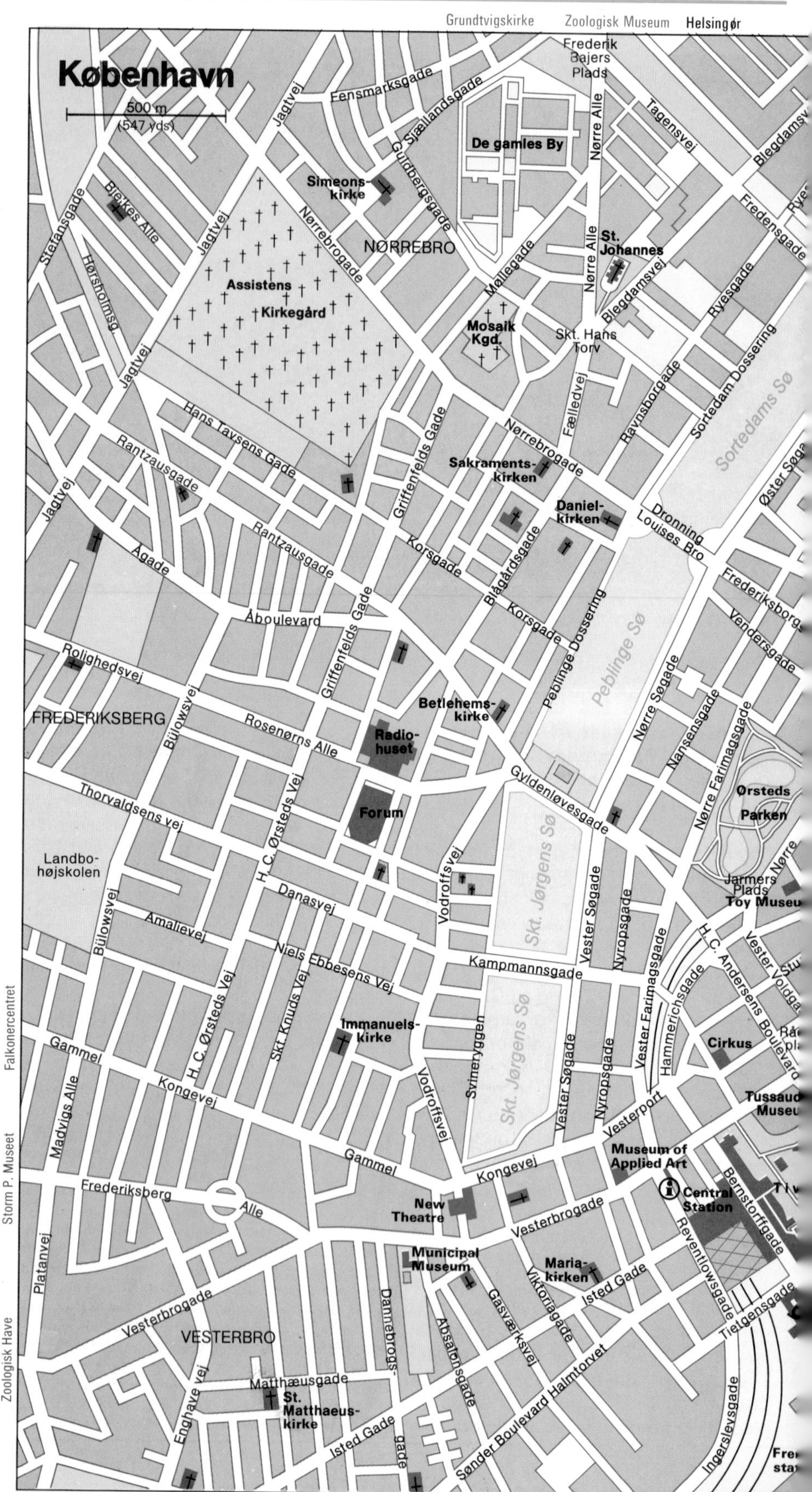
København
500 m
(547 yds)
Grundtvigskirke
Zoologisk Museum
Helsingør
Frederik Bajers Plads
De gamles By
Simeons-kirke
NØRREBRO
Assistens Kirkegård
Mosaik Kgd.
St. Johannes
Skt. Hans Torv
Sakraments-kirken
Daniel-kirken
Sortedams Sø
Dronning Louises Bro
Peblinge Sø
Betlehems-kirke
Radio-huset
Forum
FREDERIKSBERG
Landbo-højskolen
Skt. Jørgens Sø
Ørsteds Parken
Jarmers Plads
Toy Museum
Immanuels-kirke
Cirkus
Tussaud Museum
Museum of Applied Art
Central Station
New Theatre
Municipal Museum
Maria-kirken
VESTERBRO
St. Matthaeus-kirke
Falkonercentret
Storm P. Museet
Roskilde
Zoologisk Have
Rødby
Rødby
Fensmarksgade
Sjællandsgade
Guldbergsgade
Jagtvej
Nørrebrogade
Nørre Alle
Tagensvej
Blegdamsvej
Fredensgade
Ryesgade
Møllegade
Fælledvej
Ravnsborggade
Sortedam Dossering
Stefansgade
Brokes Alle
Hørsholmsg.
Hans Tavsens Gade
Rantzausgade
Ågade
Åboulevard
Griffenfelds Gade
Korsgade
Blågårdsgade
Peblinge Dossering
Frederiksborggade
Vendersgade
Rolighedsvej
Bülowsvej
Rosenørns Alle
Thorvaldsens vej
H.C. Ørsteds Vej
Gyldenløvesgade
Nørre Søgade
Nansensgade
Nørre Farimagsgade
Danasvej
Vodroffsvej
Amalievej
Niels Ebbesens Vej
Kampmannsgade
Vester Søgade
Nyropsgade
Vester Farimagsgade
Hammerichsgade
H.C. Andersens Boulevard
Vester Voldgade
Skt. Knuds Vej
Svineryggen
Gammel Kongevej
Madvigs Alle
Vesterport
Frederiksberg Alle
Platanvej
Vesterbrogade
Bernstorffgade
Reventlowsgade
Viktoriagade
Gasværksvej
Istedgade
Absalonsgade
Dannebrogsgade
Tietgensgade
Matthæusgade
Enghavevej
Søndre Boulevard
Halmtorvet
Ingerslevsgade

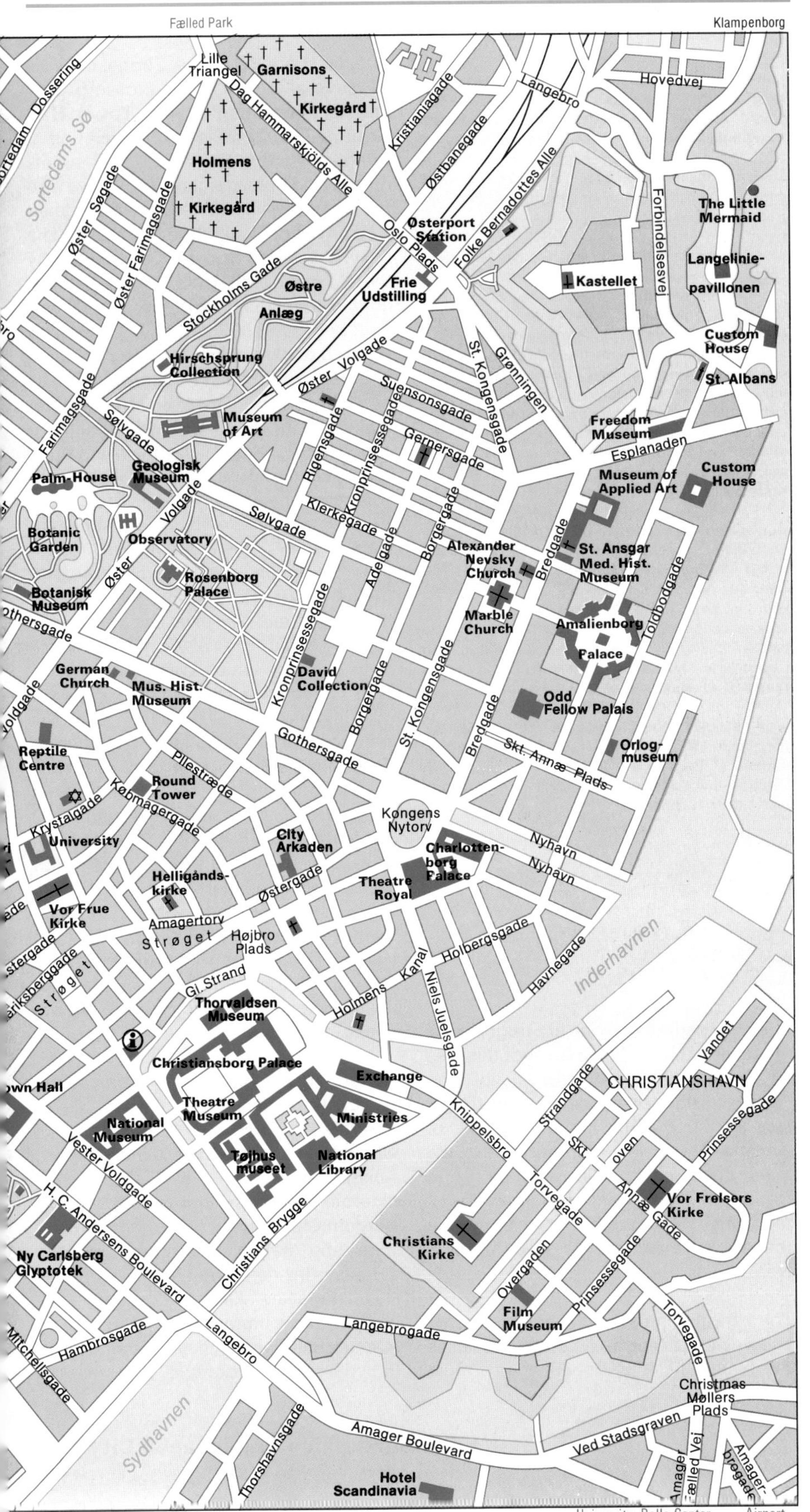
Fælled Park
Klampenborg
Lille Triangel
Garnisons Kirkegård
Holmens Kirkegård
Dag Hammarskjölds Alle
Kristianiagade
Østbanegade
Langebro
Hovedvej
Sortedams Sø
Øster Søgade
Øster Farimagsgade
Stockholms Gade
Østre Anlæg
Østerport Station
Oslo Plads
Folke Bernadottes Alle
Forbindelsesvej
The Little Mermaid
Langelinie-pavillonen
Kastellet
Frie Udstilling
Custom House
St. Albans
Hirschsprung Collection
Øster Volgade
Suensonsgade
St. Kongensgade
Grønningen
Farimagsgade
Sølvgade
Museum of Art
Gernersgade
Freedom Museum
Esplanaden
Geologisk Museum
Palm-House
Rigensgade
Kronprinsessegade
Museum of Applied Art
Custom House
Botanic Garden
Observatory
Volgade
Sølvgade
Klerkegade
Borgergade
Adelgade
Alexander Nevsky Church
Bredgade
St. Ansgar Med. Hist. Museum
Toldbodgade
Botanisk Museum
Rosenborg Palace
Marble Church
Amalienborg Palace
Gothersgade
German Church
Mus. Hist. Museum
Kronprinsessegade
David Collection
Borgergade
St. Kongensgade
Bredgade
Odd Fellow Palais
Orlog-museum
Skt. Annæ Plads
Reptile Centre
Pilestræde
Gothersgade
Round Tower
Købmagergade
Krystalgade
University
Kongens Nytorv
City Arkaden
Charlotten-borg Palace
Nyhavn
Nyhavn
Helligånds-kirke
Østergade
Theatre Royal
Vor Frue Kirke
Amagertorv
Strøget
Højbro Plads
Holbergsgade
Havnegade
Inderhavnen
Gl. Strand
Holmens Kanal
Niels Juelsgade
Strøget
Thorvaldsen Museum
Christiansborg Palace
Exchange
Vandet
CHRISTIANSHAVN
Theatre Museum
Ministries
Knippelsbro
Strandgade
Prinsessegade
National Museum
Vester Voldgade
Tøjhus museet
National Library
Skt. Annæ Gade
Vor Frelsers Kirke
Torvegade
H. C. Andersens Boulevard
Christians Brygge
Christians Kirke
Ny Carlsberg Glyptotek
Overgaden oven Vandet
Prinsessegade
Film Museum
Langebrogade
Torvegade
Hambrosgade
Langebro
Mitchellsgade
Sydhavnen
Thorshavnsgade
Amager Boulevard
Ved Stadsgraven
Christmas Møllers Plads
Amager Fælled Vej
Amager-brogade
Hotel Scandinavia
University, Bella Center,
Airport

became the capital. The heavily fortified town was provided with fine buildings in the time of the popular King Christian IV (1588–1648) and successfully resisted attacks by the Swedes in 1658 and 1659 and by the combined English, Dutch and Swedish fleets in 1700. The old town of Copenhagen was destroyed in 1728 and again in 1795 by fire, and in 1807 suffered considerable damage by bombardment from the British Royal Navy.

Under Christian VIII (1839–48) the city received a comprehensive statute of self-government. After the change from an absolute monarchy into a constitutional government was made, Copenhagen became, in 1849, the seat of the new government and the function of the city as the political hub of the country was made stronger. Copenhagen then reached out beyond its defensive walls. In 1867 the fortifications were demolished and several parks arose on the area where the ramparts had been. The opening of a free port in 1894 gave a boost to Copenhagen's economy and transport and the inauguration of Kastrup Airport in 1924 had a decisive impulse.

During the First World War many refugees came to Copenhagen, especially after the Russian Revolution in 1917. At the beginning of the Second World War Denmark declared itself neutral, but in 1940 the country was occupied by German troops. Resistance organisations were formed, which were especially concerned that Danish Jews, living principally in Copenhagen, were able to escape to Sweden, via Korsør. On the evening of 4 May 1945 the German capitulation was announced. The first post-war years were difficult for the city because of heavy destruction, but in 1948 the Marshall Plan brought relief. At the end of the 1950s there was a boom. In 1962 "Strøget" became one of the first traffic-free pedestrian streets in Europe.

Sightseeing in Copenhagen

The busy pedestrian zone of Strøget forms the centre of the city. To the S of this area lie Tivoli and the "Castle Island" (an island surrounded by canals). On the far side of the harbour is the district of Christianshavn. The northern part of the inner city extends as far as Langelinie at the entrance to the port. On either side of the lakes which border the inner city on the west are the districts of Frederiksberg, Nørrebro and Bispebjerg.

The 1.8 km (1 mile) long pedestrian zone, known as ****Strøget** (= lines), traverses the inner city. It is Copenhagen's most popular shopping venue. Strøget consists of several roads criss-crossing one another, beginning at the **Town Hall Square** (*Rådhuspladsen*) and ending at Kongens Nytorv. Some adjoining streets on the N (Købmagergade, etc.) have also been pedestrianised. The streets are lined by many shops, boutiques and cafés. The busy Town Hall Square is dominated by the ****Town Hall** (*Rådhus*; open daily; guided tours; admission fee) which was built between 1892 and 1905 and which is based partly on the Italian Renaissance and partly on medieval Danish architecture. The tower is 106 m (350 ft) high. The building is richly adorned with sculpture and painting. Above the main entrance can be seen a figure of Bishop Absalon in gilded copper and in the Great Hall are busts of Martin Nyrop, the architect who designed the building (d. 1921), the sculptor Bertel Thorvaldsen (1770–1840), Hans Christian Andersen (1805–75) and the physicist Niels Bohr (1885–1962). The *World Clock* at the main entrance which was designed and constructed by Jens Olsen (1955) shows not only the time and the date but various astronomical constellations (it is open to the public). On Town Hall Square stands the *Dragon Fountain* (sculpture "Contest of the Bull with the Lindwurm" by Joachim Skovgaard, 1923), a memorial to Hans Christian Andersen and, in front of the Palace Hotel on a stone column 12 m (40 ft) high, two *Lurplayers* in bronze by Siegfried Wagner (1914). NE of Town Hall Square Strøget widens out and forms the Gammeltorv and Nytorv squares. On the latter can be seen old patrician houses of about 1800.

Continuing along Strøget we come to the ***Church of the Holy Ghost** (*Helligåndskirke*); and the *Helligåndshus* which formerly belonged to a monastery. Amagertorv No. 6 is believed to be the oldest in the town; it was built in 1616 by Burgomaster Hansen in Dutch Baroque style and has a beautiful sandstone gateway. Inside is the showroom of the Royal Porcelain Factory. No. 10 is the well-known Illums Bollinghus store (Danish handwork and handicrafts. Passing the Stork Fountain one reaches

Fountain outside Copenhagen City Hall

**Kongens Nytorv (King's New Market), a large square laid out at the end of the 17th c. In the centre of the square stands an equestrian statue of Christian V. On the S side of the square is the *Theatre Royal* which was erected in Late Renaissance style between 1872 and 1874. In front of the main entrance are bronze memorials to the Danish comic dramatist Ludwig Holberg (1684–1754) and the tragic dramatist Adam Dehlenschläger (1779–1850).

A good starting-point for a walk round the old town is Nytorv. In the square are the former *Law Courts* which are considered to be the finest work of Danish Classicism. N from here by way of Gammeltorv and Nørregade we come to the **Church of Our Lady** (*Vor Frue Kirke*). The present church is the sixth to be built on the same site. After the fifth church was burned down by the bombardment of the town in 1807 the architect Christian Friedrich Hansen created the present classical building in 1811–29. In the vaulted two-storeyed interior can be seen numerous works by Thorvaldsen; behind the altar his well-known figure of Christ and along the walls the Twelve Apostles. The font has a figure of a kneeling angel. The characteristic square tower with a flat roof is topped by a gleaming cross. To the N of the church beyond Bispetorv is the main building of the ***University**, founded by Christian I in 1479. The present building, which is influenced by the style of English university buildings, was erected by Peter Malling between 1831 and 1836. The assembly hall, with historic paintings, and the entrance hall with frescoes by Constantin Hansen (mythological themes) dating from about 1850 are interesting. On the other side of Nørregade stands one of the oldest churches of Copenhagen, *St Peter's*, originally Late Gothic and restored in 1816. It has a 78 m (255 ft) high tower. Inside the church and in the herb garden there are a number of tombs.

From Nørregade narrow lanes lead into *Fiolstræde*, a parallel street with many bookshops and antique-dealers. In Krystalgade can be seen the *Synagogue*, built in 1833 in yellow brick. Passing this we come into *Købmagergade* (shopping street) with the ***Round Tower** (*Rundetårn*), 36 m (120 ft) high and 15 m (50 ft) in diameter, which was built as an observatory in 1642 and which contains a small collection of material relating to the 16th c. Swedish astronomer Tycho Brahe (see Notable Figures). The platform on the top from which there is a magnificent panorama of Copenhagen is reached by a wide spiral ramp. The tower is the one referred to in Hans Andersen's story "The tinder Box": "eyes as big as the Round Tower . . .". We continue the walk by way of Skindergade and Kejsergade to Gråbrødretorv, one of Copenhagen's most charming squares with brightly coloured old houses. From here it is a short distance back to Nytorv by way of Strøget.

Starting from Town Hall Square and crossing H. C. Andersens Boulevard we come to the famous amusement park ****Tivoli**, "the world-famous pleasure gardens which many towns have tried unsuccessfully to copy. It is best to enter by the main gate in Vesterbrogade, especially in the evening and at night to

The Chinese Tower, Tivoli

Strøget: Pedestrian precinct

Tivoli: main entrance

get the full effect of its illuminated grounds with their flower-beds and lake, but it is equally a delightful place to go to during the day when it is very quiet and peaceful, perhaps to have an omelette in Faergekroen which, more or less, sits in the lake. Or if you prefer to go in the evening, go early so that you can enjoy all the pleasures on offer, so many that it is impossible to enjoy everything in one visit: the open-air concerts held each afternoon and evening opposite the main entrance, the brass-band concerts in front of the Opera Hall, both of which start the evening off from time to time with the "Champagne Galop" which was written by one of the former conductors and starts with a loud "plop" to the great joy of all present. The Concert Hall Orchestra plays every evening often free of charge, while the orchestra gives way to a large symphony orchestra on Tuesdays or to plays, opera and ballet, often with world-famous artists. Week nights at 7 and 10.30 (10 on Saturdays and Sundays) you can watch a magnificent programme of musical/circus turns on the open-air stage of "Plaenen" which lies almost half-way between the main entrance and "Concerthallen". There are seats for which you must pay, but the vast majority stand gasping as daring acrobats walk the swaying tightropes over their head. Whatever you are doing, hurry back to the Mime Theatre in time to watch the last Commedia dell'Arte show in Europe at 7.45 or 9.45. You will be very lucky if you can find a seat for there are very few and those are usually reserved for the elderly and infirm with children crowding every space in front. The performance is a sheer delight from the moment when the peacock's fan folds to start and throughout the next half hour which is enchanting. As the show is in mime it does not matter what language you speak; you can enjoy the antics of the Clown, the dancing of Columbine and Harlequin or laugh at some other comedy because you, like time, will be standing still and be back in Fairyland.

Every Saturday and Sunday and sometimes on Wednesdays the Tivoli Boy Guards march round and through the park accompanied by a band and, if you begin to feel tired, there is a little train which wanders through the gardens and past the illuminated flower-beds, fountains and lake to give you a rest. If you are hungry, there is a wealth of restaurants from the de luxe to the modest where you can find anything from an epicure's meal to hot

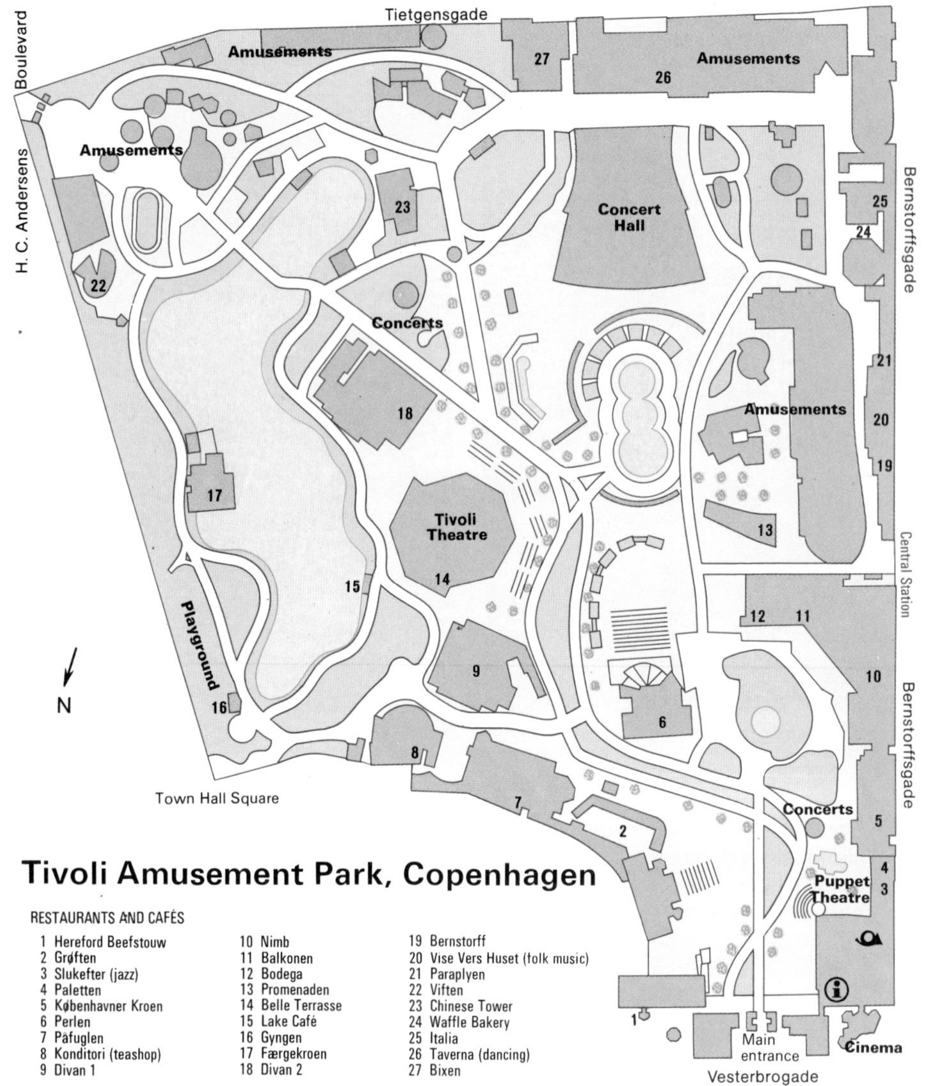

Tivoli Amusement Park, Copenhagen

RESTAURANTS AND CAFÉS

1 Hereford Beefstouw
2 Grøften
3 Slukefter (jazz)
4 Paletten
5 Københavner Kroen
6 Perlen
7 Påfuglen
8 Konditori (teashop)
9 Divan 1
10 Nimb
11 Balkonen
12 Bodega
13 Promenaden
14 Belle Terrasse
15 Lake Café
16 Gyngen
17 Færgekroen
18 Divan 2
19 Bernstorff
20 Vise Vers Huset (folk music)
21 Paraplyen
22 Viften
23 Chinese Tower
24 Waffle Bakery
25 Italia
26 Taverna (dancing)
27 Bixen

dogs or beer and sandwiches. If you prefer the noise of a fair-ground, then you can find that, too, for, at the side of the alleys leading from the entrance in Bernstorffsgade right round the back of the park behind Concerthallen and ending roughly at the entrance at the corner of Tietgensgade and H. C. Andersens Boulevard, there are every kind of fair-ground entertainment from the "Big Dipper" to the roundabouts, hall of mirrors and chambers of horrors to shooting-galleries and games of chance all to the sound of music. Every Wednesday night at 11.15 and Saturdays and Sundays at 11.45 everyone waits for the firework display to provide a wonderful finale. All of which adds point to the story, no doubt apocryphal, of the man who, when asked if he knew anything about Denmark, replied, "Not much. All I know is that it is a country in the north with a capital called Tivoli."

In the new entrance from H. C. Andersens Boulevard can be found three other attractions (Hans Christian Andersen Castle). ***Louis Tussaud's Waxworks** (open: daily 10 a.m.–4.30 p.m.; in summer until midnight; admission fee) are housed in the entrance building. Here can be seen representations of Danish and foreign personalities. In Hans Christian Andersen Castle can also be found a *Holograph*

Tivoli Amusement Park

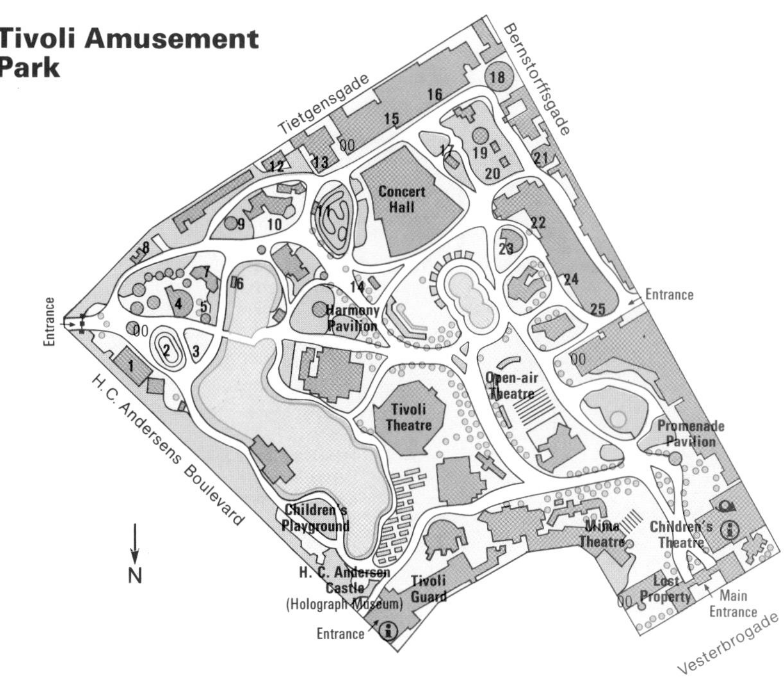

AMUSEMENTS
1 Flying Carpet
2 "Ladybird"
3 Children's Giant Wheel
4 "Caterpillar"
5 The Viking
6 Boating-pool
7 "Mini Go-Go"
8 Glass House
9 "Traffic Roundabout"
10 Woodland Roller
11 Vintage Cars
12 "Red Dragon" swing
13 Haunted House
14 Tram, line 8
15 Dodgems
16 Blue Cars
17 "Little Flyers"
18 Roundabout
19 Odin Expressway
20 Merry-go-round
21 Galleys
22 Tub track
23 Balloon Swing
24 Slide
25 "Devil's Fire"

Museum ("Hologramme"; three-dimensional effects are obtained by means of special lighting technique). Artists and scientists from all over the world have co-operated in the permanent exhibition (Holograph World; open: daily 1 May–15 Sept. 10 a.m.–midnight; rest of year 11 a.m.–8 p.m.; admission fee).

To the S at Vesterbrogade 8 stands a many-storeyed house where Danish craftsmen and craft firms have conducted a shop for 50 years under the name of ***"den permanente".** Today the undertaking is run on a completely commercial basis. At Vesterbrogade 59 can be found the *Municipal Museum* (Kobenhavns Bymuseet; open: 1 May–30 Sept. Tues.–Sun. 10 a.m.–4 p.m.; 1 Oct.–30 April Tues.–Sun. 1–4 p.m.) in which the visitor can gain a general idea of the history of the city. Room 14 contains the Soren-Kierkegaard Collection which was inaugurated in 1960.

From Tivoli H. C. Andersens Boulevard leads SE to Dante Square (Dante Plads). Here stands the ****Ny Carlsberg Glyptothek** (open: 1 May–31 Aug. Tues.–Sun. 10 a.m.–4 p.m.; 1 Sept.–30 Apr. Tues.–Sat. noon–3 p.m., Sun. 10 a.m.–4 p.m.; Wed. and Sun. admission free), in front of which rises the *Dante Column*, a gift from the city of Rome. The museum contains the collections of Carl and Ottilia Jacobsen (Carlsberg Brewery), who presented them for public exhibition in 1888. The building was erected in two phases, the first part in 1892–97 with three wings and a richly decorated façade facing Dante Square, the second in 1901–06. The central feature, known as the Winter Garden, is a pillared marble hall in the style of an ancient temple court. The front building contains the *modern collection*. To the left of the entrance hall are rooms containing works by Danish sculptors, particularly by two pupils of Thorvaldsen – H. V. Bissen

MAIN FLOOR: ANTIQUITIES

GROUND FLOOR: MODERN COLLECTION

Ny Carlsberg Glyptothek

MAIN FLOOR: ANTIQUITIES
Entrance through Winter Garden

1–4	Egyptian art
5	Ancient Oriental art
6–9	Greek Archaic, classical and Hellenistic art
10	Greek portraits
11–17	Roman portraits

GROUND FLOOR: MODERN COLLECTION
Entrance through Entrance Hall or Winter Garden

33–37	French sculptors (Carpeaux and Rodin)
38	Cafeteria
39	Catalogues, postcards
40	Lift
41–42	Danish sculptors of 19th and 20th c. (H. V. Bissen, J. A. Jerichau)
47, 47a	Works by G. Henning

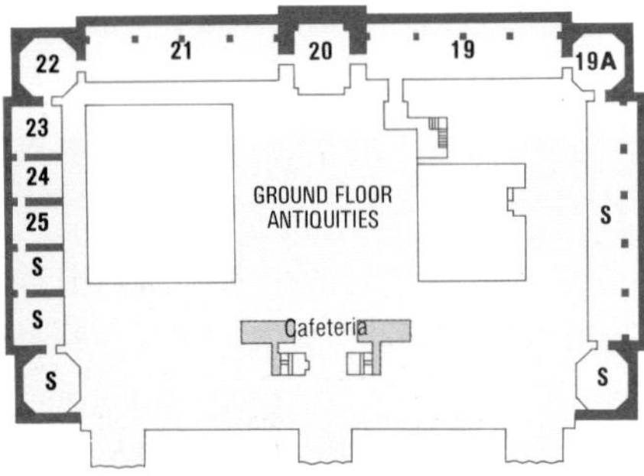

GROUND FLOOR: ANTIQUITIES
Entrance through Central Hall

19–23	Etruscan art
24–25	Palmyra collection
S	Study collections

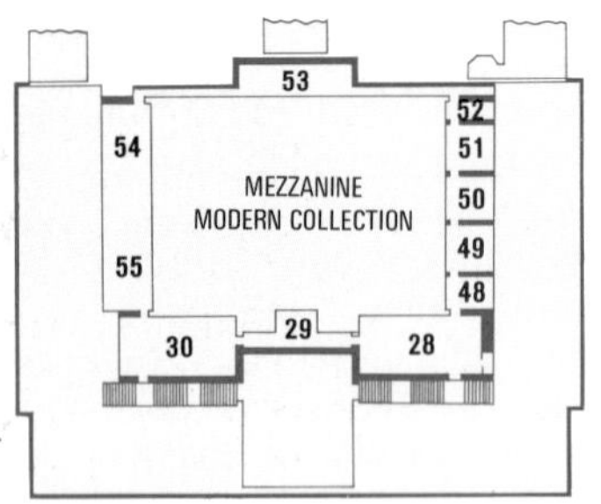

MEZZANINE: MODERN COLLECTION
Stairs from Entrance Hall or lift from Room 40

28–30	French Impressionists and their followers
48–52	Danish painting from J. Juel to W. Marstrand (18th–19th c.)
53	Sculpture by H. E. Freund
54–55	Danish painting from T. Philipsen to N. L. Stevns and E. Weie, K. Isakson and G. Henning (19th–20th c.)

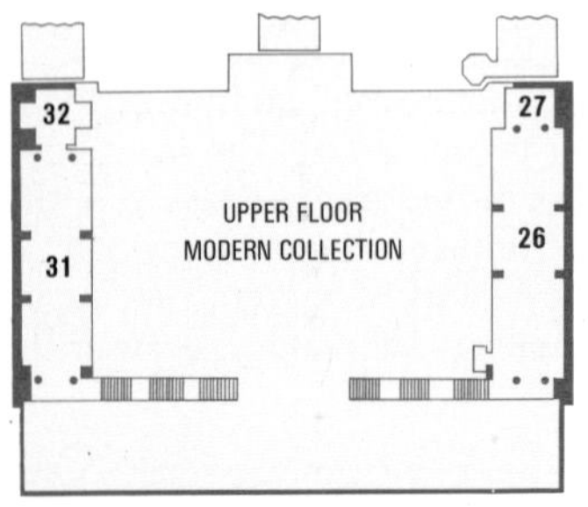

UPPER FLOOR: MODERN COLLECTION
Stairs from Entrance Hall or lift from Room 40

26	French painting from David to Manet; Degas bronzes
27	French sculpture
31–32	French painting from Gauguin to Vuillard; Rodin bronzes

Christiansborg Palace

(1798–1868) and J. A. Jerichau (1816–83); the rooms to the right are devoted to French sculpture with a collection of Rodin's work (1840–1917). The mezzanine and upper floor of the building contain further sculpture, including an important collection of bronzes by Edgar Degas and a collection of pictures by Danish artists of the 19th and 20th c. (Impressionists). In the Winter Garden are further sculptures, among them a fountain group "The Water Mother and her Children", by Kai Nielsen (1882–1924).

The *collection of antiquities* in the rear building was assembled with the help of the German archaeologists W. Helbig and P. Arndt and is one of the finest of its kind north of the Alps. It possesses many Roman portraits and busts. The Egyptian and Etruscan collections are also very fine. Every period of Egyptian sculpture is represented in the Egyptian collection; and the Greek sculpture includes outstanding examples of the 6th and 5th c. B.C., Archaic art and some of the best work of the time of Phidias, Polycletus, Praxiteles and Lysippus.

Along Vester Voldgade, opposite the Glypotothek, we come to the ****National Museum** (*Nationalmuseet*; open: 16 June–15 Sept. Tues.–Sun. 10 a.m.–4 p.m.; 16 Sept.–15 June Tues.–Fri. 11 a.m.–3 p.m., Sat., Sun. noon–4 p.m.), the buildings and departments of which are bordered by Ny Vester Gade and the Frederiksholms Kanal. The museum has a notable collection illustrating Danish history, including an old "sun chariot" (cult object in the form of a cart) more than 2000 years old, Romanesque and Gothic church fittings as well as Danish porcelain and silver. In addition there are collections of antiquities and coins. In the collection of Danish Peasant Culture of the 18th and 19th c. (open: 16 June–15 Sept. Tues.–Sat. 1–4 p.m., Sun. 10 a.m.–4 p.m.; 16 Sept.–15 June Tues.–Sat. 1–3 p.m., Sun. noon–4 p.m.) costumes, houses and tools are exhibited. The ethnographical collection of the museum, including items from Greenland, give an excellent impression of the life of the Polar regions. Incorporated in the National Museum is the *Prince's Palace* (1741–44), the earliest Danish Rococo palace, which was influenced by the French style of the period.

From here we cross the Frederiksholms Kanal on to the island of Slotsholm upon which stands ****Christiansborg Palace**, seat of the Danish Government and Parliament (*Folketing*). The building also houses the Foreign Ministry, the Supreme Court and the Queen's Audience

Gammel Strand, Copenhagen

Chambers. The Parliament and the Royal Rooms can be visited on guided tours. The palace occupies the site on which Bishop Absalon built the earliest fortifications of the city in 1167; remains of these can be seen under the present building. The foundation-stone of the first palace erected on the site of the original castle was laid by Christian VI in 1733, but the building was not completely finished and was destroyed by fire in 1794. Of the huge palace of four wings in Viennese Baroque style there survives only the Riding-School (Ridebane). A new palace was built by Frederik VI in the first 20 years of the 19th c. but was only rarely used as a Royal Residence; in 1849 it became the home of the new Parliament. This palace was also burned down in 1884. Among the parts which survived the fire was the palace church (dome with figures of angels by Thorvaldsen). The "third" Palace of Christiansborg was erected between 1907 and 1928 to the design of Thorvald Jørgensen. The façade consists of dressed Bornholm granite. In the courtyard is an equestrian statue of Frederik VII. There are conducted tours of the Royal Apartments and Parliamentary Rooms. Within the Riding-School complex, where the royal horses are exercised every morning, stands the old Court Theatre, now the Theatre Museum; and in the middle of the Riding-School is a monument to Christian IX.

On the other side of Tøjhusgade we come to the **Arsenal** (*Tøjhus*) which houses the *Military Museum* (collection of weapons and uniforms). Near the Arsenal in a park is the **Royal Library** (1.7 million volumes; 52,000 manuscripts), in which exhibitions are also held. Immediately NW of Christiansborg Palace is the ****Thorvaldsen Museum** (open: 2 May–30 Sept. Mon.–Sat. 10 a.m.–4 p.m.; 1 Oct.–30 Apr. Mon., Wed.–Sun. 10 a.m.–3 p.m.) with works by Bertel Thorvaldsen (1770–1844), the greatest Danish sculpture. The building in Neo-classical style was constructed to designs by Gottlieb Bindesbøll (1839–48). On the exterior facing the canal are frescoes depicting Thorvaldsen's return from Rome in 1838. In addition to Thorvaldsen's works the museum contains his own art collection. In Gammel Strand, on the opposite side of the canal, is the statue of an **old fishwife* (Fiskerkone). Every morning by the statue fishwives can be seen selling their wares.

Christiansborg Palace from the air

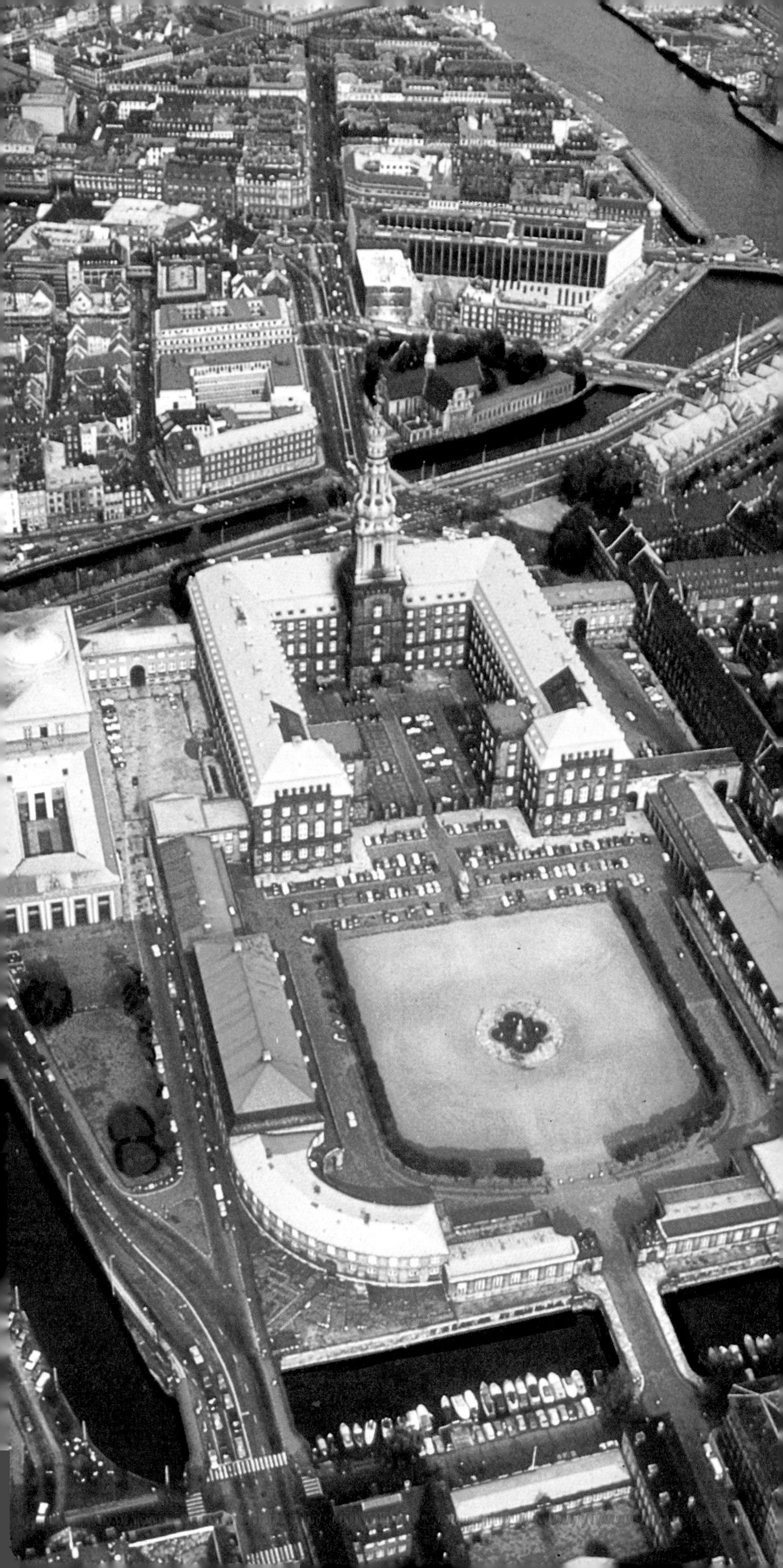

SE of Christiansborg, facing the harbour, stands the **Exchange** (*Borsen*, 1619–20), a picturesque building in Dutch Renaissance style with a tower 54 m (177 ft) high, the spire of which is formed by the intertwined tails of four dragons. This and the green patina of the copper roof are characteristic of the building. The tower is not open to the public.

On the opposite side of the canal stands the early 17th c. ***Holmen Church** which was intended for the use of seamen. The "Royal Doorway" was brought here from Roskilde Cathedral. Fine features of the interior are a Baroque altar of unpainted oak and a carved pulpit by Abel Schrøder the Younger, both dating from about 1660. In a side chapel are various tombs including that of the naval hero Nils Juel (d. 1697).

From Børs Gade a bascule bridge, the Knippelsbro, with a span of 29 m (95 ft), leads into the district of CHRISTIANSHAVN on the island of Amager. The older part of this district, transversed by a number of canals, has something of the atmosphere of Amsterdam. There are pretty houses fronting the waterside by which stands the Christians Kirke, flanked by two pavilions. The ***Church of Our Saviour** (*Vor Freiser Kirke*) in Skt. Annæ Gade, has a splendid Baroque altar, a beautiful font and a richly carved organ. The characteristic spire, with an external spiral staircase and a figure of Christ standing on a globe, affords extensive views. Since it was at Christianshavn originally that the Royal Fleet was to be protected, military establishments were set up. In 1971 the old barracks in Bådsmands Stræde were vacated. Drop-outs, members of the "alternative society" and hippies moved into the building and proclaimed it the "free State of Christiana". After protests by the Danish public this establishment was recognised as a "social experiment". Christiana still exists today.

Charlottenborg Palace on the E side of Kongens Nytorv, has been the headquarters of the Royal Academy of Art since 1754. To the rear of the palace runs ***Nyhavn** ("New Harbour"; picture p. 41) which is flanked by old-fashioned gabled houses. The streets which run alongside the water also bear the name of Nyhavn. At the end of the waterway can be seen an anchor as a memorial to Danish sailors who lost their lives during the Second World War. Nyhavn was once a disreputable quarter of the city but now, with its many brightly coloured little houses on the left-hand side of the canal, it is a very charming part of Copenhagen. From Nyhavn there is a hydrofoil service to Malmö in Sweden and it is also one of the stopping-places for the sightseeing canal boats. Bredgade leads northwards from the upper end of Nyhavn to the ***Marble Church** (begun in 1749, completed in 1894). It is also known as the Frederiks Church. Features of the interior include an ivory Crucifix, a German carving in oak and a seven-branched golden candelabrum. The church has a dome 84 m (275 ft) high and the façade is decorated with statues of great figures in Biblical and ecclesiastical history, including St Ansgar, the Apostle of the North, and the religious reformer Grundtvig.

Frederiksgade leads from the church to ****Amalienborg Palace**, the residence of the Queen. It was built by Niels Eigtev about 1750 under King Frederik V. The spacious octagonal Palace Square is surrounded by four separate but linked palaces, one of which is used by the Queen, the second the residence of the Heir to the throne, a third kept for use of visiting royals and the fourth houses the administrative offices of the throne; in the middle of the square stands an *equestrian statue of Frederik V* (1771). The palace originally provided residences for noble families including Counts Christian Frederik Levetzau and Adam Gottlob Moltke, Baron Joakim Brockdorff and the Counsellor Severin Løvenskjold. When Christianborg Palace was burned down in 1794, the King took over Amalienborg as his residence. The Danish kings continued to use the palace from time to time. Queen Margarethe II and her family today occupy the upper storey of the Schack Palace (formerly Løvenskjold). The Moltke Palace is used for official purposes. (The palaces are not open to the public.) The soldiers of the royal guard with their bearskins and blue uniforms (on festive occasions red, white and blue uniforms) are a symbol of the city. When the Queen

The Exchange

The "Little Mermaid"

is in residence in the palace, the changing of the guard takes place at noon.

By following Bredgade from the Marble Church in a northerly direction we come to the Russian *Alexander Nevski Church*, which has three gilded onion domes, and to *St Ansgar's Church*, the oldest Roman Catholic church in Copenhagen and, since 1942, of cathedral status; on the façade is a beautiful sculpture of St Ansgar. A Rococo building near St Ansgar's Church houses the ***Museum of Applied Art** (*Kunstindustrimuseet*; open: Tues.–Sun. 1–4 p.m.). The collections in the museum comprise European applied art from the Middle Ages to the present day and also objects from China and Japan. The emphasis is on furnishing of living quarters (carpets, porcelain, ceramics, etc.). Bredgade ends on the Esplanade; to the left is the Nyboder residential quarter which was built for sailors in the 17th and 18th c. In Churchill Park near the Esplanade can be found the *Freedom Museum* (documents concerning the Danish resistance against the Nazis from 1940 to 1945). Close by stands *St Alban's Church*, the English church of the Anglican colony in Copenhagen. Next to the church is a great fountain, the ***Gefion Springvandet**, erected in 1908; according to legend the goddess Gefion with her oxen ploughed Zealand out of Swedish ground.

Langelinie, the landing-place for a promenade along the shore begins at the Gefion Fountain. From here one comes to ***Kastellet**, the former Citadel of Frederikshavn, the oldest parts of which date from 1625. When in 1658 Denmark lost her possessions on the eastern side of the Øresund, Copenhagen became, therefore, a frontier town and the defences were strengthened. The buildings within the Citadel are well maintained and include two gates, the Zealand Gate and the Norwegian Gate. From the Citadel it is only a short distance to the **"**Little Mermaid**" (*"Den lille Havfrue"*) on the Langelinie; the official emblem of Copenhagen. The bronze sculpture was created by Edward Eriksen in 1913 based on the theme from one of H. C. Andersen's stories.

Going west from the Citadel and passing *Østerport* Station and the *Free Art Exhibition* (Den frie Udstilling) we come to

Østre Anlæg Park. On the N side (Stockholmsgade 20) is the ***Hirschsprung Collection** (*Hirschsprungske Samling;* open: Wed.–Sun. 1–4 p.m.), bequeathed to the city by a well-known Copenhagen cigar-manufacturer. Its principal items are Danish painting and sculpture of the 19th c.

In the southern part of Østre Anlæg stands the ***State Museum of Art** (*Statens Museum for Kunst* (1891–96); open: Tues.–Sun. 10 a.m.–5 p.m.). It consists of a main building with rooms for painting and sculpture and a print department, as well as an annexe for special exhibitions.

In the *painting collection* are works representative of European art from the 13th to the 18th c. In the Italian department can be seen important works including paintings by Titian and Tintoretto; the Dutch and Flemish schools are represented by Rubens and Rembrandt. The German collection includes Lucas Cranach the Elder and his successors. The museum also possesses a comprehensive collection of Danish Biedermeier painting as well as works of the first decades of the 20th c., but very little modern work. The museum also houses a notable private collection with works by Braque, Matisse and Picasso. The Print Collection which has been removed from the Royal Library contains some 100,000 items.

Adjoining the Østre Anlæg on the S lies the **Botanic Garden** (*Botanisk Have;* open: daily 8.30 a.m.–4 or 6 p.m.) which, like other parks, was laid out on the remains of former fortifications. the principal features are the Palm House, the Botanic and Geological Museums, an artificially arranged biotope devoted to the wild plants of Denmark, and an Alpine Garden. In a park to the E of the Botanic Garden stands ****Rosenborg Palace** (*Rosenborg Slot;* open in summer: daily 10 or 11 a.m.–3 p.m.; admission fee), built by Christian IV between 1610 and 1626 as a summer palace and used by the Danish Royal Family from the middle of the 18th c. as a spring and autumn residence. In 1833 the palace was opened to the public as a museum. It contains the *private collections of Danish kings* (furniture, paintings and sculptures); in addition the insignia of the kingdom, including the Crown Jewels, are on show. Of particular interest are the *Marble Room,* a Baroque reception room, and the *Knights' Hall* with the Coronation Throne which was used from 1871 to 1940. Porcelain is also exhibited ("Flora Danica" service). The adjoining park, *Kongens Have* or Rosenborg Have, was laid out in the time of Christian IV. Here can be seen many statues, including one of Hans Christian Andersen.

Vesterbrogade leads from the inner city to the district of FREDERIKSBERG in the W. In the S of the extensive park of Frederiksberg Have stands the *Palace of Frederiksberg,* built in Italian style with an ochre-yellow façade. To the W of the palace we come to the ****Zoological Garden** (*Zoologisk Have;* open: daily 9 a.m.–4, 5 or 6 p.m.), one of the largest zoos in Europe. Its great speciality is the breeding and rearing of musk-oxen. Visitors are able to see seals, apes, lions and other animals being fed. At the entrance to the zoo stands an observation tower. A tunnel leads to the children's zoo. In the adjoining district of VALBY, to the S, stand the large buildings of the ***Carlsberg Brewery.** The entrance in Ny Carlsberg Vej is in the form of an *Elephant Tower;* actually a cooling tower resting on four massive granite elephants. Guided tours (Mon.–Fri. 9, 11 a.m., 2.30 p.m.) take the visitor through the various parts of the brewery including the fermenting cellar, the store-rooms and the brewery museum. Every visitor is given the opportunity of tasting the product.

In *Nørrebro,* a working-class complex N of Frederiksberg, lies the great ***Assistens Cemetery** (*Assistens Kirkegard*). Here several celebrated Danish figures are buried, including Hans Christian Andersen, Søren Kierkegard and Martin Andersen Nexø, the novelist of the working classes. On 1 May 1984 a *Workers' Museum* was opened in Copenhagen in the district of Nørrebro (Rømersgade 22). The museum is devoted to the cultural history of the workers' movement from 1850 (open: Mon.–Thurs. 11 a.m.–4 p.m., Sun. 2–5 p.m.; admission fee).

Following Jagtvej in a northerly direction from Nørrebro, we come to the ****Zoological Museum** (*Zoologisk Museet;* open: 1 May–30 Sept. daily 10 a.m.–5 p.m.; 1 Oct.–30 Apr. Mon.–Fri. 1–5 p.m., Sat., Sun. 10 a.m.–5 p.m.) on the university campus. The museum is divided into two sections, the "Fauna of Denmark" and "From Pole to Pole" (animals of the

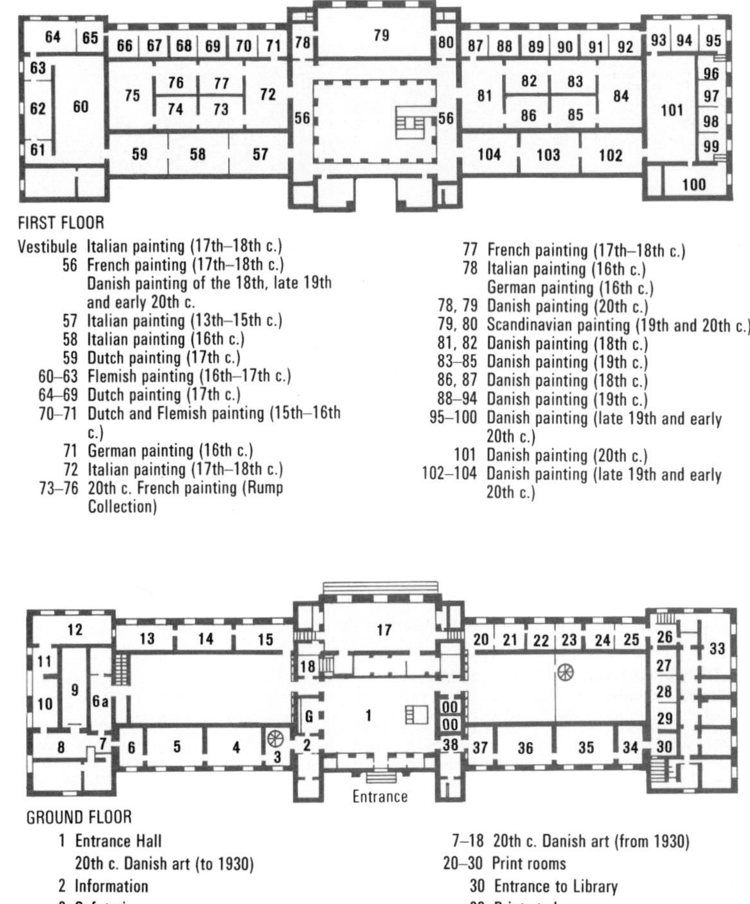

world). Animals can be seen here in their natural habitat.

Half-way between Nørrebro and the Zoological Museum Tagensvej diverges from Jagtvej NW to the district of *Bispebjerg* where stands the ****Grundtvig Church** (*Grundtvigs Kirke*), built between 1921 and 1940 by Peter Wilhelm Jensen Klint and named after the founder of the Folk High School movement. Inspired by the style of the typical country churches of Denmark, the architect designed a taller mighty church building of yellow brick. The W front resembles a gigantic organ. Indeed, the church houses one of the largest organs in Scandinavia. In the lofty interior concerts are given.

SURROUNDINGS. – The most southerly part of Copenhagen lies on the *island of **Amager** (Music Festival with church concerts Sept.–Oct.) which is joined to the inner city by a great lift bridge (Langebro); when a ship passes this can be raised and lowered in a very short time. On Amager is situated the modern exhibition and congress centre, *Bella Center* and – to the S of Kastrup – the international *Kastrup Airport* (Københavns Lufthavn Kastrup. The little town of **Dragør** (hotel: Dragør Færgegård, 46 b.) lies on the E coast of the island; this is a popular holiday resort which has retained its character as a rural and fishing community (over 50 houses are protected monuments). A Maritime Museum is of considerable interest. *Store Magleby* in the S of the island was once known as "Dutch Town", as the first inhabitants of the town were Dutch who settled here in the 16th c. and who drained and cultivated the island. A half-timbered 18th c. building houses the *Amager Museum* (paintings and costumes of the Dutch immigrants). Off the island of Amager is the island of Saltholm, a bird sanctuary (ferry).

Lyngby Open-air Museum

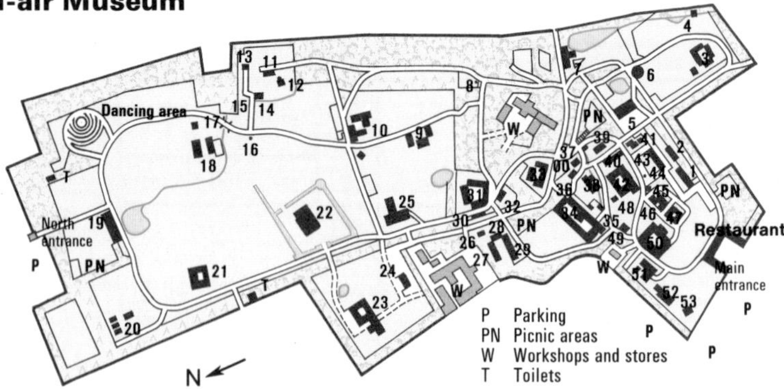

1 Fisherman's house, Agger, N Jutland
2 Seaman's house, Fanø
3 Farmhouse (early 19th c.), Øster Larsker, Bornholm
4 Water-mill, Pedersker, Bornholm
5 Peasant house (end of 16th c.), Ostenfeld, S Schleswig (Germany)
6 Tower windmill, erected on its present site in 1832, in use until 1906 (no access)
7 Water-mill (before 1800), Ellested, Funen (Fyn)
8 Boundary stone (1734), Løve, Central Jutland
9 Farmhouse (*c.* 1850), Karup Heath, Central Jutland
10 Farmhouse (from 1736), Læsø, Kattegat
11 Peasant house (1866), Múla, Bordoy, Faroes
12 Store hut, Viderejde, Vidoy, Faroes
13 Buckwheat mill for domestic use, Sandur, Sandoy, Faroes
14 Buckwheat drying kiln, Múla, Bordoy, Faroes
15 Stone used in weight-lifting contests, Múla, Bordoy, Faroes
16 Milestone (2nd half of 17th c.), Holstebro district, W Jutland
17 Stone bridge (2nd half of 18th c.), Smedevad, near Holstebro, W Jutland
18 Farmhouse (from 1770), Vemb, W Jutland
19 Barn (originally *c.* 1600) from a farm at Fjellerup/Djursland, E Jutland
20 Fishermen's houses, Nymindegab, W Jutland
21 Farmhouse (1803), Lønnestak, W Jutland
22 Peasant house (1653), Eiderstedt, SW Schleswig (Germany)
23 Farmhouse (originally 17th c.), Sønder Sejerslev, N Schleswig
24 Pillow-lace-making school (19th c.), Nørre Sejerslev, N Schleswig
25 Crofter's house (18th c.), Rømø
26 Fuel shed, Sode, NE Schleswig
27 Barn (17th c.), Øsby, NE Schleswig
28 Barn (1605), Grønninghoved, NE Schleswig
29 Peasant house (1766), Barsø, NE Schleswig
30 Small farmhouse from Dyndred (2nd half 18th c.); Alsen, N Schleswig
31 Peasant house with shoemaker's workshop, Ødis Bramdrup, near Kolding, E Jutland
32 Farmhouse (18th c.), True, E Jutland
33 Potter's workshop (1844), Sorring, E Jutland
34 Farmhouse (originally 2nd half of 17th c.), Halland (Sweden)
35 Double farm (18th c.), Göinge, Skåne (Sweden)
36 Drying kiln, Småland (Sweden)
37 Two-storey storehouse, SE Småland (Sweden)
38 Small water-mill, W Småland (Sweden)
39 Smallholder's steading (18th c.), Dörröd, Skåne (Sweden)
40 Weaver's house, Tystrup, Zealand
41 Houses of country craftsmen (17th–19th c.), Kalvehave, Zealand
42 Farm worker's house, Englerup, Zealand
43 Farmhouse (before 1800), Pebringe, Zealand
44 Almshouse (1710), Greve, Zealand
45 Boundary stone (1757), Virum, Zealand
46 Fire station (*c.* 1850), Kirke Såby, Zealand
47 Small farm (19th c.), Årup, Funen (Fyn)
48 Small farmhouse (19th c.), Kirke Søby, Funen (Fyn)
49 Village green with place of assembly
50 Village smithy (*c.* 1845), Ørbæk, Funen (Fyn)
51 Farmhouse (1747), Lundager, Funen (Fyn)
52 Small farmhouse, Dannemare, Lolland
53 Small farmhouse (before 1800), Tågense, Lolland
54 Post-mill (*c.* 1662), Karlstrup, Zealand (no access)

Along *Lyngbyvej* (motorway) we come to *Lyngby* (hotels: Eremitage, 182 b.; Fortunen, 28 b.; Frederiksdal, 117 b.; restaurants: Duetten; Oasen). There, in a park, stands *Sorgenfri Palace*, built in the 18th c. and since 1789 the property of the Royal Family (entrance to the southern part of the park).

Near Lyngby is also the extremely interesting ***Open-Air Museum** (*Frilandsmuseet;* open: 15 Apr.–30 Sept. Tues.–Sun. 10 a.m.–5 p.m.; 1 Oct.–14 Apr. Sun. 10 a.m.–3 p.m.; admission fee), an annexe of the National Museum. Within its area of 35 ha (86 acres) are farmhouses, dwellings and mills from all parts of Denmark and some from the Faroes. Each building is furnished with old utensils. There are also old houses from Schleswig-Holstein and Sweden. Not far from the Open-Air Museum in *Brede* there is an Ethnological Museum which is also a department of the Danish National Museum. The exhibits here are concerned with daily life (furniture, clothes, tools, etc.).

Leaving Copenhagen by Østerbrogade and Strandvej we come to Hellerup, N of the port installations. Here is the ***Tuborg Brewery** which is now merged with the Carlsberg Brewery. On the brewery site stands the largest "beer bottle" in the world (26 m (80 ft) high), originally constructed for the Nordic Industrial Exhibition in 1888; it has a lift to take visitors to the top.

A short distance to the N in Charlottenlund we come to Denmark's ***Aquarium** (open: 1 Mar.–31 Oct. daily 10 a.m.–6 p.m.; 1 Nov.–28 Feb. Mon.–Fri. 10 a.m.–4 p.m., Sat., Sun. 10 a.m.–5 p.m.; admission fee) with about 3000 brightly coloured fish and other denizens of the deep from all the seas of the world. There is also a trotting-course.

Finally one comes to ***Dyrehaven**, a large park with a game reserve where deer can be seen grazing. Also in the park is the Royal hunting-lodge, the *Eremitage* (built in 1736 in Rococo style), which is still in use, and from it there is a fine view over the Øresund to Sweden. In the S part of the park lies the pleasure centre of ***Bakken** (pony-rides for children, etc.) and near by is Klampenborg (restaurant: Peter Lieps Hus) with villas and good bathing. On the E4 NW of the park lies the little village of Nærum (Nerum) with *Sommers Oldtimer Museum* (Nærum Hovedgade 1; open: Sun.–Fri. 9 a.m.–5 p.m., Sat. 9 a.m.–1 p.m.). The collection consists of 26 vintage cars (1923 Bugatti, 1925 Bentley, 1937 Jaguar, etc.) and over 300 old model cars.

Esbjerg

Jutland
District: Ribe amt
Population: 80,000
Postal code: DK-6700
Telephone code: 05

Turistbureau
Skolegade 33;
Tel. 12 55 99.
British Consulate
Grimsbyvej;
Tel. 13 08 11
Turistbureau
Kirkegade 3
DK-6840 Oksbøl
Tel. (05) 27 18 00
Turistbureau
Torvet 5
DK-6800 Varde
Tel. (05) 22 32 22

HOTELS. – *Ansgar Missionshotel*, Skolegade 36, 90 b.; *Bangs Hotel*, Torvet 21, 137 b.; *Bell-Inn*, Skolegade 45, 60 b.; *Britannia*, Torvet, 121 b.; *Esbjerg*, Skolegade 31, 58 b.; *Olympic*, Strandbygade 14, 174 b.; *Palads Hotel*, Skolegade 14, 77 b. – YOUTH HOSTEL. – CAMP SITE.

RESTAURANTS. – *Den Røde Okse*, Tarphagevej 9; *Korskroen*, Skads Hovedvej 116; *Kunstpavillonen*, Havnegade 20; *Palads Restaurant*, Skolegade 14; *Parken*, Sovej 9.

EVENT. – *Fish auction for tourists* (July–Aug.).

Esbjerg, the fifth largest town in Denmark, lies on the W coast of Jutland facing the north tip of the island of Fanø. The port is the country's most important North Sea harbour and its largest fishing port; in addition it is the base for Denmark's oil and gas exploration in the North Sea.

Exports and imports and the processing of fish form the most important branches of the town's economy. The principal exports are the produce of agriculture and fishing. Passenger traffic is also significant; there are ferry services from Esbjerg to Great Britain (Newcastle, Harwich) and to the Faroes (Tórshavn).

HISTORY. – After the Treaty of Vienna (1864), under the conditions of which Denmark had to give up the Duchies of Schleswig-Holstein and Lauenburg to Germany, the ports on the W coast of Schleswig were only available to the Danes on payment of customs duties. Therefore it was decided in 1868 to build a port on the site where Esbjerg now stands, especially with a view to trading with England. The port was completed in 1878 but was later extended and modernised on several occasions. Since tides have a negligible effect in this location, the depth of water is very good. Esbjerg received its charter in 1898.

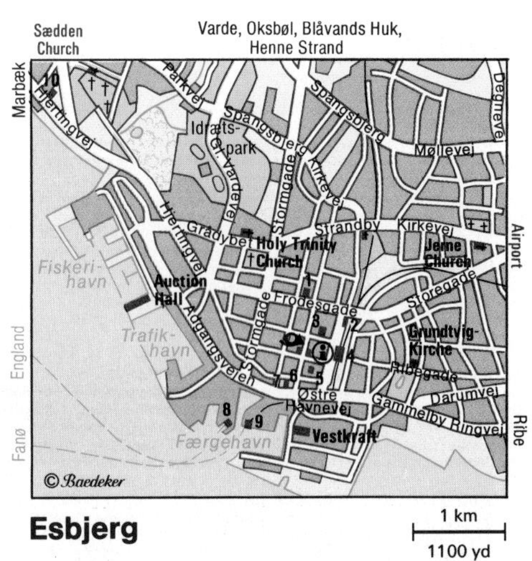

Esbjerg

1 km
1100 yd

1 Town Hall
2 Bus Station
3 Esbjerg Museum
4 Rail Station
5 Book-printing Museum
6 Art Gallery
7 Water Tower
8 Fano ferry
9 Ferry to England
10 Fishery and Maritime Museum

SIGHTS. – In the municipal park near the harbour stands the *Water Tower* (1897), the landmark of Esbjerg; near it is the *Art Gallery* (1962; open: 10 a.m.–5 p.m., Weds also 7–9 p.m.) housing a comprehensive collection of 20th c. Danish art including both paintings and sculpture. Among the exhibits are works by Harald Giersing, Wilhelm Lundstrøm, Richard Mortensen, the Jørgen brothers and Arne Haugen Sørensen. Special exhibitions and concerts of international repute take place in the Art Gallery. Exhibited in the *Esbjerg Museum* (Nørregade 23; open: 10 a.m.–4 p.m.) are objects illustrative of life during the Iron Age and the era of the Vikings. The museum also has a large collection of amber as well as costumes typical of those worn on the offshore island of Fanø.

Another interesting feature of Esbjerg is the *Museum of Book-printing* (Borgergade 6; open: 1 May–1 Oct. Mon.–Sat. 2–5 p.m.). The museum is set out like a Danish printing-works with apparatus and practice concerning the printing of books by hand. It is a working museum and the visitor can obtain finished examples of the craft. Running parallel to Borgergade is Kongensgade, a busy pedestrian zone and shopping street where there are a number of houses in art nouveau style and buildings from the last

Fishing port on the North Sea coast

quarter of the 19th c. On the quay of the fishing harbour stands the **Fish Auction Hall** (area 8000 sq. m (9570 sq. yd)); first auction on weekdays at 7 a.m. Not far N can be seen a memorial for fishermen lost at sea. This consists of a granite rotunda in which are engraved the names of Esbjerg fishermen who have lost their lives at sea since 1900.

In Tarphagevej, a short distance to the NW, is the ***Fishery and Maritime Museum** (1968). The museum houses a comprehensive collection of apparatus and vehicles connected with the fishing industry, a salt-water aquarium with fish found in the seas round the Danish coasts, and a huge open-air sea-lion basin which contains 500,000 litres (110,000 gallons) of water. There is a viewing window, 15 m (50 ft) wide, below the water. The sea-lions are fed daily at 11 a.m. and 2.30 p.m.

In Esbjerg there are a number of interesting churches. To the N of the town centre, in Grådbyet, stands *Holy Trinity Church* (Treenighedskirken) which was built in 1961 to designs by Erik Flagsted Rasmussen and Knud Thomsen. The building has four triangular gables; three have glass mosaic windows (Jens Urup) and the organ occupies the fourth. Adjoining the church on the N is *Vognsbøl Park*. Still farther N, in Fyrvej we come to *Sædden Church*, designed by the architects I. and J. Exner and dedicated in 1978. It is an impressive building with unique lighting. The altar and the font stand in the middle of the church. There are two other notable churches in the town; the *Grundvigs Church* in Grundvigsallé, built 1868–69 by Ole Nielsen with a roof constructed in the form of a V, and the Romanesque *Jerne Church* which was mentioned as early as 1306. The latter is built of granite and was later provided with a brick tower; inside are an altar of 1634 and a granite font.

SURROUNDINGS. – By way of Hjerting, an attractive coastal suburb of Esbjerg with a view of Ho Bay, a road leads to the *Marbæek Nature Park*, some 12 km (7 miles) NW of the town. Heather and scrub are a feature of the landscape. Two Iron Age settlements have been excavated here. The steep coasts at Ho Bay are impressively picturesque and there are lakes with a multitude of birds. The Marbæekgård, with an agricultural exhibition and a restaurant, is situated in the centre of this area. To the NE of Marbæek Nature Park is an 18-hole golf-course.

20 km (12 miles) N of Esbjerg lies the busy industrial township of **Varde** (pop. 10,000; hotel: Højskolehjemmet, 22 b.), with old houses, St Jacob's Church

Memorial to sailors lost at sea

(12th–13th c.), a well-stocked provincial museum with a Viking collection and a large open-air theatre. A model of old Varde, scale 1:10, can be seen NW of the town centre in the Arnbjerg complex. *Varde Sommerland*, a large leisure park for young and old, has mini-golf, a climbing-tower, a suspension railway and animals among its attractions (open: 25 May–25 August 10 a.m.–6 p.m.).

13.5 km (8 miles) W of Varde we come to *Oksbøl* (Strandhotel in Vejers Strand, 64 b.; restaurant: Turisthotel); in the Romanesque Ål Church are 13th c. wall-paintings. Farther SW at Blåvands Huk, the most westerly point in Denmark, stands a lighthouse. Driving NW from Varde we come to the seaside resort of **Henne Strand** (hotels: Pension Feriegarden, apartments, in Henneby; Henne Kirkeby Kro, 12 b.; Motel Udsigten, apartments) at the foot of the 64 m (210 ft) high *Blåbjerg shifting dunes*. To the N extends the Blåbjerg plantation and to the S, in a nature reserve, the Fil Lake.

Fåborg

Funen
District: Fyns amt
Population: 18,000
Postal code: DK-5600
Telephone code: 09
(i) **Turistbureau**
Havnegade 2
Tel. 61 07 07

HOTELS. – *Faborg Fjord*, Svendborgvej 175, 80 b.; *Korinth Kro*, Reventlowsvej 10, in Korinth, 52 b.; *Strandgade*, Strandgade 2, 22 b. – YOUTH HOSTEL. CAMP SITES.

RESTAURANTS. – *Det Lille Apotek*, Torvet 17; *Mosegård*, Nabgyden 31; *Ved Brønden*, Torvet/Tårngade 5.

Fåborg, an attractive little town, lies in the S of Funen on the Fåborg Fjord. In the W extends the peninsula of Horneland with the ferry port of Bøjden, from where boats ply to Fynshav on the island of Als.

HISTORY. – In the Middle Ages Fåborg belonged at different periods to the Kingdom of Denmark and the Duchy of Schleswig. It was fortified and had a castle which is mentioned in 1377. During the "Counts' Wars" (1534–36) the fortifications were destroyed with the exception of the West Tower (Westtor). In the 19th c. the merchants of the town were engaged in the cereal trade. In the middle of the 19th c. Fåborg had a regular boat service to Copenhagen. In 1880 the railway arrived.

SIGHTS. – There are some well-preserved streets and houses. The *West Gate* in Vestergade, a medieval town gate with a passage for vehicles, and a bell-tower on the Lille Tårnstræde are impressive. The museum *"Den gamle Gård"* (The old Farm) houses local collections. The ***Fåborg Museum** (open: 1 Apr.–31 Oct. daily 10 a.m.–4 p.m.; 1 Nov.–31 Mar. Sat. and Sun. 11 a.m.–3 p.m.) is especially worth seeing, as it contains a comprehensive collection of works by painters from Funen of about the period 1900. It was Mads Rasmussen, a prosperous merchant, who had the initiative to found the museum which was constructed to plans by the architect Carl Petersen. The Danish sculptor Kai Nielsen (1882–1924) created a statue of Mads Rasmussen which can be seen in the museum.

SURROUNDINGS. – 2 km (1¼ miles) stands a watermill *Kaleko Mølle* (now a museum) which was renovated in 1968. From Fåborg road A8 leads E to the so-called Funen Alps; on the left is the *Lerbjerg* (126 m (413 ft)). In 9 km (5½ miles) we come to *Brahetrolleborg Castle* (15th c. but rebuilt on several occasions) with a large park at the entrance to which lies Humlehaven, a restaurant in which exhibitions of art and antiquities are mounted (entrance to the park daily 9 a.m.–5 p.m.). By continuing along the A8 we come to the ***old manor-house of Egeskov** (musical matinées in Knights' Hall, July–Aug.) situated on the left away from the road. It was built on oak piles from 1524 to 1554 and is one of the best-preserved moated houses in Europe. The house is surrounded by a large park. In an annexe can be found the *Oldtimer Museum* with old cars and aircraft (house, park and museum open in May and September daily 10 a.m.–5 p.m.; gardens and automobile collection also June to Aug. daily 9 a.m.–6 p.m.). A short distance to the E lies the village of Kværndrup (Kverndrup) (hotel: Kværndrup Kro, 23 b.).

Falster

District: Storstrøms amt
Area: 514 sq. km (198 sq. miles)
Population: 45,000

(i) **Turistbureau**
Østergade 2
DK–4800 Nykøbing
Tel. (09) 85 13 03

Turistbureau
Langgade 61
DK–4874 Gedser
Tel. (03) 87 90 41
(open only in summer)

Turistbureau
DK–4850 Stubbekøbing
Tel. (03) 84 13 04
(open only in summer)

The island of Falster lies between the two larger islands of Lolland (west) and Zealand (north), to which it is joined by bridges. Gedser Odde, the southern tip of the island is the most southerly point in Denmark. On the E coast there are beautiful sandy beaches.

From Lolland the Frederik IX Bridge crosses the Guldborg Sound to the largest town on Falster, **Nykøbing** (pop. 26,000; hotels: Baltic, 130 b.; Motel Liselund, in Sundby, 50 b.; Teaterhotel, 37 b.; camp site; restaurants: Stegepanden; Taghaven), beautifully situated on the E side of the Sound. At the end of the 12th c. fortifications were set up on a peninsula on the Guldborg Sound for protection against the Wends, and these were later converted into Nykøbing Castle. The town grew up round the fortifications. After the Reformation the castle was the residence of widowed Danish queens. Since several queens of German descent resided here, many Germans came to the town. In 1787 the castle was sold and later pulled down. As there was no longer any income from the Court, the inhabitants began to play a greater part in trade and industry. Today there are tobacco, margarine and cement factories in Nykøbing Falster. A few beautiful half-timbered houses of the old town still remain, including the *Ritmestersgård* in Store Kirkestræde, the old corn merchant's house in Slotsgade and the buildings in Langgade, where No. 18 is the oldest house in the town. A notable building is the *Franciscan church* (Gråbrødrekirke), built about 1500 in Gothic style as part of a monastery; after the Reformation it became the Town Church. It contains a picture (1514) by Lucas Cranach the Elder. In the herb garden near the church, orginally laid out by Franciscan monks, medicinal herbs have again been cultivated for a number of years. The **Falster Museum** is housed in the so-called Czarens Hus (1700) in which Peter the Great lived during his visit to Denmark. In addition to material about the island of Falster and its people, ceramics and articles of copper and pewter are displayed.

12 km (7 miles) W of the town *Corselitze Castle* stands in a park; the main wing dates from 1777 and the park of 7 ha (17 acres) was laid out at the same time with ponds and canals (park open daily Apr.–Oct.; main wing can only be viewed by parties from May to Sept. by prior arrangement). From the park a main road leads to the coast near *Tromnæs*

Egeskov Mansion, built on oak piles

Beach on the coast of Falster

Storstrøm Bridge

(Tromnes) where an 18th c. garden pavilion can be seen. The longest coastal woodland of eastern Denmark extends northwards from Tromnes.

Near **Bøtø** in the S of Falster lies the leisure centre *"Familienland Falster"*, a large area with many facilities for sports and pleasure including a water-chute, a model boat pond and a bob-track for go-carts (open: 31 May-20 June 10 a.m.–6 p.m.; 21 June–10 Aug. 10 a.m.–8 p.m.; 11 Aug.–16 Sept. 10 a.m.–6 p.m.; admission fee).

16 km (10 miles) from Nykøbing Falster, in the extreme S of the island, lies the little port of **Gedser** (Højvang Petit Motel, in Gedesby, 22 b.; Marinakroen Restaurant at the Yacht Harbour). There are ferry services from here to Lübeck–Travemünde in the Federal Republic of Germany (3 hours) and to Rostock–Warnemünde in the German Democratic Republic (1 hour 50 minutes). In autumn large flocks of birds can be seen flying over this part of Falster on their way south.

A2 runs NW from Nykøbing through fertile arable country and pasture land to *Nørre Alslev* (Orehoved Hotel, in Orehoved, 20 b.; Motel Volieren, in Øster Kippinge, 24 b.). In the Gothic church can be seen a frieze with heraldic figures. In Nørre Alslev a road branches off E to **Stubbekøbing** (pop: 7300; hotel: Elverkroen, 80 b.; camp site), an ancient little town beautifully situated on the Grøn Sound, with the oldest church on the island (*c.* 1200); attractive views from the tower. A ferry crosses in 12 minutes to **Bøgø** from where a bridge leads on to the island of Møn (see entry).

To the N of Nørre Alslev the **Storstrøm Bridge** (3211 m (3500 yd)) crosses the Storstrøm to the little island of *Masnedø* and from there the road continues over a bascule bridge to Vordingborg on the island of Zealand. The E4 coming from Lolland leads NE from Nørre Alslev over the *Farø–Falster Bridge* (1726 m (1888 yd)), the centre section of which can be opened, to the island of **Farø** and from there over the *Zealand–Farø Bridge* (1596 m (1746 yd)) to Zealand. The two bridges, opened in 1985, form a relief route for the Storstrøm Bridge and together are known as the Farø Bridges.

Fanø

District: Ribe amt
Area: 55 sq. km (21 sq. miles)
Population: 2800
Turistbureau
Havnepladsen
DK–6270 Nordby
Tel. (05) 16 26 00

The popular North Sea island of Fanø lies off the coast of South Jutland to the south of Esbjerg, from which it is reached by ferry in 20 minutes.

On the island of Fanø

The chief place on the island is the fishing village of **Nordby** (hotel: Krogården, 32 b.; restaurant) on the E coast. In the local museum are models of Danish trading vessels and costumes. The *Fanø Museum* exhibits a typical Fanø house showing how the people lived 300 years ago; it contains curiosities which were brought home by sailors who lived on the island. There are many models of ships in the 18th c. church. About 3 km (2 miles) SW of Nordby lies the resort of **Fanø Vesterhavsbad** with an attractive beach extending S along the W coast of the island, whereas the interior is largely wooded. The southern tip of the island at **Sønderho** (Sønderho Kro, 14 b.; camp site; festival in July) can be reached by car from Nordby in 15 minutes. The village has pretty thatched fishermen's houses; Hannes Hus (*c.* 1770) houses a local museum. Many model ships hang from the roof of the little church.

Faroe Islands/ Færøerne/Føroyar

Autonomous Island Group
Total area: 1400 sq. km (540 sq. miles)
Population: 45,000
Turistbureau
Box 368
DK–3800 Tørshavn

Bay on Mykines Island, with "Bird Rocks"

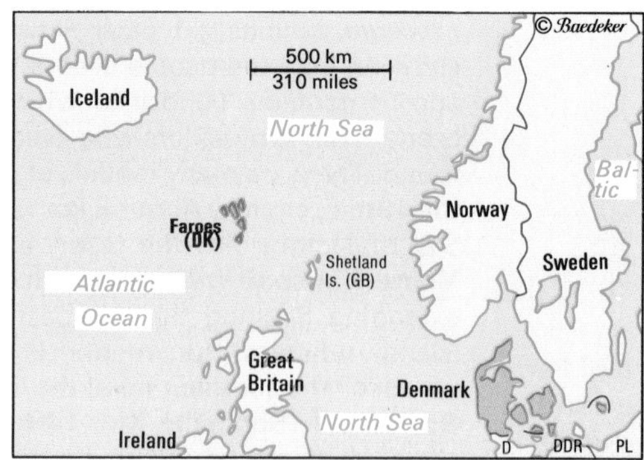

Position of the Faroes in the North Atlantic

Flag of the Faroes

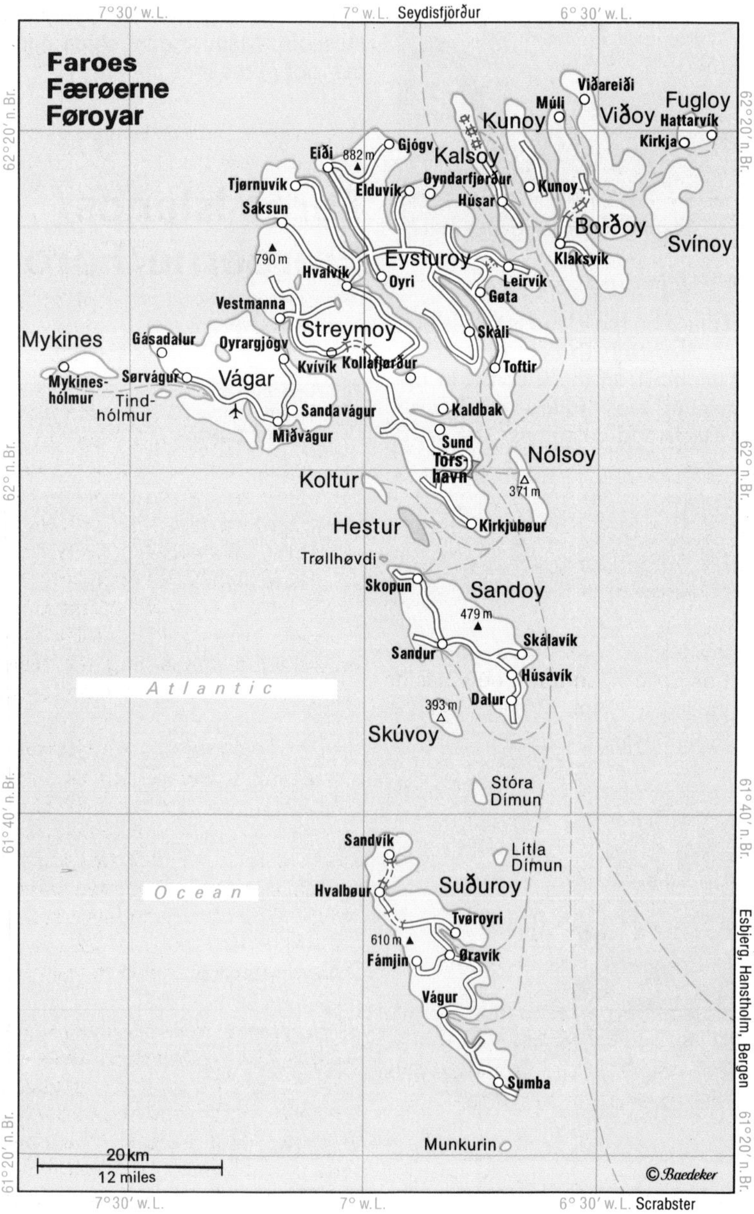

Faroes
Færøerne
Føroyar

7°30′ w.L. 7° w.L. Seydisfjörður 6° 30′ w.L.

62°20′ n.Br. 62° n.Br. 61°40′ n.Br. 61°20′ n.Br.

Viðareiði
Múli
Fugloy
Viðoy
Hattarvík
Kunoy
Kirkja
Gjógv
Eiði
882 m
Kalsoy
Tjørnuvík
Elduvík
Oyndarfjørður
Kunoy
Saksun
Húsar
Borðoy
Svínoy
Klaksvík
790 m
Eysturoy
Hvalvík
Oyri
Leirvík
Gøta
Vestmanna
Streymoy
Skáli
Mykines
Gásadalur
Oyrargjógv
Kvívík
Kollafjørður
Toftir
Mykines-hólmur
Sørvágur
Vágar
Tindhólmur
Sandavágur
Kaldbak
Miðvágur
Sund
Tórshavn
Nólsoy
Koltur
371 m
Hestur
Kirkjubøur
Trøllhøvdi
Skopun
Sandoy
479 m
Sandur
Skálavík
Húsavík
Atlantic
Dalur
393 m
Skúvoy
Stóra Dímun
Sandvík
Lítla Dímun
Ocean
Hvalbøur
Suðuroy
Tvøroyri
610 m
Fámjin
Øravík
Vágur
Esbjerg, Hanstholm, Bergen
Sumba
Munkurin
20 km
12 miles
© Baedeker

7°30′ w.L. 7° w.L. 6° 30′ w.L. Scrabster

The Faroe Islands (Danish "Færoerne"; Faroese "Føroyar"), meaning "Sheep Islands", is a group of 18 islands, 17 of which are inhabited, and several skerries which together represent an autonomous part of Greater Denmark. They are situated some 600 km (673 miles) W of the Norwegian coast in latitude 62° N. The islands can be reached by air from Copenhagen, the airport being situated on the island of Vågar. In the summer months the islands are served by ferries, including ships from Esbjerg and Hanstholm.

The islands are of volcanic origin and consist of basalt with a thin layer of tufa. They have steep rocky coasts and fjords which bite deep into the land. The landscape consists predominantly of meadows, fen and heathland. Trees and bushes are only found in a few cultivated plantations. The animal life of the islands consists of birds, fish, seals and whales. Many birds live on the rocky coasts. Since the islands lie within the sphere of the Gulf Stream, precipitation is considerable (rain falls on 280 days a year; annual rainfall 1200–1700 mm (47–66 in). The proximity of the sea means summers are cool (11 °C (52 °F)) and the winters are relatively mild (3 °F (47 °F)). The influence of the Gulf Stream ensures that the sea temperature in summer and in winter varies little and the sea remains free of ice.

The language of the Faroes was originally a dialect of Norwegian but it now has its own linguistic system, Danish being a compulsory second language in the schools. Spirits, wine and beer are not sold on the open market; only a light beer is obtainable. Tourists can bring their own requirements with them or order normal beer from a local brewery (information in the hotels). Sheep-rearing has long been important on the island group which is indeed named after sheep. Today the principal source of income for the inhabitants is fishing. Some of the people work in shipyards and spinning-mills. Pullovers in beautiful colours and designs are popular souvenirs with tourists.

HISTORY. – The Faroes were settled from the 7th c. by Celts but were conquered about 800 by Norwegian Vikings and from 1035 they belonged to Norway. In 1380 both Norway and the Faroes came into the possession of Denmark. After the break-up of the union between Norway and Denmark in 1814 the Faroes remained Danish. During the Second World War the islands were occupied by British troops. In 1948 they received the status of an autonomous country under the Danish Crown (internal self-determination); the Danish parliament is responsible only for their interests in the fields of foreign policy and defence (23 March 1948). The Faroes have their own coat of arms and their own flag. They do not belong to the European Economic Community. The legislative body of the country is the parliament (Lagting), consisting of elected representatives. Executive power is in the hands of the government (Landsstyret), the members of which are appointed by the Lagting. The Faroes send two members to the Danish parliament.

SIGHTS. – The chief islands of the Faroes are Streymoy, Esturoy, Suduroy, Sandoy and Vágar.

Tórshavn (hotels: Borg, 216 b.; Hafnia, 105 b.), the port and chief town of the Faroes, lies on the S coast of the island of *Streymoy*. It has only 13,000 inhabitants and is the smallest capital in Scandinavia. The oldest part of the town, with many wooden houses, is on a spit of land in the harbour area. At the tip of this peninsula, at *Cape Tinganes*, the Vikings established their first "thingstead", probably about 930. Near the peninsula stands a memorial to Niels Ryberg Finsen (1860–1904) who was born in Tórshavn and won the Nobel Prize for Medicine in 1903 (see Notable Figures). Also of interest is the fortress of *Skansen* (*c.* 1580), from which in former times entrance into the town was defended. In the *National Museum* (boats, ethnological collections, etc.) information concerning the history and culture of the Faroes can be found.

SW of Tórshavn lies **Kirkjubøur**, where Irish monks were living as early as the 8th c. Here stand the ruins of *St Magnus's Cathedral* (13th c.) which was never completed but which has high walls of basalt and Gothic pointed windows. *St Olaf's Church*, which has been restored, and the 900-year-old wooden "Roystovan" house are open to visitors.

Two places N of Tórshavn are worth visiting; *Kvivik*, where a house dating from the Viking Age has been excavated, and *Hvalvik* which has the oldest wooden church in the Faroes. In a deep valley about 10 km (6 miles) from here, on the NW coast of Streymoy, lies *Saksun* (good

Rural settlement on Mykines

fishing in the neighbourhood); the *Dúvugard*, a farmhouse built with boulders and turf, is furnished much as it was in the Middle Ages (open in summer 2–6 p.m.).

A runic stone can be seen near **Sandavágur** on the island of *Vágar* to the W of Streymoy. The *Bøsdalafossur Waterfall* is scenically impressive. From Sørvágur on the W coast of the island there is a boat service in summer to the little island of *Mykines*, where the bird rocks are easily accessible and exceptionally attractive. Seagulls, guillemots and puffins abound; the inhabitants catch birds for food.

E of Streymoy lies *Eysturoy*. These two islands, the largest in the group, are joined by a bridge. Between Gjógy and Eidi (Hotel Eidi, 15 b.) in the N of Eysturoy rise the highest cliffs of the Faroes, reaching 882 m (2895 ft) above sea-level. These cliffs can be climbed in clear weather and from the top there is an extensive view over the sea and the islands. At the N tip of Eysturoy the rocks of *Risin* and *Kellingin* tower up from the water.

To the N and NE of Eysturoy lie many large and small islands. **Klaksvik** (Sjømansheimid Hotel, 75 b.) on *Bordoy* is the second largest town of the Faroes; in the *Christianskirke* a Faroes boat hangs from the roof, the only one of four which came safely in a stormy winter's night in 1923. **Vidareidi** (Hotel Nord, 22 b.) on the island of *Vidoy* is the most northerly point in the Faroes, it is situated in a hilly area where there are excellent facilities for walking. From the village fine views of five islands may be enjoyed. The cliffs to the N of Vidareidi are home to immense colonies of sea-birds and here also they are trapped with nets for food.

To the S of Streymoy lie *Sandoy* and *Suduroy*, between which flows the Suduroyar Fjord. Sandoy, the flattest of the islands is used for agriculture and has excellent fishing. In the pretty village of *Húsavik* can be seen an old house with an open fireplace and chimney. Until a few years ago this house was still inhabited.

Sumba on Suduroy is the most southerly point of the islands. The road to it passes the impressive cliff mass of *Beinisvørd* on the W coast. The most modern fish-processing plant on the Faroes is to be found in *Vágur* on a bay of the E coast, and here can also be seen the votive church which was a gift from a Norwegian lady.

Fredericia

Jutland
District: Vejle amt
Population: 46,000
Postal code: DK–7000
Telephone code: 05

Turistbureau
Axeltorv
Box 68
Tel. 92 13 77

Turistbureau
Østergade 1
DK–7790 Hvidbjerg
Tel. (07) 87 14 22

HOTELS. – *Hyby-Lund*, Fælledvje 58, 24 b.; *Landsoldaten*, Norgesgade 1, 122 b.; *Postgården*, Oldenborggade 4, 155 b. – YOUTH HOSTEL. – CAMP SITE.

RESTAURANTS. – *Den Lille Hornblæser*, Jyllandsgade 53; *Handværkeren*, Vendersgade 61; *Hvilested Kro*, Fredericiavej 462.

Fredericia lies on the E coast of Jutland, north of the place where a road bridge (E 66) leads E to the island of Funen.

HISTORY. – In the middle of the 17th c. Frederik III (1648–70) had a fortress built here, with the help of which northern Jutland was protected against enemy attacks and the crossing from Jutland to the island could be made in safety. Within a semicircular rampart the fortress-builder Gottfried Hoffman laid out streets in a rectangular pattern. The name "Fredericia" dates from 1664. Fredericia was one of the few towns in Denmark where people could live who were not adherents of the Evangelical Lutheran faith. Therefore Jews could be found there from 1679 and, since the 18th c. members of the Reformed Church, many of whom were engaged in growing tobacco. In 1864 Fredericia was besieged during the Second Schleswig-Holstein War and after severe bombardments the town was evacuated. Thereafter it lost its importance as a fortress. Not until 1909, when the fortifications were demolished, did Fredericia expand.

SIGHTS. – In the course of the German-Danish War the Danes succeeded in capturing Fredericia on 6 July 1849. This victory over the forces of Schleswig-Holstein is commemorated by the bronze statue "The Valiant Soldier" in the town centre; it was created by H. V. Bissen (1796–1868), a pupil of Thorvaldsen. The *Fredericia Museum* in Jernbanegade contains a notable collection of lamps, as well as documents concerning the religious denominations who found santuary in the town in former centuries (open: daily mid June to mid August; at other times Tues.–Sat. in the afternoons). There is an enjoyable walk along the ramparts of the demolished fortifications, from which there are extensive views.

SURROUNDINGS. – N of the town on *Trelde Næs* extends a region of dunes, and still farther N on the coast lies the resort of **Hvidbjerg**, with a broad sandy beach and white dunes up to 27 m (90 ft) high.

Frederikshavn

Jutland
District: Nordjyllands amt
Population: 35,000
Postal code: DK–9900
Telephone code: 08

Turistbureau
Brotorvet 1
tel. 42 32 66

HOTELS. – *Hoffmanns Hotel*, Tordenskjoldsgade 3, 127 b.; *Jutlandia*, Havnepladsen 1, 202 b.; *Motel Lisboa*, Søndergade 248, 90 b.; *Mariehønen*, Danmarksgade 40, 72 b.; *Park Hotel*, Jernbanegade 7, 63 b.; *Sømandshjemmet*, Tordenskjoldsgade 15, 61 b.; *Turisthotel*, Margrethevej 5, 44 b. – YOUTH HOSTEL – Buhlsvje 6. CAMP SITE – Apholmenvej 40.

RESTAURANTS. – *Den Gule Pakhus*, Tordenskjoldsgade 14; *Færgekroen*, Lodsgade 8; *Hyttefad* I & II, Trindelen (fish); *La Bagatelle*, Havnegade 7; *Gastronomen*, Jernbanegade 7; *Møllehuset*, Skolvalleen.

Frederikshavn is situated on the E coast of northern Jutland. From the fortified natural harbour ferries sail to Gothenburg (Sweden), Larvik and Oslo (Norway) and to the Danish island of Læsø. Fishing (flounders, oysters) and fish-processing are important branches of the town's economy, as are shipbuilding, engineering and iron-foundries.

HISTORY. – Where the present town now stands there was in medieval times the fishing settlement of "Fladstrand", from which the inhabitants plied their trade. When in the course of the Thirty Years War a defence entrenchment was built, the place gained in importance. A fortifications specialist erected a powder-tower, surrounded by a wall. In 1818 Fladstrand received its municipal charter and the name of "Frederikshavn" after Frederik VI. In the 19th c. the citadel, apart from a few buildings, was pulled down.

SIGHTS. – In the town centre stands the former *Powder-Tower* (1688; Krudttårnet) which now contains a collection of weapons (open from April to November). The oldest part of the town, *Fiskerklyngen*, lies to the N of the fishing harbour and here a number of well-preserved 17th c. houses can be seen. 4 km ($2\frac{1}{2}$ miles) from the town centre stands a 58 m (190 ft) observation tower, *Cloostårnet* (alt. 165 m (540 ft)) from which there are extensive views of the Vendsyssel

Landing the fish

Powder-Tower

countryside and the sea. Close by, in Gærumvej (Gerumvej), are *Iron Age Cellars* (Jernalderkædrene), with material of the Early Iron Age found in the locality. 3 km (2 miles) SW of Frederikshavn, by way of Møllehus Allé, set in 50 ha (124 acres) of wooded parkland, is the manor house of *Bangsbo* (1750), now a museum (open: daily 10 a.m. – 5 p.m.; closed 1 Jan.-28 Feb. on Sat. and Sun.); in the maritime section can be seen a large collection of figureheads and models and paintings of ships. In addition the museum is the largest Resistance museum outside Copenhagen; on show are exhibits concerning the period of occupation (1940–45). Near the museum are a zoo and the *Stenhave Museum* with a collection of more than 1000 stones with carvings or inscriptions, the oldest of them dating from prehistoric times. From the *Pikkerbakken*, a range of low hills to the south of Bangsbo Manor, there are magnificent views of Frederikshavn, the surrounding countryside and the sea.

SURROUNDINGS. – 12 km ($7\frac{1}{2}$ miles) S of Frederikshavn is the fishing port and seaside resort of **Sæby** (Seby; pop. 17,500; hotel Viking, 50 b.; restaurant Henrik Ibsen; youth hostel; several camp sites). Near the beach stands St Mary's Church which originally belonged to a monastery founded in 1469. Fresco-painting (*c.* 1500) shows the mother of Mary on her natal bed, with monks playing musical instruments. The Dutch altar-table dates from 1520.

Frederikssund

Zealand
District: Frederiksborg amt
Population: 16,000
Postal code: DK–3600
Telephone code: 02

Turistbureau
Østergade 3
Tel. 31 06 85

Turistbureau
DK–3300 Frederiksvaerk
Tel. 12 30 01

Turistbureau
Nørregade 22
DK–3390 Hundersted
Tel. 33 77 88 (open only in summer)

Turistbureau
Algade 52
DK–4500 Nykobing Sjælland
Tel. 41 08 88

HOTEL. – *Isefjord* 17b.

RESTAURANTS. – *Færgekrogen Bi-Lidt*, Strandvejen 2; *Kalvø*, Kalvøen.

EVENT. – *Viking Festival* (June–July).

Sæby Harbour

The port of Frederikssund is situated in the N of Zealand on the E shore of the Roskilde Fjord.

4 km (2½ miles) S the remains of five Viking ships were recovered in 1962 from the fjord; they had probably formed part of an underwater barrier (museum in Roskilde).

HISTORY. – Since the Roskilde Fjord at Frederikssund is at its narrowest, it is here that the easiest crossing from North Zealand to the peninsular or Hornsherred can be made. Therefore there was already a ferry here in the Middle Ages. In the course of time a trading-station arose which in 1573 received the right of levying customs duties. At the end of the 16th c. a bridge of boats was built; and in the 19th c. a bridge across the sound.

SIGHTS. – Frederikssund is known particularly for the Viking plays. These plays, which do not commence until late evening are followed by a "Viking Feast". They are very popular and enjoyable, as is the food which one eats with one's fingers and washes down with a kind of mead. Tickets can be booked through a tourist office or by the hotels. Many people prefer to book with one of the tourist coaches going from Copenhagen or Roskilde rather than driving back in the dark long after midnight. Incidentally, if you go, take a rug with you and a warm jacket as the seats are wooden and sitting outdoors for several hours can be very rough.

The *J. S. Willumsen Museum* (1955–57) contains works by this artist; he had left them to the State on condition that a museum would be built to house them. J. F. Willumsen (1863–1958), born in Copenhagen, lived for many years in France and worked both as a painter and sculptor and also as an architect. He was both respected and rebuked, and he played an important role in Danish art for some 70 years. In the rooms of the museum, the first modern museum to be built in Denmark after the Second World War, 125 works by this artist are on show.

SURROUNDINGS. – On the Hornsherred spit of land 6.5 km (4 miles) W of the town stands *Jægerspris Castle* in a splendid wood. It was once the summer residence of Frederik VII. N of the castle lies the beautiful Nordskoven (the Northern Woods). Driving N from Frederikssund along the shores of the Roskilde Fjord we come to the port and industrial town of **Frederiksværk** (Frederiksverk; hotel: Sandkroen, in Asserbo, 13 b.), with an iron and steel works. On the site of the former powder and cannon factory stands the Krudtværk Museum ("krudt" is the Danish word for powder) with implements dating from the period of the establishment of the factory. To the N of Frederikssverk on the shore lie the popular resorts of *Liseleje* (hotels: Lisegården, 40 b.; Liselængen, 58 b., May–Oct.) and *Tisvildeleje* (hotels: Badepension Helenekilde, 63 b.; Rågeleje Klit Holiday Centre (apartments), in Vejby; restaurant: Bakkefrydgård Bodega). Between them extends the "Tisvilde Hegn" woodland area which was originally planted to stabilise the shifting sand of the dunes. The whole of this northern shore of Zealand stretching round from Hundested through Gilleleje and Hornbæk to Helsingør (Elsinore) is delightful. It is also very popular in summer or any holiday week-end so it is better to book in advance at those times.

To the W of Frederiksverk the fishing village of *Hundested* (Hundested Kro and Hotel, 102 b.) lies at the confluence of the Isefjord with the Kattegat. This was once the home of the Polar explorer Knud Rasmussen (1879–1933); at the Spoddsbjerg Lighthouse (view) there is a museum with souvenirs of the explorer (articles of clothing, photographs, fishing tackle). There is a ferry service from Hundested to Grenå.

Nykøbing Sjælland (hotels: Klinterkroen, in Klint, 24 b.; Rørvig Motel, 44 b.; restaurants: Apotheker–Hjørnet; Lyngkroen), on Nykobing Bay on the far side of the mouth of the fjord, is one of the oldest trading-posts in Denmark.

The Anneberg Collection (Egebergvej) is considered one of the most important collections of antique glass in northern Europe. The Oddsherreds Local Museum near the church has interiors of peasants' and fishermen's houses; adjoining is a bakery museum.

Funen/Fyn

District: Fyns amt
Area: 3482 sq. km (1344 sq. miles)
Population: 398,000

Funen, Fyn in Danish, the second largest island of Denmark, lies between Jutland and Zealand. The W coast is washed by the Little Belt, the E coast by the Great Belt. The area is generally flat; only in the SW is there a wooded moraine ridge, known as the "Funen Alps". The fertile marl soil yields an abundant harvest of agricultural produce, which has led to the island's being called the "Garden of Denmark".

Funen can be reached from Jutland by one of the two large bridges spanning the **Little Belt**. The older of the two (1935), to the S, is a reinforced-concrete structure (1178 m (1300 yd)) long; clear height above the water is 33 m (108 ft). The newer bridge (1970), within sight of the older one to the N, is Denmark's first suspension bridge (1080 m (1200 yd)) long; span 600 m (650 yd); clear height 42 m (138 ft)). Also there are many ferries between Funen and other Danish islands.

The cultural heart of Funen is Odense (see entry), the birthplace of Hans Christian Andersen. The coastal towns of Middelfart, Nyborg, Fåborg and Svendborg (see individual entries) are also worth seeing.

Greenland/ Grønland/Kalaallit Nunaat

Autonomous Territory
Area: 2,175,600 sq. km (839,782 sq. miles)
Population: 51,000
Postal code: DK–3900
Turistbureau
Skibshavnsvej B 19
DK–3900 Nuuk/Godthåb

Flag of Greenland

Greenland (Danish Grønland, Greenlandic Kalaallit Nunaat), the largest island in the world, is situated NE of the North American coast; it extends between latitude 59° 46′ and 83° 39′ N and longitude 11° 39′ and 73° 8′ W. In the W the island is separated from the Canadian Archipelago by Davis Strait, Baffin Bay and Smith Sound, in the E from Spitzbergen by the Greenland Sea and from Iceland by the Denmark Strait.

By its nature the island forms part of the Arctic; 85 per cent of the surface is covered by a gigantic sheet of ice averaging some 1500 m (4900 ft) in thickness. The ice-free area, 341,700 sq. km (131,896 sq. miles) in extent, lies principally on the coast; this is a region of fjords and skerries, the land resembling the Alps (although in the N and NW there are also plateaux), reaching heights of 1200–1500 m (3938–4923 ft). The highest point is the *Gunnbjørn Fjeld* (3733 m (12,252 ft)) in the E of Greenland. Disko Island lies off the W coast. There is an air service between Denmark (Copenhagen) and Greenland.

The people known as Greenlanders have developed from a mixture of Eskimos and Europeans. In addition there are a few pure-blooded Eskimos and Europeans. In Greenland the local language and Danish are spoken. Greenlandic is derived from the language of the Eskimos. Danish is a compulsory language in the schools.

In the parts of the country close to the edges of the ice, the vegetation consists mostly of birch and alder trees with junipers and rhododendrons. Farther north the vegetation is characterised by Polar pasture, grasses, mosses and lichens. Animals, found chiefly on the coasts, include reindeer, foxes and hares. In the N and NE there are also musk-oxen, Arctic wolves and lemmings. In the coastal waters seals, whales and walrus are found as well as about 100 species of fish. More than 200 species of birds get their food from the sea.

The principal branches of the economy are fishing and the processing of fish, together with seal-hunting and sheep-rearing. In Marmorilik lead, zinc and silver are mined. Many people work at home, producing objects of stone, wood, bone, skin and pearls and in recent years a modest tourist industry has developed in Greenland. *The Royal Greenland Trading Company* which, from 1774, supplied Greenland with imported goods and which was supported until the end of 1985 by the Danish State, has been called "Kalaallit Niuerfiat" (Greenland trade) since 1 January 1986 when its headquarters were transferred from Copenhagen to Nuuk/Godthåb. The adoption of the trading organisation by the Greenland Government means a further step for the island on the path to independence.

HISTORY. – The earliest inhabitants of Greenland were Eskimos (Inuit). In 982 Eric the Red, a Norwegian Viking, landed on the island and called it Greenland although it had been discovered in 875 by the Norman Gunnbjørn. From 1261 the island was subject to the Norwegian Crown. After the European settlers had succumbed to poor living conditions in the Middle Ages, the missionary Hans Egede landed in 1721 on the W coast of the island in the region of present-day Godthåb. Greenland again became settled by Europeans. When Norway and Denmark separated in 1814 Greenland remained Danish. A dispute about the island was settled by the International Court of Justice in The Hague in 1933 in favour of Denmark. During the Second World War the United States established air bases on Greenland. In 1953

Greenlanders

. . . and flowers of Greenland

Greenland became part of the Kingdom of Denmark with equal rights, and since the 1 May 1979 it has had internal autonomy; Denmark represents the interests of the country in the fields of foreign policy and defence. Greenland does not have full membership of the EEC but has the status of an overseas territory. The legislative body is the Parliament (Landsting) which is comprised of elected representatives. Executive powers lie in the hands of the Government (Landsstyre), chosen by Parliament. The people are also represented in the Danish Folketing by two members.

CLIMATE. – As is usual in countries with ice and tundra there are considerable differences of climate in places. In the interior and in the N of Greenland conditions of extreme Polar temperature hold sway. In the S the weather is milder but there is more precipitation. On the E coast the cold East Greenland current keeps the temperature low.

Most vacation areas are on the W coast which has the mildest climate. Prominent features of the coastal places are fishing vessels and small gaily painted wooden houses. Icebergs move into the sea from the coastal waters.

Narsarsuaq (Arctic Hotel, 110 b.; restaurant) in southern Greenland is a base for walking tours. For hotel guests excursions to sights in the vicinity are provided, including trips to ruins of the Viking period (c. 1000), to the inland ice and to fishing settlements. There is also a *South Greenland Programme* which includes a stay in *Narsaq* (hotels: Narsaq, 15 b.; Klamers Hotel, 12 b.; both with restaurants), *Qaqortoq/Julianehåb* (Hotels: Qaqortoq, 27 b.; Sømanshjemmet, 44 b.; both with restaurants) and *Nanortalik* (hotel: Kap Farvel, 12 b.; Klamers Hotel, 12 b.; both with restaurants).

A popular place is **Nuuk/Godthåb** (pop. 10,000; hotels: Godthåb, 18 b.; Grønland, 76 b.; Sømandshjemmet, 36 b.; all with restaurants), the capital of Greenland. Here the National Museum of Ethnology, Archaeology and Eskimo Art is of interest. Godthåb is the starting-point for tours of the Godthåb Fjord. Here there is a mild climate and on the cliffs grass and flowers grow (fishing is possible).

On the W coast N of Godthåb lies *Sisimiut/Holsteinsborg* (hotel: Sømandshjemmet, 82 b., with restaurant) a fishing port with wharf. E from here at the end of the fjord lies *Kangerlussuaq/Søndre Strømfjord* (KGH Transithotel, 203 b.; no prior booking) where there is the most important airport in Greenland. Between Godthåb and Søndre Strømfjord walking tours (including a visit to the inland ice) are organised and in winter there are safaris on skis.

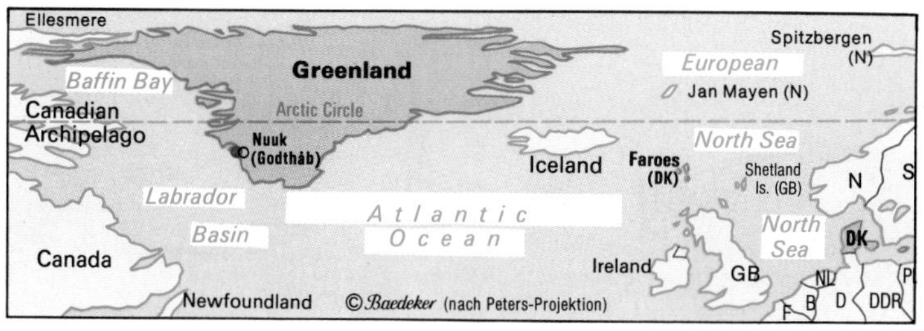

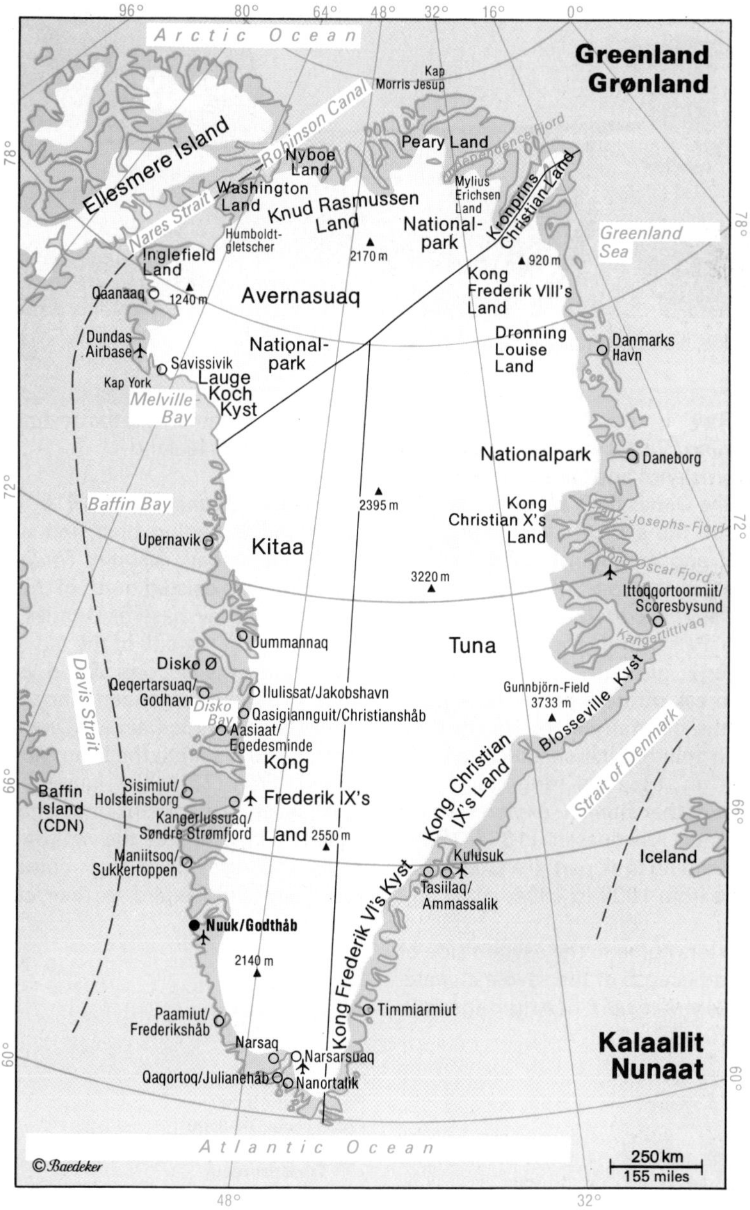

Greenland
Grønland

Arctic Ocean
Kap Morris Jesup
Peary Land
Independence Fjord
Robinson Canal
Ellesmere Island
Nares Strait
Nyboe Land
Washington Land
Knud Rasmussen Land
Humboldt-gletscher
Inglefield Land
2170 m
Mylius Erichsen Land
National-park
Kronprins Christian Land
920 m
Greenland Sea
Qaanaaq
1240 m
Avernasuaq
Kong Frederik VIII's Land
Dundas Airbase
Savissivik
Kap York
National-park
Lauge Koch Kyst
Melville Bay
Dronning Louise Land
Danmarks Havn
Nationalpark
Daneborg
Baffin Bay
2395 m
Kong Christian X's Land
Franz-Josephs-Fjord
Upernavik
Kitaa
Kong Oscar Fjord
3220 m
Ittoqqortoormiit/ Scoresbysund
Kangertittivaq
Uummannaq
Tuna
Disko Ø
Qeqertarsuaq/ Godhavn
Disko Bay
Ilulissat/Jakobshavn
Qasigiannguit/Christianshåb
Aasiaat/ Egedesminde
Davis Strait
Gunnbjörn-Field 3733 m
Blosseville Kyst
Strait of Denmark
Kong Frederik IX's Land
Kong Christian IX's Land
Sisimiut/ Holsteinsborg
Kangerlussuaq/ Søndre Strømfjord
2550 m
Baffin Island (CDN)
Maniitsoq/ Sukkertoppen
Kulusuk
Tasiilaq/ Ammassalik
Iceland
Nuuk/Godthåb
Kong Frederik VI's Kyst
2140 m
Paamiut/ Frederikshåb
Timmiarmiut
Narsaq
Narsarsuaq
Qaqortoq/Julianehåb
Nanortalik
Kalaallit Nunaat
Atlantic Ocean
© Baedeker
250 km
155 miles
96° 80° 64° 48° 32° 16° 0°
78° 72° 66° 60°

Nuuk/Godthåb, the capital of Greenland

Disko Bay is on Disko Island. In *Qeqertarsuaq/Godhavn,* the largest place on Disko Island and once a base for whalers, the Danes have set up a research station with the aim of investigating the biological and ecological conditions in the Arctic. On the coast of Disko Bay lies *Ilulissat/Jakobshavn* (hotels: Arctic, 80 b.; Hvide Falk, 46 b., with restaurant) where huge glaciers "calve", that is icebergs break off from them; these push out into the coastal waters. Vacationers can watch this natural spectacle and/or take part in trips by dog-sleigh. In Jakobshavn the Danish explorer Knud Johan Victor Rasmussen (1879–1933) was born and he took part in a Greenland expedition from 1902 to 1904.

Fewer visitors come to the eastern side of Greenland because of the severe climate. *Tasiilaq/Ammassalik* (Angmagssalik Hotel with restaurant) is the destination of short trips from Iceland.

Puffin

Rasmussen founded in 1910 in NW Greenland a trading-post and called it after the legendary island of *Thule,* which is said to have existed north of the British Isles. The US air base of Dundas, which was set up on the site of the old trading-post during the Second World War, has since 1951 been extended. The village of Thule (Greenlandic Oaanaaq) was moved 100 km (60 miles) to the N on Murchison Sound. From Thule Rasmussen undertook seven expeditions into the Arctic where he investigated the various Eskimo tribes and researched their cultural life, especially with regard to their common interests.

Grenå

Jutland
District: Arhus amt
Population: 19,000
Postal code: DK–8500
Telephone code: 06

Turistbureau
Torvet 1
Tel. 32 12 00

HOTELS. – *Grenå Strand,* Havneplads 1, 30 b.; *Hotel*

du Nord, Kystvejen 25, 240 b.; *Schloss Sostrup*, in Gjerrild, 100 b. – two camp sites.

RESTAURANTS. – *Det Gyldne Krus*, Lillegade 18; *Drop-inn*, Havnevejen 10.

The popular resort of Grenå lies on the Kattegat on the peninsula of Djursland, part of Jutland. From the town, which is important as a ferry and fishing port, car ferries leave for Hundested on Zealand and for Varberg in Sweden. There are excursion ships to the island of Anholt.

SIGHTS. – In this attractive place there are many old half-timbered houses, in one of which (dating from 1750) in the market-place can be found the *Djursland Museum*. Here articles of everyday use and handcrafted articles from the district are exhibited; there is also a collection of pipes (open: mid May–mid Sept. Tues.–Sun; otherwise variable).

SURROUNDINGS. – 6 km (4 miles) NE of the town lies **Fornæs** (Fornes), the most easterly point in Jutland. A lighthouse was erected here in 1892. 25 km (15 miles) inland from Grenå we come to *Djurs Sommerland*, a leisure park near the beautiful *Løvenholm Woods* (Løvenholm Skov). There are attractions here for young and old, including gold-panning in "cowboy country", water-chutes, an aerial cableway over the lakes and trips on the Djurs River (open: 11 May–1 Sept. 10 a.m.–6 or 8 p.m.; admission fee).

Haderslev

Jutland
District: Sønderjyllands amt
Population: 30,000
Postal code: DK–6100
Telephone code: 04

Turistbureau
Apotekergade 1
Tel. 52 55 50
Turistbureau
Kongensgade 5
DK–6070 Christiansfeld
Tel. 56 16 30 (open only in summer)

HOTELS. – *Motel Haderslev*, Damparken, 60 b.; *Norden*, Storegade 55, 64 b.; *Motel Syd*, Åbenråvej 120, 28 b. – YOUTH HOSTEL. – CAMP SITE.

RESTAURANTS. – *Hotel Harmonien*, Gåskaegade 19; *Hotel Norden*, Storegade 55.

EVENT. – *Town Festival of Duke Hans* (June).

Haderslev, an industrial and commercial town, is situated in the S of Jutland on the narrow Haderslev Fjord which penetrates inland from the E.

HISTORY. – Haderslev was founded probably in the middle of the 12th c. at a fork in the road where there was also a ford and developed into an important town and ecclesiastical centre. Because of its position the place was involved on several occasions in the wars for the Duchies of Schleswig and Holstein. Between 1864 and 1920 Haderslev belonged to the Prussian

Pack-ice on the coast of Disko Bay

Half-timbered houses in the Open-air Museum

province of Schleswig-Holstein. When the Duchy of Schleswig was divided in 1920 Haderslav became Danish.

SIGHTS. – The low houses make the town of Haderslev very pretty. The **Cathedral** (Church of Our Lady; *Vor Frue Kirke*), dating from the 13th–15th c., stands high on a hill. The interior is notable for the light choir, a beautiful Baroque pulpit (1636) and a bronze font (1485; cast by Peter Hansen).

In the N of the town can be found an ***open-air museum** (*Haderslev Amts Museum*) with half-timbered farms and windmills from East Schleswig and an interesting collection of excavation finds (including flint tools and cult objects found in the marshes, and an oak coffin).

SURROUNDINGS. – To the N of the Town on road A10 we come to **Christiansfeld** (hotel: Den Gamble Grænsekro, 20 b. with restaurant), founded by the Moravian Brethren with the consent of King Christian VII in 1773. The town is impressive in its simplicity and has many mementoes of the Brothers from Saxony – the Brødremenighedens Kirke of 1776, plain and undecorated, the cemetery subdivided into plots bordered by lime trees, and the *Brotherhood Museum*, in which ethnographical collections of the missionary work of the Moravian Brethren can be seen. In the cellar is housed the *Fire Brigade Museum* of South Jutland (Sønderjysk Brandværnsmuseum).

Helsingør

Zealand
District: Federiksborg amt
Population: 56,000
Postal code: DK–3000
Telephone code: 02

Turistbureau
Havnepladsen 3
Tel. 21 13 33
Turistbureau
Hovedgade 6B
DK–3250 Gilleleje
Tel. 30 01 74 (open only in summer)

HOTELS. – *Hamlet*, Bramstræde 5, 60 b.; *Marienlyst*, Nordrej Strandvej 2, 425 b.; *Skandia*, Bramstræde 1, 80 b.; – YOUTH HOSTEL. – CAMP SITE.

RESTAURANTS. – *Færgegården*, Stengade 81B; *Hos Anker*, Bramstræde 1; *Klostercafeen*, Skt. Annægade 35.

EVENTS. – Fishing Competition (Gilleleje; Apr.); Sailing Regatta "Round Zealand" (June); Music in the Bastions of Kronborg Castle (every Sat. June–Aug.); Fishing Competition (Aug.), and an occasional performance of "Hamlet".

The old Danish port and trading town of Helsingør (more familiar in English as Hamlet's "Elsinore") lies on the NE coast of the island of Zealand only 4.5 km (3 miles) from the Swedish town of Helsingborg on

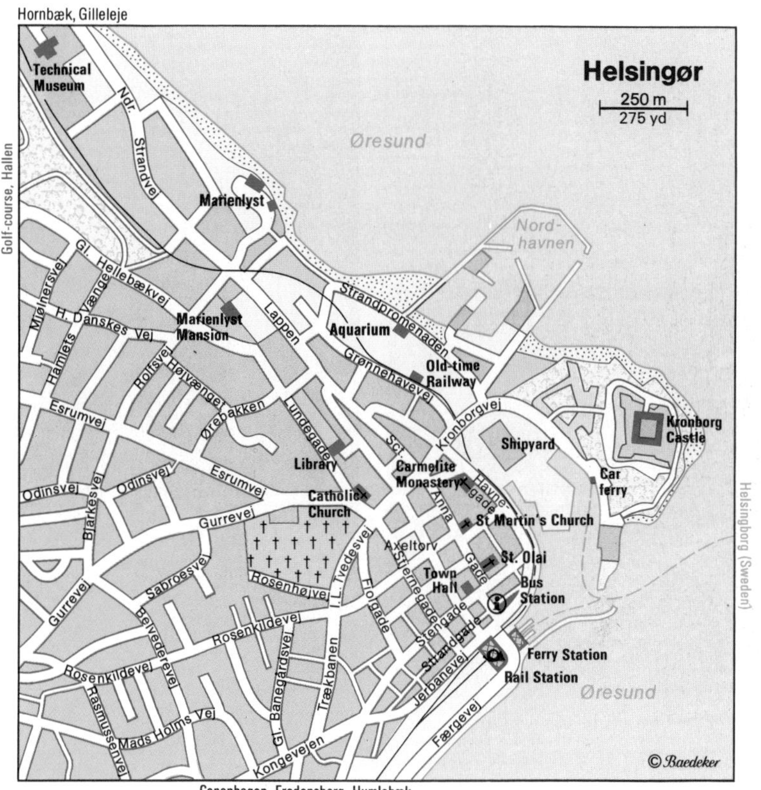

the other side of the Øresund. Helsingør possesses a productive shipyard as well as engineering, brewing and textile industries. A rail ferry plys over the Øresund to Helsingborg.

HISTORY. – The rise of the town can be traced back to the first half of the 13th c. After the Norwegians had burned down the settlement in 1288, King Eric of Pomerania began, in about 1420, to build a new castle on the outermost spit of land; this castle was called "Krogen" or "Ørekrog". The town obtained its charter in 1426, Eric introduced tolls for vessels passing through the Øresund. Both banks of the channel then belonged to Denmark and every ship which sailed through the Sound had to pay a toll accordingly. The King made the town an ecclesiastical centre; three monasteries were founded. When in 1658 the easterly provinces of the country, Schonen, etc., fell to Sweden, Helsingør lost much of its former importance. During the 17th c. several epidemics led to a decline of the population. At the end of the 18th c. English and Scottish merchants settled in Helsingør; the town obtained a land link with Copenhagen. In 1857 tolls in the Sound were abolished. Since the end of the 19th c. many holiday villas have sprung up between Helsingør and Copenhagen and tourism has benefited the town.

SIGHTS. – The town is divided into an inner area, a north-western and a north-eastern area where stands Kronborg Castle on a pensinsula. In the Inner Town the railway station lies opposite the terminal of the Danish Railways' ferry; and adjoining it on the N extends the port with the *Swedish Pillar* (Danish/Sveasøjlen; 11.75 m (39 ft) high) set up there in 1947 as an expression of gratitude to Sweden for taking in Danish refugees at the beginning of the Second World War. Many of these refugees were able to flee across the Øresund. To the NE runs *Stengade*, the main street of Helsingør and the axis of a pedestrian zone. The street is lined with fine old houses. The **Town Hall** (1855) has glass mosaics in the Council Chamber; these have motifs depicting the history of the town; they date to 1936–39 and are by Poul and Fanny Sæbye. Not far NE stands *St Olaf's Church* (foundation-stone laid about 1200; completed 1480–1559), with a notable Baptistery; the church has been a cathedral since 1961.

Well worth seeing is *St Mary's Church*, about 150 m (164 yd) farther N in Skt. Annagade. The church, which was built in

View of Helsingør

Chapel in Kronborg Castle

the Middle Ages, has a fine interior and a magnificent organ. It was here that the composer Dietrich Buxtehude (1637–1707) was organist between 1660 and 1668; he lived at Skt. Annagade, No. 6. St Mary's Church forms the southern wing of a *Carmelite monastery* built in 1430 and restored between 1902 and 1905. The courtyard, enclosed on all sides by open arcades, the church and the chapter-house, is the venue for concerts and lectures (guided tours through the church and monastery daily at 2 p.m.; 14 Apr.–15 Sept. also at 11 a.m.). To the W of Skt. Annagade we come to the *Axeltorv*, the hub of the town. Here stands a memorial fountain (Einar Utzon-Frank, 1926) to King Eric of Pomerania who gave Helsingør its charter. A market is held on the Axeltorv on Wednesdays and Sundays and from May to October on Fridays an antique market is also held here (1.30–6 p.m.). In *Strandgade*, the eastern boundary of the pedestrian zone, can be seen, as in Stengade, beautiful old houses, including Nos. 77–79, the *Old Pharmacy* (1577 and 1642) and Nos. 72–74, the *Court-house* (*c.* 1520).

From the Axeltorv we proceed in a north-westerly direction through Nygade and Marienlyst Allé to the Mansion of *Marienlyst*. Originally conceived as an observation pavilion overlooking the Sound, it was reconstructed in 1760 by Nicolas Henri Jardin for Queen Juliane Marie, the widow of Frederik V. Today the mansion, which is surrounded by an old park, serves as the *Municipal Museum of History*; it contains items on the history of the town, Louis XVI furniture, sculpture, etc. In the park is a commemorative grave for the Danish Prince Hamlet, a granite sarcophagus which was produced by the sculptor Einar Utzon-Frank and erected here in 1926.

In Nordre Strandvej (No. 23) is the **Danish Museum of Technology** (Danmarks Tekniske Museum; open: daily 10 a.m.–4 or 5 p.m.), to which a transport museum is annexed. This important museum portrays in two sections the development of natural science and technology as well as transport from its origins to the present day. On show are old models of aircraft, railways, trams and buses, including the Danish "Hammelvognen" (1886) and Ellehammer's aeroplane (1906). The museum also mounts special exhibitions. From *Grønnehave* in the northern part of the port the Old-time

Historic vehicles in the Technical Museum

Railway runs in summer (June–September on Sundays) to Gilleleje (24 km (15 miles)). The *Øresund Aquarium* can be found on the esplanade to the E of Grønnehave. In 10 biotopes marine animals from the Øresund are on show (open: daily in summer).

In the NE of the town on a peninsula in the Øresund rises ****Kronborg Castle** (see cover picture) which is a landmark from far off. Originally a fortress, built about 1420 by Eric of Pomerania, stood here. The new castle was built between 1574 and 1584 under King Frederik II by the Dutch architects Hans van Paescheng and Anthonis van Opbergen. After a catastrophic fire in 1629 Christian IV had the castle rebuilt between 1635 and 1640, finance being provided by raising the tolls for ships passing through the Øresund. From 1785 until 1922 the castle served as a garrison; in 1924 it was renovated. In the S wing is the *Castle Chapel* which survived the fire of 1629; it has a magnificent Renaissance interior, including wood-carving by German masters. The N wing houses the 63 m (69 yd) long *Knights' Hall*. The *Danish Commercial and Maritime Museum* is also to be found

Kronborg Castle, Helsingør

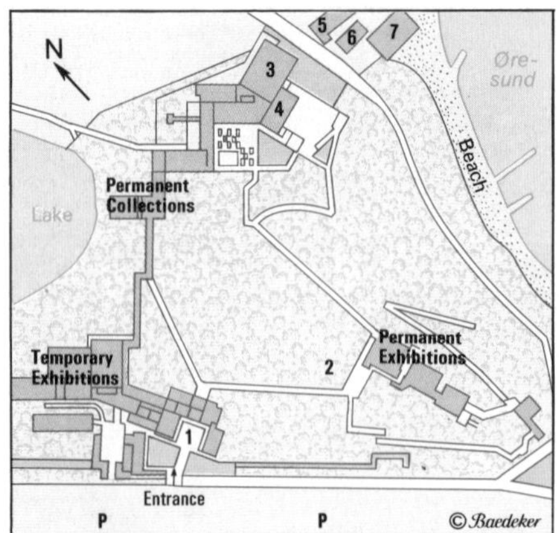

Louisiana Museum

1 Old Villa
2 Sculpture Garden
3 Concert Hall
Theatre
4 Cafeteria
5 Guest-house
6 Guests' Studio
7 Utility Building

P Car parking

in the castle. The collection illustrates the history of Danish maritime trade and seafaring (open daily). In the casemates (fortified walls) below the inner ramparts is a seated statue by H. P. Pedersen-Dan of the sleeping *"Holger Danske"*, the national hero, who, according to legend, will only awaken in the country's hour of need. From the SW tower (Telegraftårnet; 145 steps) there is a magnificent **view* and a walk along the outer bastions can be recommended. The *Flag Battery* is "the platform before the castle" on which, in Shakespeare's "Hamlet", the ghost of the Danish King appears striding past the guard.

SURROUNDINGS. – 10 km (6 miles) S of Helsingør, on the coast road, lies the village of *Humlebæk* (Humlebek). Here the ****Louisiana Museum** (open: daily 10 a.m.–5 p.m., Wed. 10 a.m.–10 p.m.; admission fee), founded in 1958 by the merchant and art-lover Knud W. Jensen, stands in a park with a view of the Øresund. It has a good international collection of modern painting from 1950 until the present day, and in the beautiful old park stand exceptionally fine sculptures, including works by Hans Arp, Alexander Calder, Max Ernst, Alberto Giacometti, Henry Moore and Jean Tinguely. Every year there are special exhibitions, sometimes of contemporary works and sometimes examples of older cultures. In addition there are concerts and poetry festivals. For trips on the Old-time Railway from Helsingør to Gilleleje (24 km (15 miles)) see pages 102-3.

Sculptures in the park of the Louisiana Museum

Fredensborg Castle

The road runs past many seaside resorts to the northern tip of Zealand. Leave Helsingør on the Strandvej, passing the Mansion of Marielyst in 1.5 km (1 mile) and Julebæk (beautiful beach) in another 2.5 km ($1\frac{1}{2}$ miles); then via Hellebæk through a stretch of woodland along the coast to the popular resort of **Hornbæk** (Trouville Hotel, 99 b.; camp site) with a beautiful beach only 50 m (55 yd) from the town.

The road continues through the resorts of *Villingbæk* and *Dronningmølle* (camp site). 2 km ($1\frac{1}{2}$ miles) S, on a hill on the Villingerød–Esrum road, are a park and museum (open: 1 Mar.–31 Oct. Tues.–Sun. 9.30 a.m.–5 p.m.; admission fee) containing works by the painter and sculptor Rudolph Tegner (1873–1950; some 200 pictures and 200 sculptures). Shortly before Gilleleje, on a high cliff to the right of the road, is the *Nakkehoved Lighthouse* (54 m (177 ft)) with extensive views (camp site). From here it is 4 km ($2\frac{1}{2}$ miles) to **Gilleleje** (hotels: Pension, 36 b.; Strand, 43 b.; restaurants: Gilleleje Havn; Karen og Marie; camp site) an old fishing village (fish auction daily) which is also a popular holiday resort. From the breakwater there are good views of the Kattegat, extending to the Swedish coast. Items of local interest, fishing equipment, costumes, etc. can be seen in the Gilleleje Museum (Rostgaardsvej 2; open: 15 June–15 Sept. Tues.–Sun. 2–5 p.m.). About 1 km ($\frac{1}{2}$ mile) W is *Gilbjerg Hoved*, the most northernly point on Zealand.

Continuing in a south-western direction on road A6 we come after 15 km (9 miles) to *Fredensborg* (Country House Hotel, 40 b.) with ****Fredensborg Castle** (1719–22; open: July daily 1–5 p.m., admission fee) which is the summer residence of the Royal Family (except in July). King Frederik IV named the castle "Fredensborg" as a memorial to the peace which ended the Nordic War (1700–20). The ***park** extending NW to Lake Esrum has fine avenues of birches and is one of the most impressive in Denmark. It is only open to the public in July.

Herning

Jutland
District: Ringkøbing amt
Population: 56,000
Postal code: DK-7400
Telephone code: 07

(i) **Turistbureau**
Bredgade 2
Tel. 12 44 22

HOTELS. – *Eyde*, Torvet 1, 163 b.; *Motel Herning*, Vardevej 9, 184 b.; *Herning Missionshotel*, Skolegade 1, 77 b.; *Østergårds Hotel*, Silkeborgvej 94, 160b. – YOUTH HOSTEL – CAMP SITE.

RESTAURANT. – *Hotel Hammerum*, Jernbanegade 8–10.

The town of Herning in Jutland between Ringkøbing and Silkeborg is the centre of the Danish textile industry.

HISTORY. – There were nine farms here at the end of the 17th c. and in 1840 there were only 21 inhabitants. The town developed very quickly to become an important centre of communications and in 1868 it got its own market. Industrial firms settled here.

SIGHTS. – In the *Municipal Museum* (Museumsgade) the life of the once-poor people of the heathland is presented by means of reconstructed farmhouse interiors and wax figures clothed in old costumes. The *Textile Museum* gives an impression of the development of the textile industry by means of tools from simple examples to modern processing works. In addition there are mementoes of Steen Steensen Blicher (1782–1848), the poet of the local heathland.

3 km (2 miles) E of the town centre lies the *Angligården*, the building of a textile factory which was closed in 1973. This was planned as a combination of industrial plant and art collection. To plans by Carl Theodor Sørensen and Christian Frederik Møller the house had a circular layout; in the inside courtyard is a 200 m (650 ft) long ceramic frieze "Phantasy Playing round the Wheel of Life" by Carl Henning Pedersen. The *art collection* has works by Danish masters, including Asger Jorn, Paul Gadegaard and Richard Mortensen, as well as pictures by foreign artists (open: Tues.–Sun. 10 a.m.–5 p.m.). In the adjoining park can be seen sculptures by Svend Dalsgaard, Robert Jacobsen, Henry Heerup, etc. Near this complex stands a *museum* which was opened in 1976, exhibiting works by Carl-Henning Pedersen and Else Alfelt. Here, too, the external wall is decorated with a ceramic frieze by Pedersen. This is reflected in a moat which surrounds the building.

SURROUNDINGS. – By following the main road A18 and branching off right after 5 km (3 miles), we come on the edge of the woods to the Romanesque *Rind Church* (Rind Kirke) which is about 800 years old. 12 km (7½ miles) west of Herning, near Havnstrup, is *Jutland's Minizoo* (open: Easter–Oct. 10 a.m.–6 p.m.).

Hillerød

Zealand
District: Frederiksborg amt
Population: 33,000
Postal code: DK–3400
Telephone code: 02

Turistbureau
Torvet 1
Tel. 26 28 52

HOTEL. *Missionshotel*, Slotsgade 5A, 36 b.

RESTAURANTS. – *Slotsherrens Kro*, Frederiksborg Slot 5; *Slotskroen*, Slotsgade 67.

The town of Hillerød, a railway junction, is in the N of Zealand.

HISTORY. – In the early Middle Ages Hillerød became a settlement. Some years later a nobleman built a mansion on an island in the present castle lake; this house was inherited by Frederik II (1559–88) who wanted to use the area for hunting. In 1562 the King built a castle and called it "Frederiksborg". The castle lake was formed by damming. The King's son, Christian IV (1588–1648), had the castle pulled down and a new one built between 1602 and 1620 in Renaissance style. In the period of Absolutism all Danish kings were anointed in the castle church, the last being Christian VIII (1840). The town of Hillerød also came into being in the time of Christian IV. In 1658 during the war with Sweden King Frederik III and Karl X Gustav of Sweden met at Frederiksborg. On their departure the Swedes sacked the castle and, among other things, they took away the fountain of Adrian de Vries. Later the castle was used only as a summer residence. When the members of the Royal Family gave preference to Fredensborg (see Helsingør) the heyday of Frederiksborg was past. There has been a stud in Hillerød since 1720 and the Frederiksborg horse has always been important in Danish breeding.

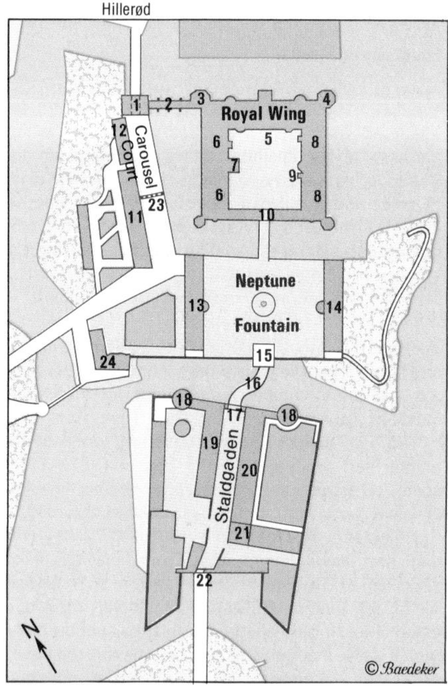

Frederiksborg Castle

1 Audience Chamber
2 Long Corridor
3 Mint Tower
4 Jægerberg Tower
5 Great Gallery
6 Chapel Wing
7 Chapel Tower
8 Princesses' Wing
9 Kitchen Well
10 Terrace Wing
11 Store-room Wing
12 Tea-rooms
13 Castellan's Lodging
14 Chancery
15 Gatehouse Tower
16 South Bridge
17 Christian VI's Gateway
18 Frederick II's Round Towers
19 Royal Stables
20 Hussars' Stables
21 Herluf Trolle's Tower
22 Town Gate
23 Former Carousel Gate
24 Restaurant

Frederiksborg Castle

SIGHTS. – The ****Castle of Frederiksborg** (open: 10 or 11 a.m.–3, 4 or 5 p.m.; admission fee) lies on three islands in the little Frederiksborg Lake. The castle, which was restored in its original style after a fire in 1859, is considered to be the finest Danish Renaissance building. Since 1888 the main courtyard has had a copy of the Fountain of Neptune by Adrian de Vries (1623) which was taken to Sweden in 1658.

The actual castle is situated on the third island. Since 1877 it has been furnished as a *Museum of Natural History* with the help of financial assistance in accordance with the scientific and artistic aims of the Carlsberg Fund. The museum gives an over-all view of Danish history and culture by means of pictures, portraits, furniture and *objets d'art*. The *castle church* in the west wing, which remained unharmed by the fire of 1859, has pews with inlaid work, a magnificent pulpit, an oratory and a fine wooden organ-case; concerts are given in the church. Interesting rooms in the castle are the Knights' Chamber with groined vaulting, a stucco frieze, carved chests and cabinets, the Summer and Winter Apartments and the Knights' Hall.

Adjoining the castle on the N by the lake lies the park, with terraces and avenues bordered by lime trees; it is considered one of the finest Baroque layouts in the north.

In Jægerbakken Park by the lake is the *North Zealand Regional Museum*; the *Museum of the History of Currency* can be found in the Frederiksborg Bank, Slotgade 16. Readers who wish to visit Frederiksborg in summer are advised to go during the week as it is a very popular outing, not only with Danes, but foreigners also and becomes very crowded at week-ends. A delightful day can be spent going by car or coach from Copenhagen, first for a brief visit to Fredensborg and then, by an easy road, to Frederiksborg.

Having spent an hour or two in the castle, walk or drive on the road which runs round the lake until opposite the castle: here is the place to picnic on the grass or to take photographs – it is one of the most beautiful sights in Denmark.

SURROUNDINGS. – In the direction of Frederiksværk, 6 km (4 miles) W of the town, we come to the *Æbelholt Monastic Museum*, housed in the ruins of a monastery; it contains human skeletons dating from the Middle Ages.

Himmelbjerg (in the foreground the steamer "Hjejlen")

Himmelbjerg

Jutland
Altitude: 147 m (482 ft)

The Himmelbjerg (Heaven Mountain), which has long been considered the highest hill in Denmark, overlooks Lake Julsø in Central Jutland. From the observation tower a splendid **view* of the surrounding forests and lakes may be enjoyed. Various other viewpoints can be found along the footpaths. Many political and religious meetings took place here during the 19th c., commemorated by several monuments. The paddle-steamer "Hjejlen" sails on the lake to Silkeborg.

Hjørring

Jutland
District: Nordjyllands amt
Population: 34,000
Postal code: DK-9800
Telephone code: 08

Turistbureau
Akseltorv 5
Tel. 92 02 32
Turistbureau
Vrenstedvej 6
DK-9480 Løkken
Tel. 99 10 09

HOTELS. – *Kirkedal*, Mårup Kirkevej 30, 33 b.; *Marinella*, Strandvejen 85–89, 211 b, both in Lønstrup; *Phønix*, Jernbanegade 6, 120 b. – YOUTH HOSTEL. – CAMP SITES.

RESTAURANTS. – *Messing Jens*, Jernbanegade 19; *Skammekrogen*, Østergade 38.

The old town of Hjørring, the principal place in Vendsyssel in North Jutland, is an industrial centre.

HISTORY. – The hill, which still forms the central point of the town, was a place of assembly during the whole of the Middle Ages; it was here that the "Thing" (Council) of Vendsyssel was held. The oldest known privileges of the town date from 1243. When assemblies of the "Thing" ceased at the beginning of the 16th c., a period of decline set in. In the 19th c. the fortunes of Hjørring improved; the economy thrived and industries came to the town (dyeworks, iron-foundries, etc.). In the middle of the 19th c. the roads to Hjørring were improved and in 1871 the town was linked to the regional rail network.

SIGHTS. – There are 18th c. half-timbered houses in the vicinity of the pedestrian zone. *St Catherine's Church* (*c.* 1250), a Romanesque red-brick building, stands in Kirkestræde. Of interest are the 13th c. Gothic Crucifix and an altar-panel with Baroque scrollwork dating from 1650. The **Historical Museum of Vendsyssel** (*Vendsyssels Historiske Museum*; open: 1 June–15 Sept. 10 a.m.–5 p.m.; 16 Sept.–31 May 1–4 p.m.) in Museumsgade 2 is housed in several old buildings, including a rectory; the garden is surrounded by prehistoric tombstones and medicinal plants. On view are items from the prehistoric epoch up to present-day popular art. In the *Museum of Art* can be seen paintings by artists from Vendsyssel (open: Tues.–Sun.)

SURROUNDINGS. – N of the town on the Skagerrak lies the port of **Hirtshals** (hotels: Fyrklit, 1024 b., apartments, restaurant; Hirtshals Kro, 45 b., restaurant; Skagerak, 22 b.). From the harbour, which was constructed between 1919 and 1930, there is a ferry service to Norway. The fish-processing industry is of considerable importance. In Hirtshals there is a *North Sea Museum* devoted to fishing and marine biology. It also has salt-water pools for seals and bottle-nosed dolphins (open: Mon.–Fri. 9 a.m.–4 or 8 p.m.; Sat. and Sun. 10 a.m.–5 p.m.; admission fee).

Driving W from Hjørring to the coast, we reach *Lønstrup*, a fishing village with good bathing. In the *Mårup Church* near by can be seen the anchor of a stranded English frigate, a memento of the many shipwrecks in Jammer Bay. The shifting sands in this area have caused much damage. The Sandflugtsmuseum at the *Rubjerg Knude*, a steeply sloping bank, gives details of the movement of the sands. To the S on Jammer Bay lies the popular resort of *Løkken* (hotels: Furreby Motel, 32 b., Apr.–Oct.; Grønhøj Strand, in Ingstrup, apartments; Løkken Badehotel, apartments; Løkkenshus, 43 b.; Løkkens Vejkro, 18 b.; restaurant: Peter Bådsmand), with a fine wide beach on which it is possible to drive to *Blokhus*, about 16 km (10 miles) away. Attention should be paid to the speed limit!). Near Saltum, between Løkken and Blokhus, the *Fårup Sommerland* leisure centre has facilities for various sports, from riding to go-carting (open: 1 May–31 Aug., 10 a.m.–6 or 8 p.m.).

It is worth while visiting the **Premonstratensian Monastery of Børglum**, some 6 km (4 miles) E of the coast. This dates from the 12th and 13th c. and well into the 12th c. was a Royal Court. Part of the building was converted about 1150 into a diocesan centre. In the middle of the 18th c. the entire complex was restored by the Danish architect Laurids de Thura and reconstructed into a Baroque mansion. Visitors can see the courtyard and the monastic church which was left unaltered and is a good example of Early Gothic. The church has remarkable Rococo furnishings (open: daily end of June–mid August 10 a.m.–5 p.m.; at other times by arrangement).

Historical Museum in Hjørring

Enclosing rampart of the Viking Castle of Fyrkat

Hobro

Jutland
District: Nordjyllands amt
Population: 14,000
Postal code: DK-9500
Telephone code: 08
(i) **Turistbureau**
Adelgade 26
Tel. 52 56 66
Turistbureau
Kirkegade 4 B
DK-9550 Mariager
Tel. 54 13 77

HOTELS. – *Alpina*, Ålborgvej, 34 b.; *Motel Hobro*, Randersvej 56–60, 48 b. – YOUTH HOSTEL. – CAMP SITE.

RESTAURANT. – *Teaterrestauranten*, Vestergade 4.

The old town of Hobro lies at the W end of Mariager Fjord in North Jutland, surrounded by heath and farmland.

HISTORY. – Hobro arose at a place where a bridge crosses the fjord; this can be seen on the town arms of 1584. In the 18th c. the town became important for maritime trade and from 1859 Hobro had a regular link with Copenhagen by ship. After the deepening of the harbour (1910–13) Hobro developed into an industrial town (foodstuffs, engineering).

SIGHTS. – The *church* (Adelgade) was built 1851–52 to plans by Gottlieb Bindesbøll who was also responsible for the Thorvaldsen Museum in Copenhagen. The mosaic of Christ by Joakim Skovgaard is notable. Near the church (Vestergade) is the *Hobro Museum* where can be seen a collection of silver and porcelain as well as objects which were found in the nearby Viking site.

SURROUNDINGS. – 3 km (2 miles) SW of the town (follow the sign "Vikingeborgen Fyrkat" lie the ****remains of a circular stronghold** dating from about 960. The Danish National Museum has reconstructed the circular rampart (Fyrkatborgen) and a Viking house about 1000 years old (open: Tues.–Sat.). It is planned to build a complete Viking village near Fyrkat. Near *Snæbum*, a short distance W of Hobro, can be seen "corridor graves" of the New Stone Age (about 3000 B.C.). To the E of Hobro, on the S bank of the Mariager Fjord, lies the township of *Mariager* (Hotel: Postgården, 16 b.; restaurant: Landgangen), one of the smallest towns in Denmark. The picturesque townscape is characterised by numerous half-timbered houses and an abundance of roses ("town of roses"). In the church which once belonged to the Convent of St Bridget (founded 1430), can be seen the so-called "coffin of Christ", a carved chest with a figure inside. The museum is housed in an old merchant's dwelling. Every Sunday a museum train runs to Handest (17 km ($10\frac{1}{2}$ miles)). S of the town rises the barrow of Hohøj.

Holstebro

Jutland
District: Ringkøbing amt
Population: 37,000
Postal code: DK-7500
Telephone code: 07
Turistbureau
Brostræde 2
Tel. 42 57 00. Telex 66 458

HOTELS. – *Bel Air*, Den Røde Plads, 114 b.; *Krabbes Hotel*, Stationsvej 18, 27 b.; *Schaumburg*, Nørregade 26, 65 b. – YOUTH HOSTEL. – CAMP SITE.

RESTAURANTS. – *Laksen*, Den Røde Plads; *Rådhuskælderen*, Kirkestræde; *Søens Perle*, Tujavej 20; *Tinghuset*, Store Torv.

EVENT. – *International Jazz Festival* (Sept.).

Holstebro is an old commercial and industrial town on the Storå in north-west Jutland.

HISTORY. – The place, first mentioned in 1274, grew up at the spot where there was a crossing over the Storå River where many roads converged. The oldest municipal privilege dates from the year 1552 and in the 16th c. merchants from Holstebro traded with the Netherlands. The 17th c. saw an economic decline. In the 19th c. there was a renewal of industrial activity helped by the extension of the port in Stuer, a new road system and rail link (1866) as well as the setting up of various industries.

SIGHTS. – Round the *Store Torv* (Market-Place), set in the town centre, the roads form a pedestrian precinct with shopping streets and specialist shops. The fountains and works of contemporary art are impressive; these include the sculptures "Women on the Cart" by Alberto Giacometti erected in 1966 in front of the *Old Town Hall* and, farther northwards in Nørregade, "Water Art" ("Vandkunsten") by Helge Bertram (1975), a high stone wall surrounded by water-basins. S of the Market-Place by the River Storå is *Red Square* (Røde Plads) with a fountain which was unveiled in 1977.

There are many museums in Holstebro which is the cultural centre of West Jutland. Exhibits on the history of the local regiment of Dragoons, including uniforms and details of the Resistance movement in this region, can be seen in the **Dragoon and Freedom Museum** in Asylgade (open: 1 May–30 Sept. Mon.–Fri. 2–4 p.m.; 1 Oct.–30 Apr. Thurs. 2–4 p.m.). Weapons from 30 countries (from the period 1848 to 1945) are contained in the historic weapon collection in Sønderlandsgade No. 8; in addition the collection includes literature, weapons and other things from the period of occupation and Danish Resistance (1940–45; visitors admitted by arrangement). S of Sønderlandsgade at Sønderbrogade No. 2 can be found the **Holstebro Museum of Art**. It exhibits Danish painting and sculpture, including works by Henry Heerup, Laurits Hartz and Ejler Bille, as well as international prints of the 20th c. and collections of non-European art, including pre-Columbian ceramics from Peru, and African art (open: 15 June–15 Aug. daily 11 a.m.–5 p.m.; 16 Aug.–14 June Tues.–Fri. noon–4 p.m. and Sat., Sun. 11 a.m.–5 p.m.).

E of the Inner City at Museumsvej No. 1, the *Holstebro Museum* (a local museum of historical and cultural collections) is situated in a lawned area. Here, together with finds from the Stone Age, the Viking era and the Middle Ages, is a collection of silver cutlery, a pipe and cigar collection and a collection of dolls.

Outside the town on the N at Døesvej No. 1 stands the *Nørreland Church* (dedicated in 1969), a building designed by the architects Inger and Johannes Exner. The church is circular in form so that the worshippers and minister can congregate round the altar and the font. Near the main building is a steel mast carrying the belfry. There are 44 bronze bells which can be operated both manually and electronically. In the vicinity of this church, at Nørrebrogade No. 1, we find the *Jens Nielsen and Olivia Holm-Møller Museum* (Jens Nielsen og Olivia Holm-Møller Museet; open daily 10 a.m.–5 p.m.) which was also designed by Inger and Johannes Exner. As well as works by Jens Nielsen and Olivia Holm-Møller the museum includes paintings by Kirsten Lundsgaardvig and sculptures by Niels Helledie. It is intended to obtain works with religious themes for the museum.

SURROUNDINGS. – Some 18 km (11 miles) W of Holstebro lies the village of Vemb, and not far S the Mansion of *Nørre Vosborg*. Thatched houses surround the courtyard which has a belfry. The main building of four wings, the oldest part of which goes back to 1552, can be visited (open: June–Aug. daily 11 a.m.–6 p.m.; Easter–end Oct. Sat. 1–6 p.m., Sun 11 a.m.–6 p.m.).

Horsens

Jutland
District: Vejle amt
Population: 56,000
Postal code: DK–8700
Telephone code 05
(i) **Turistbureau**
Kongensgade 25
Tel. 62 31 32
Turistbureau
Odelsgade 17
DK–7130 Julesminde
Tel. 69 33 13

HOTELS. – *Bygholm Parkhotel*, Schüttersvej 6, 130 b.; *Dagmar*, Smedegade 68, 53 b.; *Danica*, Ove Jensens Allé, 48 b.; *Jørgensens Hotel*, Søndergade 17, 48 b.; *Postgården*, G1. Jernbanegade 6, 70 b.; *Motel Thorsvang*, Vejlevej 58, 16 b. – YOUTH HOSTEL. – Two CAMP SITES.

RESTAURANTS. – *Eydes Kælder*, Søndergade 17–19; *Kronborg*, Åboulevarden 4–6; *Lille Heimdal*, Rædersgade 8–10; *Los Chicos*, Smedetorvet 8–10.

The important industrial town of Horsens lies on the E coast of Jutland at the head of Horsens Fjord.

HISTORY. – The oldest privileges granted to the town go back to the year 1442. Many churches and monasteries were established which were used after the Reformation for other purposes. In the 16th c. landed gentry from the surroundings moved into the town and built houses there. After Horsens had suffered in the 17th c. from the effects of war, in the 18th c. trade, especially with Norway, experienced a revival. About 1859 a new port was constructed and Horsens developed into an industrial town. The explorer Vitus Bering (1680–1741), after whom the Bering Strait between Alaska and Cape Deshnew in Asia is named, was born in Horsens.

SIGHTS. – In the market-place stands the **Church of the Redeemer** (*Vor Frelser Kirke*), built at the end of the 12th c. and restored 1935–36. Inside is a beautifully carved pulpit and a notable triforium. A figure of Christ (1950) by Einar Utzon-Frank adorns the altar. The *friary church* in Borgergade is the only surviving feature of a 13th c. Franciscan foundation. It was restored in 1892 when efforts were made to revise the Late Gothic form of the building. The carved altar dates from about 1500 as do the choir-stalls and the triumphal cross. The pulpit has cartouche and scrollwork of about 1650. There are 18th c. tombstones in the churchyard.

In Søndergade, where influential merchants once operated, a rebuilt half-timbered house in Baroque style can be seen (No. 17). In this so-called *"**palais**" there lived from 1780 to 1807 the sisters of Ivan, the heir to the Russian throne, who was deposed in 1740. Later Queen Charlotte Frederike, the mother of Frederik VII, resided here from 1810 to 1829. Today the building is a hotel. Another hotel is situated on the western edge of the town in a beautiful park. This one is housed in the ruins of *Bygholm Castle*, built at the beginning of the 14th c.; the present main building dates from 1775. By the harbour in the S of the town are a number of small houses dating from the 1890s, and here also stands the former municipal electricity power-station which has been converted into a workers' and industrial museum.

SURROUNDINGS. – SE of Horsens, on a spit of land which divides Horsens Fjord on the N from Vejle Fjord on the S, is the little resort of *Juelsminde* (hotel: Juelsminde; restaurant: Liniepavillion), from where there is a ferry service to Kalundborg on Zealand.

Jutland

District: Sønderjyllands amt, Ribe amt, Vejle amt, Viborg amt, Nordjyllands amt.

Jutland (Danish Jylland), a peninsula in northern Europe is the largest part of Denmark. The Jutland Peninsula, also known as the "Danish Continent", is bounded to the N of Flensburg by the German province of Schleswig-Holstein, and extends N surrounded by the North Sea, the Skagerrak and the Kattegat. The distance from Cap Skagen in the N to the German–Danish frontier in the S is some 310 km (193 miles) and the distance from the W to Grenå in the E 172 km (107 miles). The southern part of the peninsula which was ceded by Germany to Denmark in 1920 is called Sønderjylland in Danish. Heath and woodland are characteristic of the landscape as are long beaches on the coast.

Formerly devoted exclusively to farming and fishing, Jutland now has well-developed industries, though agriculture still plays an important part in its economy. Industrial concerns are found principally in the coastal towns. Jutland has a low density of population.

There are many places on the E coast, including Århus (see entry), the second largest town in Denmark, with an open-air museum. In the surroundings of Ålborg (see entry) are burial sites dating from the Viking times. The town of Esbjerg (see entry) on the west coast is the most important North Sea port in the country. Also worth seeing are the cathedral in Ribe (see entry), the miniature town "Legoland" near Billund (see entry) and the runic stones of Jelling near Vejle (see entry). The towns in the interior, including Silkeborg and Viborg (see entries), are also worth a visit. A region of especial natural beauty is the Limfjord (see entry) in North Jutland where fishermen and boating enthusiasts will find excellent sport. Limfjord oysters are specially good.

Church of Our Lady in Kalundborg

Kalundborg

Zealand
District: Vestsjaellands amt
Population: 19,000
Postal code: DK-4400
Telephone code: 03
(i) **Turistbureau**
Volden 12
Tel. 51 09 15

HOTEL. – *Ole Lunds Gård*, Kordilgade 1–3, 29 b. – Two CAMP SITES.

RESTAURANTS. – *Fjorden*, Banegården; *Slotskælderen*, Kordilgade 40.

EVENT. – Lerchenborg Music Festival, July–Aug.

Kalundborg, an important industrial town, lies on the fjord of the same name on the W coast of Zealand. From the harbour there are ferry services to Jutland (Juelsminde, Århus) and to the island of Samsø.

HISTORY. – Near the place where the fleet used to assemble before embarking on campaigns of war, there arose in the 12th c. the fortified Kalundborg which was surrounded on all sides by walls and had two fortresses. In the 13th c. Kalundborg carried on extensive maritime trade. The oldest privileges of the town date from 1485. From 1658 to 1660 Swedish troops occupied the town and the castle was taken by them and blown up. From 1684 ships have been sailing twice a week between Kalundborg and Århus; from 1874 a rail link was established between Copenhagen and the ferry terminal. At the end of the 19th c. various industries were set up in Kalundborg.

SIGHTS. – The landmark of the town is the five-towered ***Church of Our Lady** (*Vor Frue Kirke*) in Adelgade, which was built about 1170. The plan of the church is in the form of a Greek cross with a central tower and four corner towers. Inside is a finely carved Baroque altar-piece (1650) and a granite font which dates from the time of the foundation of the church. The old Mansion of Lindegard, to the W of the Church of Our Lady, houses the *Municipal Museum*; here can be seen traditional costumes, implements for craftwork and peasants' rooms. In addition temporary exhibitions are arranged. In Skolegade stands *Folen*, a tower which survived when the Swedes destroyed Kalundborg Castle in 1659.

SURROUNDINGS. – About 5 km (3 miles) S of the town on the peninsula of Asnæs is the Baroque ***Mansion of Lerchenborg**, built between 1743 and 1753 for General Lerchen. The mansion also has a park and a rose-garden. During the summer concerts take place in the Rococo Knights' Hall. (As the house is now privately owned visitors should inquire in Kalundborg before visiting it.) Two memorial rooms in a wing of the house are dedicated to Hans Christian Andersen who was often a guest here. 1 km (½ mile) W of Kalundborg on the Gisseløre Peninsula stands the radio transmitter of Kalundborg (masts up to 143 m (470 ft) high).

Køge

Zealand
District: Roskilde amt
Population: 35,000
Postal code: DK–4600
Telephone code 03
(i) **Turistbureau**
Vestergade 1
Tel. 65 58 0
Turistbureau
DK–4660 Store Heddinge
Tel. 70 33 69

HOTELS. – *Centralhotel*, Vestergade 3, 26 b.; *Hvide Hus*, Strandvejen 111, 224 b. – YOUTH HOSTEL. – two CAMP SITE.

RESTAURANTS. – *Richters Gård*, Vestergade 16; *Rio Bravo*, Skt. Gertrudsstræde 2.

Køge, a busy and attractive little port with notable industry, is situated on Køge Bay on the E coast of Zealand.

HISTORY. – The town was probably founded because of the profitable catches of herring in the Øresund and the associated fishing trade; it received its first privileges in 1288. Although until the end of the 16th c. trade was principally with the North German towns, the Dutch now became more prominent; in addition there were in Køge wood-carvers, goldsmiths, and shoemakers; Køge beer was celebrated. The town suffered severely in the war of the 17th c. The Danish maritime hero Niels Juel inflicted considerable damage on the Swedish fleet in Køge Bay in 1677. The town experienced an upswing in the 19th c.

Street scene in Køge

SIGHTS. – The central part of the town is old, with many pretty timber-framed houses of the 16th and 17th c.; the oldest, dating from 1527, is in Store Kirkestræde. In Nørregade lies the *Town Museum* where local collections are on view, including traditional costumes, agricultural implements, articles associated with the guilds and old furniture. Also of interest is *St Nicholas's Church*, built 1450–1500, with wood-carving of the 16th and 17th c.

SURROUNDINGS. – About 7 km (4 miles) S of the town stands the *Castle of Vallø*, a distinguished Renaissance building, originally a royal palace with two impressive towers. It was established as a home for unmarried ladies of noble rank by Queen Sophie Magdalene who added another wing, the White Foundation, at the same time. For many years its mistress was always a lady of royal birth. In 1893 its interior was gutted by a huge fire and after it was restored the occupants, though usually of noble birth, could be chosen from the ranks of high-born, though not necessarily noble, women. It is surrounded by a wide moat and 40 acres of parkland and is well worth visiting in the spring when it has a wonderful show of bulbs. Travelling SE from Køge we arrive at the Stevens Peninsula and in another 22 km (14 miles) reach the little country town of *Store Heddinge* where there is a typical church built originally in 1200 and later altered. 6 km (4 miles) to the E ***Stevns Klint**, a chalk escarpment, extends along the shore and from it there is a magnificent view over the sea. The high white crag near *Højerup* (alt. 41 m (135 ft)) is particularly beautiful, and here there stands a little church of 1357 in the choir of which is a still older chapel. According to legend this was built by a fisherman who had been rescued at sea. Since the sea has constantly eroded the chalk cliffs, the church, so the legend continues, moves backwards a fraction on each New Year's night towards the land, so that it does not fall into the sea! About 1928 the choir collapsed and the rest of the church has now been made safe.

Kolding

Jutland
District: Vejle amt
Population: 56,000
Postal code: DK–6000
Telephone code: 05
(i) **Turistbureau**
Helligkorsgade 18
Tel. 53 21 00

HOTELS. – *Kolding*, Akseltorv 5, 80 b.; *Møllegården*, Dyrehavevej 198, 16 b.; *Saxildhus*, Bånegardspladsen, 148 b.; *Scanticon Kolding*, Skovbrynet, 320 b.; *Tre Roser*, Byparken, 220 b. – YOUTH HOSTEL. – several CAMP SITES.

RESTAURANTS. – *Bacchus Bistro*, Akseltorv 5; *Kryb-i-ly Kro*, Landevej 160.

Koldinghus Castle

Castle church

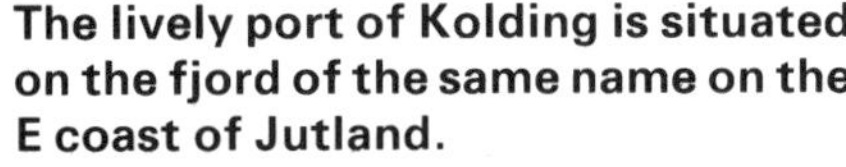

The lively port of Kolding is situated on the fjord of the same name on the E coast of Jutland.
Kolding is Denmark's largest export market for cattle. As well as abattoirs the town has textile, engineering and iron industries.

HISTORY. – The oldest privileges of the town date from 1321. Where the little Kolding Au flows into the fjord, several roads from the interior met in the Middle Ages. In 1248 the Danish King had Koldinghus Castle erected here and this was later rebuilt on several occasions. In the 16th and at the beginning of the 17th c. the cattle trade in Kolding was very profitable. The customs boundary with the Duchy of Schleswig ran immediately S of the town. During the 17th c. Kolding suffered severe damage through the effects of war. In the 19th c. the castle was burned down. In both the wars against Schleswig-Holstein Kolding was occupied by German troops. After the Treaty of Vienna in 1864 a new customs boundary between Denmark and Germany was drawn. In the second half of the 19th c. the harbour was reconstructed and industry came to the town.

SIGHTS. – In the centre of the town stands **Koldinghus Castle**, built in 1248 and destroyed by fire in 1808. The tower was re-erected between 1934 and 1936. In the restored ground floor of the north wing is an *historical and cultural museum* (open: daily 1 May–30 Sept., 10 a.m.–5 p.m.; 1 Oct.–30 Apr., Mon.–Sat. noon–3 p.m., Sun. 10 a.m.–3 p.m.), where exhibits concerning the history of the town and the surrounding area, weapons and handcrafted articles (porcelain, stoneware, silver) are displayed. The S and E wings of the castle have also been rebuilt.

The neo-Romanesque *Town Hall* (1873–75) stands in the market-place; immediately opposite is *Borchs gård*, a beautiful timbered house, formerly a pharmacy, with carved beams of 1535. Also worth seeing is the *Geographical Garden* (Geografiska Have og Rosehave), in the S of the town, which is adjoined by a rose-garden. This garden was laid out by Axel Olsen, owner of a tree nursery, and now has about 2000 species of trees and shrubs from all parts of the world, which are laid out according to geographical principles. In the garden can be seen the longest bamboo hedge in northern Europe.

SURROUNDINGS. – Inland, W of the town, lies *Vejen* (hotel: Vejen Gæstgivergård, 18 b.) which is chiefly visited for a museum which houses works by the sculptor N. Hansen Jacobsen, and because of the amusement park of Billingland. Here visitors can play with remote-controlled ships. There are also a shipping museum, a pirates' stronghold, a model train and a miniature racecourse. Near Vejen is situated the well-known *Askov People's High School* (1895), the model for these institutions in Denmark and other Scandinavian countries.

Korsør

Zealand
District: Vestsjaellands amt
Population: 21,000
Postal code: DK–4220
Telephone code: 03

(i) **Turistbureau**
Nygade 7
Tel. (03) 57 08 03
Turistbureau
Algade 1–7
DK–4230 Skælskor
Tel. (03) 59 53 74

HOTELS. – *Klarskovgård*, Bonderupvej 101, 184 b.; *Tårnborgkroen*, Tårnborgvej 16, 23 b.

RESTAURANTS. – *Skovhuset*, Skovvej 120; *Sølyst*, Havnepladsen 13.

EVENT. – *Fishing competition in the harbour* (June).

The port of Korsør lies on the W coast of Zealand overlooking the Great Belt. To the E stretches the Korsør Nor (a coastal lake). Korsør is a passenger traffic port with ferry services to Funen, Langeland and Kiel, a fishing port and it also has shipyards.

HISTORY. – There was a castle here as early as the middle of the 12th c. as a fortification against attack by the Wends. A new fortress was built by the Nor at the beginning of the 14th c. and this consisted of a tower surrounded by a wall. Korsør developed in the safety of the castle. The oldest town privileges date from 1425. In 1661 Korsør together with Copenhagen became an official trading centre. The railway between Korsør and Copenhagen was completed in 1856. Ships from Kiel which until then had called at Copenhagen now sailed to Korsør. In the second half of the 19th c. industry was set up in the town, including glass-manufacture.

SIGHTS. – Of the old fortress by the harbour only the *14th c. tower* has survived; from it there is a fine view over the town and the Belt. In Adelgade stands the *King's House* (Kongegården), a half-timbered house of 1761. In former centuries it was here that the kings stayed when they passed through the town. The façade is decorated with figures of four persons representing the Seasons. Also of interest is a monument near the port which is dedicated to the Danish writer Jens Baggesen (1764–1826), who was born in Korsør.

SURROUNDINGS. – On Skælskør Fjord, S of the town, lies the township of **Skælskør** (Kobæk Strand Hotel, 101 b.; Hesteskoen Restaurant; Trade and Industry Fair in Oct.) with old timber-framed houses and St Nicholas's Church, dating from the 13th c. 2 km (1¼ miles) S of Skælskør stands *Borreby Manor-house* (16th c.), one of the best-preserved fortified country houses of the Renaissance; it is surrounded by a rampart and a ditch. The interior of the house, which

Korsør Harbour

lies in a park, was rstored in 1884. The working quarters date from the 17th c. (entrance to the park and working quarters: 1 May–31 Oct. daily 9 a.m.–8 p.m.; 1 Nov.–30 Apr. daily 9 a.m.–4 p.m.; the main buildings can be seen by arrangement).

From Borreby Manor-house the road goes E to *Ørslev*, which has an interesting church (frieze with a representation of a medieval round dance). From there we go on to **Holsteinborg Castle** (17th c.), a Renaissance building with four wings, situated in a beautiful park with a long avenue of limes by the waterside (Holsteinborg Nor). Since 1707 the castle has been owned by the Holstein ducal family. Hans Christian Andersen stayed there on several occasions (entry to the park daily 9 a.m.–7 p.m.)

Læsø

District: Nordjyllands amt
Area: 116 sq. km (45 sq. miles)
Population: 28,000

Turistbureau
Havnegade 6
DK–9950 Vesterø Havn
Tel. (08) 49 92 42

The island of Læsø lies in the northern Kattegat. There is a car ferry between Vesterø Havn on Læsø and Frederikshavn on the coast of Jutland (duration about 1½ hours).

Two thirds of the island consists of uncultivated land, principally of fen and heath. In the N lies the Højsande area of dunes which reaches a height of 28 m (92 ft). The S of the island has low-lying meadows on the shore. The eastern point, with Danzigmand Dune, is an attractive area; the dune was named after a ship ("Danzig") which was stranded there. The Knotten Peninsula is a bird reserve.

Farmhouses with their roofs covered in seaweed are a feature of the chief place **Byrum** (Wilsens Hotel, 50 b.). The Læsø local museum is housed in a half-timbered homestead of four wings with a seaweed-covered roof; here silver and costumes are on show. In the 13th c. church there is a limewash painting of St George and the Dragon and an altar of 1450.

Langeland

District: Fyns amt
Area 185 sq. km (71 sq. miles)
Population: 23,000

Turistbureau
Bystrædet 3
DK–5900 Rudkøbing
Tel. (09) 51 14 44

Typical farmhouse in Byrum

Sailing-boats in Rudkøbing Harbour

The island of Langeland, some 50 km (31 miles) long and 3–9 km (2–6 miles) wide is situated to the SE of Funen in the Great Belt. The island can be reached by car or by ship. From Svendborg on Funen a huge bridge (1967) leads on to the island of Tåsinge and from the southern side of this island a causeway and a bridge (1962) over the little islet of Siø form a link with Langeland. As well as the ferry services to other Danish islands, there is a service between Kiel and Bagenkop.

Langeland is a long and narrow island popular for vacations with many beautiful beaches, magnificent beech woods and a multitude of holiday activities.

On the W coast lies the capital **Rudkøbing** (hotels: Rudkøbing, 12 b.; Skandinavien, 15 b.; restaurants: Æventyrmøllen; Degnehaven; youth hostel; camp site), a picturesque place with winding streets and stately merchants' mansions. Old houses can be seen, especially in Brogade and Smedegade and in the Gåsetorv. The *old pharmacy* in Brogade No. 15 (pharmaceutical equipment of three centuries) is the birthplace of the physicist Hans Christian Ørsted (1777–1851) who established the theory of electromagnetism. The *church* is interesting; its oldest part is Late Romanesque (*c.* 1100) and the tower dates from 1621. In the *Langeland Museum* (Jens Winthersvej 12) archaeological and local collections are exhibited, including swords and armour from Viking graves.

In the southern part of the island near road No. 26, lies Hennetved, and not far to the S the *Skovsgård Mansion* with a wagon collection (old horse-drawn wagons; open 15 June–31 Aug. 10 a.m.–3 p.m.). *Skovsgård Mill* (restored 1983) is a protected monument. In Humble, also in the S of Langeland, can be seen an impressive Megalithic grave, *"Kong Humbles Grav"*. 12 km (7½ miles) N of Rudkøbing **Tranekær Castle**, the oldest and largest castle in Langeland, stands on a hill. The angular building, which was reconstructed in 1863 (tower of 1859), contains the remains of a medieval royal castle. From the car park on the road to the S of the castle a path runs round the castle lake (entrance to the park outside the castle moat).

In Lohals, a resort in the N of the island, *Tom Kundsen's Safari Museum* is worth seeing. On show here are hunting trophies and an ethnographical collection from Africa.

Turistbureau
Fiskergade 2
DK–7600 Struer
Tel. (07) 85 07 95
Turistbureau
Store Torv
Det gamle Rådhus
DK–7700 Thisted
Tel. (07) 92 19 00

Limfjord

Jutland
Districts: Viborg amt and Nordjyllands amt

ⓘ **Turistbureau**
Torvet
DK–9370 Hals
Tel. (08) 25 14 50
Turistbureau
Bytorvet
DK–7730 Hanstholm
Tel. (07) 96 12 19
Turistbureau
Toldbodgade 4
DK–7620 Lemwig
Tel. (07) 82 03 72
Turistbureau
DK–9670 Løgstor
Tel. (08) 67 20 10
Turistbureau
Havnen 2
DK–7900 Nykøbing Mors
Tel. (07) 72 04 88
Turistbureau
Østerbro 7
DK–7800 Skive
Tel. (07) 52 32 66

The Limfjord, 180 km (112 miles) long, between the North Sea and the Kattegat, divides the Nørrejyske Ø, the island of North Jutland from the rest of the peninsula. With its beautiful scenery and calm water it offers ideal sailing conditions. A "vacation on the water" is made particularly attractive by the presence of many little towns with harbours and mooring-places.

A brochure "Limfjord and the Sea Coast" can be obtained at all local tourist offices and in it every mooring-place is listed. Car-drivers should note that the Limfjord can be crossed only at certain places; there are bridges over the Oddesund, Vilsund and Sallingsund (island of Mors) and over the Aggersund as well as a bridge and a tunnel at Ålborg. In addition several ferries cross the fjord in a few minutes, including one at the W and one at the E end.

Tranekær Castle

A fishing boat in the Limfjord

The western entrance to the Limfjord from the North Sea is the *Thyborøn Canal* (ferry), on the N side of which extends the popular holiday area round *Agger* and *Vestervig*. In the 11th c. Vestervig was the seat of the Bishop of Vendsyssel the most northerly part of Jutland. Today it is a little village with less than 1000 inhabitants. The church today reminds us of its proud past even if the once-magnificent three-aisled basilica suffered in the course of centuries by rebuilding and restoration. Renovation in the 1920s brought the church back into something like its original condition. It contains a number of Romanesque tombstones, including the oldest ones in Denmark (1210).

Vestervig lost its importance when its harbour silted up, and the same is true of many other places on this stretch of the coast. The silting alternated with storm tides which did further damage to the soil and a number of towns disappeared. The tiny Church and Beacon Tower of *Lodbjerg*, isolated in the dunes, bear witness to this destruction. Today the *Agger Tange* promontory is protected by dikes and breakwaters as has been done in the Netherlands.

On the S shore of the *Nissum Bredning*, a lagoon at the S end of the Limfjord, lies **Lemvig** (pop. 6500; hotels: Industriehotel, 30 b.; Nørre Vinkel, in Vinkelhage, 52 b.; Scandinavian Holiday Centre, apartments, in Vinkelhage; Marina Restaurant), an attractive town in a hilly area. The church, with an "onion tower" of 1936, has a corresponding Rococo interior. In the local museum are items concerning the history of life-saving at sea. With expanses of woodland; bog and heath and the sand-dunes of the W coast, the surroundings of Lemvig are a paradise for nature-lovers; in addition many rare waterfowl can be observed. 12 km (7 miles) W of the town a steep cliff, the 43 m (141 ft) high *Bovbjerg Klint*, borders the sea.

The little industrial township of *Struer* (Humlum Kro, 7 b.; City Restaurant) is situated on Venø Bay; in the local museum is an interesting collection of model ships. To the N and W of Struer, near *Kilen*, we come to a strange moraine landscape (nature reserve) with tunnel valleys.

In Limfjord itself there are many islands both small and large, the most important of which **Mors** (*Morsø*) is reached by bridges over the Sallingsund to the S and the Vilsund to the N, or by ferries across the Neessund and the Feggesund. The charm of Mors lies in its magnificent scenery. Especially interesting is the *Hanklit*, a 65 m (200 ft) high crag which falls almost vertically to the sea and contains animal and plant fossils of the Tertiary period. Ice Age glaciers have ground the rock into fantastic shapes. At the northern tip of Mors lies *Feggeklit*; this is the place where, according to legend, Hamlet is said to have killed his stepfather, Fegge. The chief town on Mors is **Nykøbing** (pop. 10,000; hotels: Bendix, 80 b.; Parkhuset, 36 b.; Sallingsune Færgekro, 76 b.; event: Pearl Festival, May–June), a smallish town which is known for the culture of oysters and for herring-fishing. In a restored wing of the former *Dueholm Abbey* (1370) is housed the Historical Museum (Morslande Historiske Museum) with a good collection including excavation finds, *objets d'art* and regional costumes. To the S of Nykøbing Mors a visit is recommended to the *Jesperhus Flower Park*, a large area with half a million plants and an aquarium (tropical fish; open Easter–Oct.).

E of Mors lies the little island of *Fur* with moler deposits and sandstone in the N. About 1120 a sandstone church was built in *Nederby*. In the *Fur Museum* can be seen fossils and geological curiosities. A

By the Limfjord

panoramic view of the island's beautiful natural scenery can be had from the *Stendalshøj*.

Going E from Struer we come to **Skive** (pop. 17,000; hotels: Gammel Skivehus, 120 b.; Hilltop, 125 b.; Eldorado Restaurant; two camp sites) on the fjord of the same name, a southern arm of the Limfjord. Here the *old church* (Gamle Kirke, 12th c.) is a Romanesque building with wall-paintings of 1522. The historical and cultural exhibits in the *museum* include an impressive collection of amber from Greenland. In a wood behind the harbour stands *Krabbesholm Manor*, dating from the 16th c., which has been a People's High School since 1907. In the main wing can be seen a finely furnished Knights' Hall in the style of Jutland Rococo dating from 1759 (viewing by arrangement).

In the W of the Salling Peninsula stands ***Spøttrup Castle**, one of the best examples in Denmark of medieval fortress architecture. It was built in the 15th c. for the Bishops of Viborg and is surrounded by a double moat with a dividing rampart. For a long time it was considered impregnable; to the E of the castle lies a garden with medicinal plants and spices (viewing May–Sept. 10 or 11 a.m.–6 p.m.). SW of Skive (accessible via Vinderup; Vinderup Hotel, 32 b.; Sevel Kro Restaurant), lies the *Hjerl Hede* nature park (1000 ha (2500 acres)) on the Flynder Lake. The chief attraction here is the ***open-air museum**, "the old village" (open: Apr.–Oct. daily 9 a.m.–5 p.m.) with a smithy, shops, mills, churches, etc.; near by is a Stone Age settlement (occupied in July) and a museum containing tools used in forestry and peat-digging. SE of Skive Fjord is the town of Viborg (see entry).

The road from Skive continues along the Limfjord, sometimes at a distance from the shore. By taking a side turning near Gedsted we reach *Ålestrup* (Hvide Kro, 32 b.) in the western Himmerland. Here is situated the Danish Bicycle Museum, containing about 200 bicycles from 1860 to 1970 as well as a collection of sewing-machines and radio apparatus (open: 1 May–31 Oct. Tues.–Sun. 10 a.m.–6 p.m., Fri. noon–6 p.m.). The *Jutland Rose Park* has 200 varieties of roses (open: end June–Oct.). The town of *Løgstør* (Aggersund Kro, 25 b., May–Oct; Town and Fjord Festival) lies on the Aggersund, a narrow part of the Limfjord, across which there has been a bridge since 1942. The *Limfjord Museum* (Limfjordsmuseet), is housed in the former residence of the Canal Supervisor, and here there is a collection of fishing gear and items concerned with shipping and ferries. On the northern bank of the fjord, about 7 km (4 miles) distant, stands the *Viking Castle of Aggersborg*, partially reconstructed.

From Struer (see p. 120) the A11, on the N bank of the fjord, comes to **Thisted** (pop: 11,000; hotels: Ålborg, 48 b.; Klitmøller Kro, 35 b.; Limfjorden, 38 b.; Missionshotel Merci, 50 b.; camp site), an industrial town on a bay of the Thy Peninsula. In the old cemetery with its church of about 1500 can be found the grave of the writer Jens Peter Jacobsen (1847–85) whose psychological novel "Niels Lyhne" is well known both in Denmark and abroad. On the E side of the cemetery in Jernbanegade stands the local museum with an interesting historical collection and mementoes of Jacobsen who was born in Thisted. There is a memorial of him as well as an open-air theatre in the municipal park. The fishing port of *Hanstholm* (hotels: Hanstholm, 162 b., restaurant; Hanstholm Sømandshejm, 54 b.; Pension Vigso-Bugt, 40 b.) is situated 22 km (14 miles) N of Thisted; it has a lighthouse 22.5 m (74 ft) high, with the most powerful beam in the country. From the lighthouse a road along the dunes leads to the resort of *Klitmøller* (12 km (7 miles)). Continuing along the coast to the S we reach the fishing village of Nørre Vorupør where the *North Sea Aquarium* will be of interest to visitors (open: daily June–mid Sept.).

In *Fjerritslev* (hotels: Pension Havblik, 46 b., Mar.–Nov.; Klitrosen, 98 b.; restaurant: Fjerritslev Kro), a town between the Limfjord and Jammer Bay, there is a *brewery museum* and a local museum both of which are housed in an old brewhouse (Gamle Bryggeregård; Østergade). On Jammer Bay to the N, between the flint rocks of *Skarreklit* in the W and *Sletterstrand*, extends a beautiful coastal area with dunes and chalk banks. To the E of Fjerritslev the A11 continues to *Åbybro* (Birkelse Kro, 11 b.) then continues SE to Ålborg (see entry). The town lies on the Langerak, a continuation of the Limfjord with the Bay of Ålborg. In *Hals*, an attractive resort on Ålborg Bay, are the remains of the old fortifications – magazine and arsenal. A ferry connects Hals with the S shore of the Limfjord.

Spøttrup Castle on Salling Peninsula

Lolland

District: Storstrøms amt
Area: 1241 sq. km (479 sq. miles)
Population: 85,000

(i) **Turistbureau**
Danmarksgade 1
DK-9690 Fjerritslev
Tel. (08) 21 16 55

Turistbureau
DK-4930 Maribo
Tel. (03) 88 04 96

Turistbureau
Axeltorv 6
DK-4900 Nakskov
Tel. (03) 92 21 72

Turistbureau
Adelgade 65
DK-4880 Nysted
Tel. (03) 87 19 85

Turistbureau
Havnegade 19
DK-4970 Rødby
Tel. (03) 90 50 43

Turistbureau
Torvegade 4
DK-4990 Sakskøbing
Tel. (03) 89 56 30
Sept.-May: (03) 89 45 72

The island of Lolland lies to the W of Falster, facing the German Baltic coast. Lolland is the third largest Danish island (not counting Greenland), coming after Zealand and Funen. The islands of Lolland, Falster and Møn, together with the nearby smaller islands, are known by the Danes as the "South-Sea Islands".

Lolland is still an area with little industry. The largest undertakings are concentrated round Nakskov. The most important branch of the economy is the growing of sugar-beet, with sugar refineries at Nakskov and Sakskøbing. Fishing has declined in importance. Lolland has been opened up for tourism with the network of ferries.

The E4, the shortest connection between the Federal Republic of Germany and Copenhagen, runs through Lolland; its southerly section is called the Fugleflugtsline ("As the crow flies" line). Two bridges over the Guldborg Sound lead from Lolland to Falster. The S of the island is reached by ferry which runs from Puttgarden in Germany to Rødbyhavn (in summer reservations are necessary in order to avoid delay). A second ferry service from Tårs, near Nakskov, links Lolland with Langeland and Funen.

Tour of Lolland. – From *Rødbyhavn* (Danhotel, 20 b.) the E4 leads towards Copenhagen and as far as Sakskøbing it is a motorway and thereafter a good main road until, at Rønnende on Zealand, it becomes a motorway again. Observing the Danish speed limits (exceeding them is expensive!) a motorist can cross Lolland in about half an hour. From Rødbyhavn following the E4 and then taking a side turning, we come to **Rødby** (pop. 5000; hotels: Eggerts, 12 b.; Landmandshotel, 10 b.) which was once a port. Visitors can still see a half-timbered warehouse beside which boats were moored. The town, however, was often flooded and a comprehensive scheme of dikes cut off Rødby from the sea. A *flood column* in Nørregarde shows the high-water mark of the great flood of 1872. About 6 km (4 miles) NW of Rødby stands ***Tirsted Church**, a Romanesque brick building with a fine tower and beautiful 15 c. frescoes.

From Rødby the E4 continues and in about 10 km (6 miles) comes to Maribo; in the S of the town the A9 diverges to the left towards Nakskov. On this road we pass the *Ostofte Church*, a Romanesque brick building with a Gothic tower and porch, 15th c. vaulting in the nave and a transept of 1656. In the choir can be seen well-preserved frescoes (*c.* 1400) of scenes from the Old Testament. In *Stokkemarke* the monumental tower of the church is impressive.

In *Halsted* is a 12th c. monastery which was later almost completely destroyed and converted in the 19th c. into a mansion. We then reach **Nakskov** (pop. 16,000; hotels: Harmonien, 61 b.; Thompsen, no restaurant, 46 b.; Vinkælderen Restaurant; Cod Festival, Aug.) on the Nakskov Fjord, an industrial town with a shipyard and Denmark's largest sugar refinery. The town has retained its medieval plan; narrow lanes and old houses between the harbour and Axeltorv, the market-place, in which is an old pharmacy. *St Nicholas's Church* is Gothic and dedicated to the patron saint of sailors; it has a three-tier Baroque altar. Along the S coast of Lolland are the finest beaches on the island, from Maglehøj Strand to Drummeholm. They are primarily sandy beaches with pebbles at the waterline.

In Knuthenborg Safari Park

Maribo Cathedral

To the N of Nakskov is *Løjtofte Church*, a small Romanesque church without a tower; it contains a magnificent font and a sandstone sculpture (1100) by the Gotland artist known as the "Master of the Christ in Majesty". The road continues to *Kong Svends Høj*, a Neolithic passage grave. S of here near Pederstrup the *Reventlow Museum* is housed in a mansion in the elegantly furnished rooms of which can be seen portraits of important personalities who took part in the great Land Reform of 1788 (the museum is open May–Sept. at various times; the adjoining park all year). From Kong Svends Høj we can drive along the coast to *Kragenæs*, from where ferries serve the islands of Fejø and Femø (good sailing). Instead of continuing to Kragenæs, we can bear right along the main road past the Castle of *Ravnsborg*, an old ruin with an attractive view of Smålandsfarvand. 13 km (8 miles) farther on is *Bandholm* (car ferry to Askø), the port of Maribo. An old steam-train with old-fashioned carriages runs on summer week-ends between Maribo and Bandholm. S of Bandholm lies *__Knuthenborg Safari Park__ (open: 11 May–15 Sept. daily 9 a.m.–6 p.m.), the largest manor-house park in Scandinavia (600 ha (1500 acres)), laid out in the 19th c. in English style and converted to its present use in 1970. The park which is surrounded by a wall 8 km (5 miles) long with four gates, contains a unique collection of about 500 species of deciduous and coniferous trees from all over the world, seven miniature castles and Denmark's largest collection of antelopes, giraffes, zebras, camels, rhinoceroses, elephants, ostriches and monkeys. A motor road runs across the park and through an enclosure containing Bengal tigers. There is also a children's zoo with pony-rides.

Shortly after leaving Knuthenborg the road joins the A9 which leads back to Maribo. **Maribo** (pop. 5000; hotels: Dana, 18 b.; Ebsens, 34 b.; Hvide Hus, 128 b.; youth hostel; camp site) has a beautiful setting in the heart of Lolland on the Sønder Lake. The town grew up round *Maribo Abbey* in the 15th c. Only ruins remain of the abbey in a garden immediately N of the church (beautiful view of the lake). *Maribo Cathedral* was built between 1413 and 1470 as the church of a Brigittine abbey and has two choirs, one for monks and the other for nuns. The plan of the church is roughly similar to that of the church designed by St Bridget for the mother house (principal church) of her Order at Vadstena in Sweden: Maribo was the first daughter house of Vadstena Abbey. The cathedral, however, departs from the prescribed form by having a broad central aisle of greater height than that of the lateral aisles. In the S aisle are a 15th c. triumphal Crucifix and a High Renaissance painted pulpit. Maribo also has an interesting *museum* with an historical section (runic stones) and an art collection. There is also an *open-air museum* of farmhouses and other buildings reflecting the old peasant culture of Lolland and Falster. There are pleasant walks round the *Maribo Lakes*; on the N side lies *Engestofte Manor-house* and in the S Søholt with a French-style garden. Particularly beautiful is the *Røgbølle Lake* (Røgbøllesø) with old oak trees along its shores. From Maribo the E4 continues to *Sakskøbing* (pop. 4400; hotel: Saxkjørbing, 38 b.). 4 km (2½ miles) NE is the little Renaissance manor-house of *Berritsgård*, which has an octagonal tower with a copper roof. 4 km (2½ miles) NW of Sakskøbing lies *Orebygård* in a beautiful setting on Sakskøbing Fjord; this 16th c. manor-house was remodelled in Late Renaissance style in 1872–74. The motorway (highway) ends just beyond Sakskøbing, and E4 continues NE to Guldborg and over the bridge to the island of Falster (see entry).

At Sakskøbing the A9 branches off to the right and runs SE towards Nykøbing Falster. Just beyond the junction stands the Neolithic *Dolmen of Radsted* and close by the fine Manor-house of *Krenkerup*, first referred to in the time of Queen Margarethe I. Just before Nykøbing a road goes off to the right and 17 km (11 miles) SW reaches Nysted, passing on the way *Frejlev Forest* (Bronze Age remains).

Nysted (pop. 1230; hotels: Bogtrykkeriets Motel, 10 b.; The Cottage, 17 b.; Den Gamle Gård, in Stubberup, 52 b.) is the most southerly town in Denmark and one of the smallest. This attractive place on the Baltic received its charter in 1409; it grew up round Ålholm Castle, a structure resembling a pirates' stronghold.

In the Stubberupgård, near the castle is the *Automobile Museum*, Denmark's largest collection of cars, dating from the 1890s to 1936. All the cars are beautifully preserved and in running order. There is also a model railway layout 600 sq. m (700 sq. yd) in size, with scenery reproducing that of Switzerland, Italy and Germany. A train pulled by a steam-engine runs to the beach (June–Aug. daily 10 a.m.–6 p.m., otherwise at weekends). In the town itself, which has preserved its original layout, there is a 15th c. Gothic church, with a massive tower of a later date, topped by a tall copper steeple. From Nysted a road running W brings the visitor back to the motorway (highway) in 21 km (13 miles), passing through *Holeby* (Holeby Kro, 32 b.), one of the smallest townships in Denmark, but so widely dispersed that it can claim to have the country's longest main street.

Middelfart

Funen
District: Fyns amt
Population: 18,000
Postal code: DK–5500
Telephone code: 09

Turistbureau
Havnegade 10
Tel. 41 17 88

Turistbureau
Adelgade 26
DK–5400 Bogense
Tel. (09) 81 20 44
(open only in summer)

Turistbureau
Østergade 57
DK–5610 Assens
Tel. (09) 71 20 31

HOTELS. – *Byggecentrums Kursuscenter*, Hindsgavl Allé 2, 102 b.; *Grimmerhus*, Kongebrovej 42, 20 b. – CAMP SITE.

RESTAURANTS. – *Det Gyldne Marsvin*, Østergade 36; *Kongebrogården*, Kongebrovej 63.

Middelfart, an important seaport and also a resort, is situated in the extreme NW of the island of Funen on the Little Belt. From Jutland the town can be reached by crossing one of the two bridges leading from the Danish mainland to Funen.

HISTORY. – The area of Middelfart was already populated in prehistoric times. The Royal Castle of Hindsgavl (= summit of the Hintze) which stands here is mentioned for the first time in 1295, when the kings of Denmark and Norway concluded an armistice; in the 14th c. the castle passed to King Valdemar IV. Hindsgavl was destroyed in 1694 in a storm. On the site of the former castle a mansion was built in 1784. The people of Middelfart operated ferries across the Little Belt. About the year 1500 dolphins were hunted here.

SIGHTS. – **St Nicholas's Church** (*Skt. Nicolai Kirke*) by the harbour, dates from the 12th c. It has a notable pulpit (1596) and a Baroque altar-piece (1650) with a picture by Christoffer Wilhelm Eckersberg (1843). In a half-timbered house (*Henner Frisers Hus*) by the church can be found the local museum. In the Dolphin Room are pictures and articles concerned with dolphin-hunting in the Little Belt. The grounds of *Hindsgavl Mansion* on the peninsula of the same name (W of the centre) are of interest; the house was built in 1784 and has a beautiful park.

SURROUNDINGS. – About 20 km (12 miles) N of the road from Middelfart to Odense (see entry) the pretty little town of *Bogense* (hotels: Bogense, 40 b.; Bogense Kyst, apartments) lies on the N coast of Funen. In the Middle Ages this was the place where the ferries left for Jutland. In Bogense many old houses have survived; in Østergade stands Landbohjemet (17th c.) and in Adelgade the Bryggeregården with an old monastic cellar. Near Bogense are two mansions; *Gyldensteen*, a Renaissance building erected in 1640 lies 4 km ($2\frac{1}{2}$ miles) to the E (no admittance) and the estate of *Harridslevgåde*, also a 17th c. Renaissance building, 3 km (2 miles) to the S.

The old township of **Assens** (pop. 11,000; hotels: Marcussens, 13 b.; Phønix, 10 b.; Aborghus Kro Restaurant) on the Little Belt about 40 km (25 miles) S of Middelfart has a number of timbered houses dating from the 16th and 17th c. Of especial interest is *Willemoes House* (1675) which contains mementoes of the famous seafarer, Peter Willemoes, who was born in this house (Willemoes Festival, June). The church (1488), which is 60 m (197 ft) long, contains beautiful wood-carvings. There are ferries from Assens to the two islands lying NW in the Little Belt, *Bågø* (30 minutes) and *Brandsø* (1 hour 15 minutes).

Driving E from Assens on road 168 you can see on the left in 8 km (5 miles) the *Øksnebjerg* (85 m (279 ft)) with a memorial tablet to Johann von Rantzau who in 1535 defeated a force from Lübeck and a peasant army; there is also a windmill dating from 1859; on the right can be seen the Skovsbjerg (97 m (318 ft)). Farther NE rises the *Frøbjerg*, the highest hill in Funen (141 m (430 ft); beautiful view; parking place).

Møn

District: Storstrøms amt
Area: 217 sq. km (85 sq. miles)
Population: 12,000

Turistbureau
Storegade 5
DK–4780 Stege
Tel. (03) 81 44 11

The island of Møn lies at the E end of the Storstrømm, the channel which divides the islands of Zealand and Falster. It is connected with Zealand by a bridge from Kalvehave and can be reached from Falster by crossing the Farø Bridge, built 1985 (a branch to the island of Bogø), or by taking the ferry from Stubbekøbing to the island of Bogø and crossing the causeway from there to Møn.

The white chalk cliffs to the E of the island are one of the greatest tourist attractions of Denmark. In addition Møn is interesting on account of its varied landscape – heathland, fields, meadows and marshes, as well as fine bathing beaches.

There are many prehistoric remains on Møn; especially interesting are a number of Neolithic chambered tombs known as "giants' graves". Popular legend associated these tombs with two giants – the Green Huntsman, who ruled over western Møn, and the giant Upsal, king of the cliffs, to whom the E end of the island belonged. Upsal was long regarded as the protector of the island, since it was he who caused enemy ships to be shattered on the island's rocky coast.

Tour of Møn. – The bridge from Zealand crosses the *Ulvsund* to Møn. 2 km ($1\frac{1}{4}$ miles) from the bridge a side road goes off on the right and runs through beautiful scenery (a fine view of the Sound from Borren) to the Neolithic tombs known as *Kong Askers Høj* and the *Klekkende Høj* (the best-preserved passage grave (9 m (29 ft) long and 1.25 m (4 ft) high). 11 km (7 miles) from the bridge, the main road comes to the chief town on the island, **Stege** (pop. 4000; hotels: Præsterkilde, in Keldby, 30 b.; Stege Bugt, 54 b.; The Laughing Duck Restaurant; camp site; Nordic Week, midsummer). The town arose round a castle built by Valdemar I (*c.* 1175). In the 15th c. it was surrounded by

Møns Klint

walls and a moat; one of the three town gates, *Mølleporten*, has been preserved, the only surviving medieval town gate in Denmark other than one at Fåborg. *St Hans's Church* was built about 1250 and enlarged by the addition of a three-aisled choir about 1460; it has rich fresco decoration. *In Møn Museum*, an old patrician house of 1780, can be seen historic photographs, costumes, silverware, seamen's chests and finds of the New Stone Age.

From Stege a minor road leads N into the *Ulvshale Peninsula*, the first large nature reserve established in Denmark (rare birds, unspoiled natural forest). This seldom-visited part of Møn has some of the island's finest beaches.

The main road from Stege passes through *Keldby*, which has a ***church** with richly decorated frescoes, the oldest of which, in the choir, date from the 13th c.; on the walls are vividly imagined scenes from the Bible and the vaulting has paintings by the Master of Elmelunde, whose work is frequently found in the churches of Møn. His primitive paintings, full of humour, contain many details taken from everyday life, such as Joseph making gruel for the newborn Infant Jesus. S of the church, via Keldbylille we come to *Hans Hansens Gård*, a thatched square building dating from about 1800 which is furnished with its original 19th c. furniture.

The road continues to *Elmelunde*. The church, a prominent landmark for sailors, is in the style typical of eastern Denmark and contains frescoes by the Master of Elmelunde ("Childhood of Jesus", "Last Judgment", "Entry into Jerusalem", as well as ploughing and harvest scenes). 10 km (6 miles) farther on the road reaches the main attraction of the tour, the chalk cliff known as ***Møns Klint**, the highest point of which is 128 m (420 ft) above the sea. The brilliant white of the chalk standing out against the deep blue of the sea is particularly striking when the sun is shining. A toll is payable on the last section of the road (camp site). There are footpaths along the cliffs (about 1 hour), and two steep flights of steps lead from *Storeklint* and *Jydeleje* to the sea. Fossils of marine animals and plants can be found on the shore. Along the top of the cliffs an expanse of open woodland (beeches) contains rare species of plants hidden in the undergrowth. The best view is from *Sommerspiret* (102 m (335 ft)); at *Taleren* one can hear a remarkable echo. There is an archaeological and geological museum in the park.

From Møns Klint the visitor is recommended to make a short detour to the N to see the miniature manor-house of *Liselund*, built about 1795 by the Governor of the island, Antoine de la Calmette, for his wife and named after her. In the course of his wide travels, he had acquired a taste for French architecture and the "back to nature" movement of the Romantic period; the house was, therefore, designed in the style of a simple peasant house. There are many other Romantic features in the park, including artificial lakes and waterways, a "Swiss cottage" and a "Chinese tea pavilion". Hans Christian Andersen wrote his story "The Tinder Box" while staying in the Swiss cottage. Other buildings in the park were destroyed by a landslip in 1905.

The return journey is on the same road back to Stege. By diverging to the S at Magleby we come to *Klintholm*, a mansion built in 1875 in the neo-Renaissance style. There is a marked footpath in the northern part of the park (open daily) which leads into the forest and on to the cliffs on the coast. Farther to the S on Hjelm Bay lies the fishing port and sailing harbour of *Klintholm Havn*. From Stege a detour of 7 km (4 miles) S can be made to *Æbelnæs* where there is another Stone Age passage grave.

At the S end of the island is the *Grøn Jægers Høj*, the "Hill of the Green Huntsman", another burial mound. Also here is *Fanefjord*, with a ***church** containing the richest series of paintings (*c.* 1500) by the Master of Elmelunde. The paintings form a kind of "Biblia pauperum" (Bible of the Poor), but do not hold rigorously to the Biblical accounts. The themes of the representations are taken from the Old and New Testaments and from Christian legends. There are also frescoes of the High Gothic period (*c.* 1350) on the choir arch (St Christopher, St Martin, knights and emblems of the Apostles).

From the S tip of Møn we can cross a causeway to the island of *Bogø* (pop. 925) which was once known as the "island of mills". Today there is only one survivor – *Bogø Mølle*, a windmill of Dutch origin. From Bogø we can go N to Zealand (see entry) by the Farø Bridge, or S to Falster (see entry) via the Farø Bridge or by ferry from Nyby.

Fresco in Elmelunde Church

Gavnø Mansion

Næstved

Zealand
District: Storstrøms amt
Population: 45,000
Postal code: DK–4700
Telephone code: 03
(i) **Turistbureau**
Købmagergade 20A
Tel. 72 11 22
Turistbureau
Thorsvej 8
DK–4654 Fakse Ladeplads
Tel. 71 60 34
Turistbureau
DK–4720 Præstø
Tel. 79 11 90

HOTELS. – *Axelhus*, Axeltorvet 9, 30 b.; *Borgmestergården*, Købmagergade 20, 60 b.; *Vinhuset*, Skt. Peders Kirkeplads 4, 103 b. – YOUTH HOSTEL. – CAMP SITE.

RESTAURANTS. – *Det Røde Parkhus*, Riddergade 1; *Trolden*, Jernbanegade 21.

EVENTS. – International Motor Show (Mar.); Festival of St Paul (on the canals; Aug.).

Næstved, an industrial town and port, lies on the SW coast of Zealand where the River Suså flows into the Karrebæk Fjord providing a link between the town and the Bay of Karrebæksminde.

Important branches of the economy are engineering, ceramics, timber and paper industries.

HISTORY. – Næstved developed round a medieval monastery. Trade and fishing were the main occupations of the inhabitants. Until the wars with Sweden (17th c.) the town had commercial links with North Germany, Scotland and Norway. The extension of the port, which can now be used by large ships, the improvement of communications with Copenhagen and to the S of the island, as well as the arrival of various industries brought a renewed upsurge to the town in the 19th c.

SIGHTS. – The oldest part of the town is near **St Peter's Church** (*Skt. Peders Kirke*), the largest Gothic church in Denmark. Most of the church dates from the 13th c. and the building was thoroughly restored between 1883 and 1885. During this restoration wall-paintings of about 1375 were found in the choir, including a representation of King Valdemar IV and his Consort, Hedwig, kneeling at a penitent's stool. Also to be seen are a 14th c. Crucifix, a copper font basin of the 16th c. and a pulpit of 1671. In Church Square stands the old *Town Hall* and medieval brick houses with arched windows bedded in mortar. These "stone booths" ("Stenboderne") are the only remaining medieval terraced houses in Denmark. They were occupied by craftsmen (craft museum). Among the many half-timbered houses the *Apostelgård* in Riddergade is of particular interest; it has carved figures of Apostles on the beams (*c.* 1500). Adjoining is *St Martin's Church* (Skt. Mortens Kirke: 13th c.) with a notable carved altar with scrollwork and a representation of the Crucifixion by Abel Schrøder the Younger (1602–76).

The *House of the Holy Ghost* (Helligandshuset) in Ringstedgade, once a hospital, is now the Municipal Museum.

About 2.5 km (1½ miles) N of the town is a former Benedictine Monastery (*c.* 1200) which has been the *Herlufsholm* boarding-school since 1565. The church with a Gothic ivory Crucifix (*c.* 1230) and magnificent tombs is open to the public. 6 km (4 miles) SW of Næstved on the island of *Gavnø* stands a ***mansion**. The estate, a former nunnery, became privately owned in 1584 and the house was converted into a Rococo mansion between 1755 and 1758. It possesses one of the largest private picture collections in Denmark and in the portrait gallery one of the oldest portraits in the North. In the park tulips bloom in the spring and then summer flowers, ornamental shrubs and roses (open: May–Oct. daily 10 a.m.–4 or 5 p.m.).

SURROUNDINGS. – Another stately home is *Sparresholm* (17th c.) situated 14 km (9 miles) W of the town. In a former cowhouse can be seen a collection of horse-drawn vehicles of all kinds, both carriages and carts. Near by is a wheelwright's shop, a stable and a track with Olympic measurements (open: 19 June–8 Aug. daily 10 a.m.–5 p.m.; Easter–3 Oct. Sun. 10 a.m.–5 p.m.; admission fee).

25 km (16 miles) E of Næstved lies the little town of **Fakse** by a limestone hill 76 m (250 ft) high with a quarry which has been used since the Middle Ages. In the *Geological Museum* can be seen minerals and fossils which have been found in the 70-million-year-old coral reef of the Cretaceous period. In the church are fresco-paintings and wood-carvings by Abel Schrøder. 12 km (7½ miles) SE of here the resort of *Fakse Ladeplads* (Faxe Ladeplads Hotel, 28 b.; Gefion Restaurant) on the coast (Fakse Bay) is surrounded by woodland. Fakse limestone has been shipped from this port since the Middle Ages. About 8 km (5 miles) E of Fakse the *Mansion of Vemmetofte*, which has been rebuilt several times, is situated in a park; since 1909 it has been a Baroque building. In 1735 the estate became a home for ladies of the nobility; since then the deeds of the foundation have been altered so that married couples are able to reside here.

The ***Mansion of Gisselfeld** (1554), a Renaissance building which has been altered on several occasions, lies 13 km (8 miles) NW of Fakse. The house is situated in a very beautifully maintained park in the English style. There is a lake and also a grotto with a waterfall, 400 different kinds of trees and bushes, including a bamboo wood (entrance to park: Apr.–23 Oct. daily 10 a.m.–4 or 5 p.m.; 24 Oct.–Mar. Sat, Sun. 10 a.m.–5 p.m.; admission fee). *Bregentved Manor*, the largest estate in Zealand, is situated 4 km (2½ miles) NW. Since 1746 it has been owned by the ducal family of Moltke. The manor-house, the buildings of which date partly from about 1700 and partly from the 19th c., is surrounded by a large park. Some parts of the gardens are maintained in the Baroque style (entrance to the park: Wed. and Sun. 9 a.m.–8 p.m.).

25 km (16 miles) SE of Næstved the little town of *Præstø* (Frederiksminde Hotel, 50 b.; Skipperkroen Restaurant) has a charming situation on a bay. The town has a pretty 15th c. church. To the N of the town stands *Nyso Mansion* (main buildings of the 17th c.); in the garden is a studio built by Baroness Stampfe for the sculptor Bertel Thorvaldsen (1770–1844); a side wing of the manor contains a collection of the artist's works.

Nyborg

Funen
District: Fyns amt
Population: 18,000
Postal code: DK–5800
Telephone code: 09

(i) **Turistbureau**
Torvet 9
Tel. 31 02 80
Turistbureau
Strandgade 5A
DK–5300 Kerteminde
Tel. 32 11 21

HOTELS. – *Hesselet*, Christianslundsvej 119, 92 b.; *Missionshotel*, Østervoldgade 44, 25b.; *Nyborg Strand*, Østerovej 2, 400 b. – Two CAMP SITES.

RESTAURANT. – *Danehofkroen*, Slotspladsen.

The port of Nyborg is situated on the E coast of Funen on the Great Belt.

HISTORY. – The castle (11th c.) which was built to control the Great Belt was the reason for the establishment of the town. Nyborg obtained its charter in 1271. From 1354 until the beginning of the 15th c. the meetings of the Danish Court, the annual assembly of the important people of the kingdom with the king, took place in Nyborg. From 1560 until 1857 a guard-ship in the Great Belt collected tolls from all the ships which preferred this waterway to the Øresund. The war against Sweden (1658–59) led to a long impoverishment of the town. In 1869 the fortifications were pulled down but were restored between 1917 and 1923. Today Nyborg is an important centre of communications. It is planned to build a bridge or tunnel connecting with the island of Zealand.

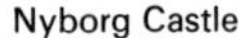

Nyborg Castle

H. C. Andersen's monument in Odense

SIGHTS. – The present ***castle** consists of only one wing, the so-called "King's Wing", and here between 1250 and 1413 the Danish kings held their Court. After restoration the medieval character of the castle (fortifications, interiors) can again be appreciated. The castle houses a collection of weapons (open: 1 May–30 Sept. 9 a.m.–6 p.m.; out of season 10 a.m.–3 p.m.). A beautiful timbered house (1601) in Slotsgade is the *Nyborg Museum*. Here exhibits illustrate the history of the town (open: in summer, daily 9 a.m.–5 p.m.). The gatehouse "*Landporten*" (1660), a 40 m (130 ft) long building with an entrance gate, stands to the N of the castle. Also of interest is the Gothic *Church of Our Lady* (Vor Frue Kirke) in Adelgade, a three-aisled building, the interior of which was reconstructed in 1973. Near the church stands the Korsbrødregård, a stone building with a Renaissance gable of 1614.

SURROUNDINGS. – About 4.5 km (3 miles) SE of the town we come to the promontory of *Kundshoved* from where ferries cross the 26 km (16 mile) wide Great Belt to Halsskov on Zealand. 2 km (1¼ miles) S of Nyborg stands **Holckenhavn**, a Renaissance building (1590–1631), which is considered one of the most magnificent mansions in Denmark. The house is surrounded by a large park with well-tended lawns, flower-beds and trees (entrance to the park daily 9 a.m.–4 p.m.).

About 40 km (25 miles) N of Nyborg on Kerteminde Bay lies the old fishing town of *Kerteminde* (pop: 10,000; hotels: Tornøes, 27 b.; Schlosspension Ulriksholm, in Kølstrup, 35 b.; restaurants: Rusen; Varmestuen; youth hostel; two camp sites) in which many old houses have been preserved. In a half-timbered house, built in 1630, can be found the Municipal Museum. The church, which was probably built about 1200, is also worth seeing. A short distance SW from Kerteminde we come to the village of *Ladby*; 1.5 km (1 mile) to the N *Ladbyskibet* (signposted), the place where a Viking ship, 22 m (72 ft) long, was found in 1935. A roof was built over the ship and the museum building constructed round it. N of Kerteminde stretches the peninsula of *Hindsholm* which, compared with Funen, has a rough climate. At first the land is hilly and then towards the N point of Fyns Hoved becomes flat. The road ends at the village of Nordskov. The peninsula has fine beaches.

Odense

Funen
District: Fyns amt
Population: 171,000
Postal code: DK–5000
Telephone code: 09
Turistbureau
Rådhuset
Tel. 12 75 20

HOTELS. – *Ansgar Missionhotel*, Østre Stationsvej 32, 70 b.; *Motol Ansgarhus*, Kirkegårds Allé 17–19, 28 b.; *Fangel Kro*, Fangelvej 55, 27 b.; *Frederik VI's Kro*, Rugårdsvej 590, 92 b.; *Golf Plaza*, Østre Stationsvej 24, 105 b.; *Grand*, Jernbanegade 18, 218 b.; *H. C. Andersen*, Claus Bergs Gade 7, 290 b.; *Motel Munkeris*, Munkerisvej 161, 134 b.; *Motel Odense*, Hunderupgade 2, 81 b.; *Odense Ny Missionshotel*, Østre Stationsvej 24, 117 b.; *Windsor*, Vindegade 45, 107 b.; *Ydes*, Hans Tausensgade 11, 39 b. – YOUTH HOSTEL. – CAMP SITES.

RESTAURANTS. – *Den Gamle Kro*, Overgade 23; *Den Grimme Ælling*, Nørregade 25; *Det Gyldne Får*, Elmegårdsvej 3A; *Målet*, Jernbanegade 17; *Næsbyhoved Skov*, Kanalvej 52; *Skoven*, Læssøegade 215; *Sortebro Kro*, Sejerskovvej 20; *Ønskebrønden*, Vestegade 57.

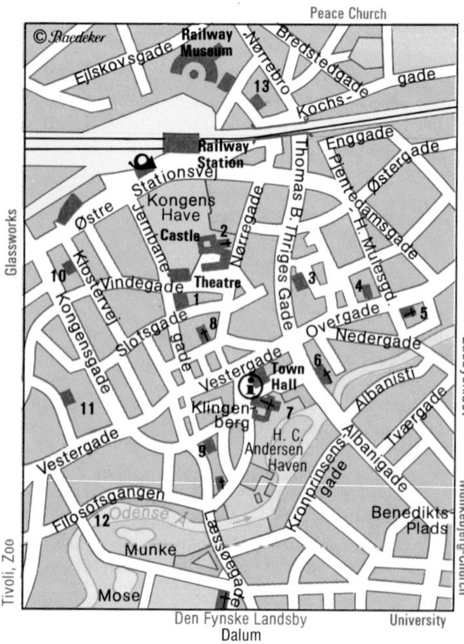

Odense

300 m
330 yd

1 Funen Museum of Art
Funen Regional Museum
2 St Hans' Church
3 H. C. Andersen's Birthplace
4 Montergarden (Museum)
5 Vor Frue Kirke (Church of Our Lady)
6 St Alban's Church
7 St Knud's Church (Cathedral)
8 Grabrodre Monastery
9 H. C. Andersen's Childhood Home
10 Falck Museum
11 Graphical Museum
12 Mooring-place for boats
13 Bus Station

EVENTS. – *Organ Festival* (June–Aug.); *H. C. Andersen Plays* (July–Aug.).

Odense, after Copenhagen and Århus the third largest town in Denmark, lies on the island of Funen on the important E66 main road from Jutland to Copenhagen; it is located on the little Odense Å which flows into Odense Fjord a short distance N of the town. Since 1966 the town has had a university.

Odense has developed into an important industrial town; the harbour is linked by a canal to the Odense Fjord on the Great Belt. It has a wharf and iron and steel, electro-technical and textile industries as well as timber-processing.

HISTORY. – The name of Odense first appears in the documents in 988, when the Bishop of the town received a letter of safe conduct from the German Emperor, Otto. No doubt it was originally a cult site devoted to the worship of Odin (Wotan); hence its name. In 1086 the Danish King Knud (Canute) was murdered in St Alban's Church here. Fifteen years later he was canonised by the Pope. An ecclesiastical headquarters and place of pilgrimage in the Middle Ages, Odense survived secularisation during the Reformation and remained an important commercial town. At the beginning of the 19th c. Kerteminde, 15 km (10 miles) away, became the port of Odense. The old town was gradually occupied by shops and businesses, so that although it has preserved its original layout it has few old buildings. Odense's most celebrated son is the fairy-tale writer Hans Christian Andersen (the initials H. C. are pronounced ho-tsay in Danish; the d in Andersen is not pronounced). He was born here on 2 April 1805, but he moved to Copenhagen, where he became famous, because he felt unappreciated in his native town.

SIGHTS. – The area of the town extends from the bank of the Odense Å in the S to the station complex in the N. In Flakhaven, a square bordering Vestergade, stands the **Town Hall** (guided tours May–Sept. Mon–Fi. 2 p.m.), the oldest part of which was built in the 19th c. and modelled on an Italian town hall. Further building took place between 1936 and 1955 and this consisted of reinforced concrete with red tiles. It contains many works of art including a sculpture, "Spring on Funen". In front of the Town Hall can be seen a statue of St Knud by Utzon Franck. To the S of the Town Hall stands ***St Knud's Church** (*Skt. Knuds Kirke*; visits May–Oct.), the cathedral of Odense. It is named after a Danish saint, Knud IV, who had begun the building which was in 1100 dedicated to his name. This church was burned down in the 12th c. After another great fire Bishop Giscio began a replacement in the 13th c. but it took almost 200 years to complete. A feature of this Gothic church is the crypt with the tombs of King Knud and his brother, Benedict. Behind the High Altar is a huge reredos with magnificent carvings by Claus Berg (*c.* 1520). There is also a bronze font of 1620 and a pulpit of 1750. The carillon in the tower is played several times a day. E of the cathedral a park named after H. C. Andersen stretches along the waterfront; in it is a statue of the well-known writer.

Crossing Albani Torv we come to *St Alban's Roman Catholic Church.* To the SW of the cathedral in Munkemøllestræde (Nos. 3–5) stands the house of Hans Christian Andersen's parents (*H. C. Andersens Barndomshjem* (H. C. Andersen's Childhood Home); open: Apr.–Sept. daily 10 a.m.–5 p.m.; Oct.–Mar. daily noon–3 p.m.); there is a memorial tablet to the writer on the gable. Andersen lived from 1807 to 1819 with his parents in one of the little apartments in this house. In 1930 the building was furnished as a museum and it is now a branch of the actual Andersen Museum in Hans Jensens Stræde (see below).

In the E of the town, on the corner of Hans Jensens Stræde and Bangs Bodor, stands a single-storey half-timbered house which is believed to have been the birthplace of Hans Christian Andersen (1805) and is now the heart of the ****Hans Christian Andersen Museum** (open: 9 or 10 a.m.–5 or 6 p.m.; winter 10 a.m.–3 p.m.). The museum houses furniture, pictures, manuscripts and books belonging to the writer. Since its foundation in 1905 the museum has been extended on two occasions because of the growth of the collection and the increase in the number of visitors. On view is a large library with Danish and foreign editions of Andersen's writings as well as a collection of illustrations to these stories. The domed hall of the museum, which was set up as a memorial hall, is decorated with scenes from the autobiographical book "Story of my Life" (frescoes by Niels Larsen Stevns).

Going S from the Andersen Museum we reach the Møntergården at Overgade Nos. 48–50. This is the *Old Mint* which now serves as a *Museum of Cultural History* (open: daily 10 a.m.–4 p.m.). The complex includes other typical houses of old Odense from the 16th and 17th c. as well as a Baroque warehouse. The buildings

Reredos in Odense Cathedral

H. C. Andersen Museum

Portrait of H. C. Andersen

contain curios of different periods as well as collections of costumes, ceramics, ecclesiastical art, silver, clocks and coins. SE of the Mint stands the **Church of Our Lady** (*Vor Frue Kirke*), a Late Romanesque single-aisled brick building with a partly preserved group of Late Romanesque round-arch windows in the E wall. The pulpit goes back to 1639 and the tower dates from the 15th c.

Jernbanegade leads from the town centre to the station and at No. 13 is the **Museum of Art** (*Fyns Kunstmuseum*; open: daily 10 a.m.–4 p.m., Wed. also 7–10 p.m.). Early Danish painting is represented by Jens Juel, Dankvart Dreyer and the painters of Funen – Peter Hansen, Fritz Syberg, Johannes Larsen and Jens Birkholm. More recent Danish painting includes works of Asgar Jorn, Richard Mortenson, Robert Jacobsen and Carl Henning Pedersen. A special exhibition of Danish Concrete and Constructive Art forms a considerable part of the collection. In the same building can be found the *Fyns Stiftsmuseum*, where the exhibits concern the prehistoric settlement of Funen and include picture strips illustrating the everyday life of reindeer-hunters as well as objects from the Bronze and Iron Ages.

Farther N near *Kongens Have Park* stands **St Hans' Church** (oldest parts of the 13th c.; choir of the 15th c.). The church was once a part of a monastery of the Order of St John of Jerusalem. On the N wall can be seen a large 15th c. Crucifix, while the font is Late Romanesque. Outside the SW wall is a pulpit which can be reached from inside the church; this is Denmark's only external pulpit. The old buildings of the monastery were converted in the time of Frederik IV into a *mansion* which lies behind St Hans' Church in Kongens Have. Frederik VII had the mansion redesigned in 1841 in the Classical style.

In the northern part of Odense near the station is the ***DSB Railway Museum** (Dannebrogsgade 24) in a semicircular building. As well as old locomotives and railway wagons a large collection of models is exhibited (open: May–Sept. daily 10 a.m.–4 p.m.; Oct.–Apr. Sun. 10 a.m.–3 p.m.). Outside the town on the N in Skibhusvej stands the *Peace Church* (Fredenskirke), a modern building

(1916–20) to the design of Jensen Klint; the design was originally intended for a church in Århus which was never built. It is an adaptation of the Gothic brick churches and was a preliminary study for Jensen Klint's famous Grundtvig Church in Copenhagen.

The *Falck Museum* (open: 1 May–31 Oct. Tues.–Fri. 10 a.m.–4 p.m., Sat., Sun. 1–5 p.m.) at Klostervej No. 28, W of the town, houses a collection of Danish fire-engines and rescue vehicles. In addition exhibits trace the history of the Falck rescue service from the opening of the first rescue station by the founder Sophus Falck in 1906 up to the present day. Then following Vestre Stationsvej from the museum in a westerly direction we come to the *Holmegaard A/S glassworks* which can be visited (Aug.–June, Mon.–Fri. 10.15 a.m.–2 p.m.; for groups of over 20 prior notice is required.

S of the Falck Museum on the third floor of Brandt Passage No. 37 is Denmark's *Graphical Museum* (open: Mon.–Fri. 10 a.m.–4 p.m., Sat., Sun. 11 a.m.–5 p.m.). The collection illustrates the development of graphics from the Middle Ages to the present day – type-setting, copper-engraving, lithography, reproduction, printing and bookbinding. In the work-rooms can be seen old machines and tools, some of which are still in use. To the S of the Odense Å is a mooring-place (Filosofengang) from which river trips can be made.

SURROUNDINGS. – There is an interesting modern church in Munkebjerg SE of the town. The *Munkebjerg Church* in Østerbæksvej was the result of an architectural competition in 1942. The winning design was for an unusual polygon structure, but local resistance prevented the construction of the church until 1962, when another team of architects took over and produced a building similar to the original plan, the unconventional style having, in the meantime, become generally accepted. The church is hexagonal, with the air of a huge tent, and has a free-standing tower. Attractions in the SW of the town are the *Tivoli Amusement Park* (open: Apr.–Sept. daily 2–11 p.m.) and the *Zoological Garden* (open: daily 9 a.m.–4 or 5 p.m.), both situated on Sdr. Boulevard.

4 km ($2\frac{1}{2}$ miles) S of the town centre we come to the **Open-Air Museum** in Hunderop Skov. This is *"Den Fynske Landsby"* (the village of Funen) with reconstructed farms and houses from the district (windmills, a brick and tile works, a school, a smithy and other workshops). Agriculture is practised according to old methods. The oldest building in the village is a barn of 1666 right at the entrance. Near by can be found a "Kro" (Krug=jug, or inn). During the summer there are often opportunities to practise weaving in the workshops, or forging or making pottery. Andersen's fairy-tales are performed annually in the open-air village theatre. *Dalum*, too, to the W of the village of Funen, is worth seeing. Its church was part of a Benedictine monastery which was moved here about 1200 from Odense. There are interesting frescoes. Not far away is the childhood home of Carl Nielsen (1865–1931), which is now a *museum* (open Apr.–Sept. 10 a.m.–5 p.m.). Here the Danish composer spent part of the youth.

Farther E is *Fraugde* with a half-timbered manor-house *Fraugdegård*; in the late 17th c. it belonged to Denmark's most celebrated ecclesiastical poet, Thomas Kingo, who later became a Bishop.

Randers

Jutland
District: Århus amt
Population: 62,000
Postal code: DK-8900
Telephone code: 06

(i) **Turistbureau**
Erik Menveds Plads 1
Tel. 42 44 77

HOTELS: – *Motel Hornbæk*, Viborgvej 100, 15 b.; *Kongens Ege*, Gl. Hadsundvej 2, 172 b.; *Randers Sømandshjem*, Østervold 42, 16 b.; *Randers*, Torvegade 11, 145 b. – YOUTH HOSTEL. – CAMP SITE.

RESTAURANTS. – *Mundskænken*, Slotscentret; *Munken*, Brødregade 23; *Storkereden*, Kirkestorvet 2; *Tronborg*, Grenåvej 2.

The industrial town of Randers is situated near the outflow of the River Gudenå into the Randers Fjord on the E coast of Central Jutland.

There have long been craftsmen of various kinds in Randers bell-founders, silversmiths, wood-carvers and shoemakers, but the town was particularly well known for its salmon; in 1820 over 1000 salmon were caught. Foodstuffs, metal-working, shoe production and wagon-manufacture are the most important branches of industry today.

HISTORY. – Since Randers was easily accessible from the interior of Jutland, the town developed at an early date into an important trade centre. There was a Royal Mint here in 1080. During the Middle Ages several churches and monasteries were founded. In the middle of the 14th c. Valdemar IV built a castle near the town. The Franciscan Monastery was converted, in 1530, into a royal palace. Between 1627 and 1629 Imperial troops under Wallenstein occupied the town

Randers: Town Hall

which suffered during the following years through the effects of the war and a great fire in 1672. During the 19th c. the quarrels about Schleswig-Holstein had an adverse effect on Randers and in the Second World War the town was occupied by German troops.

SIGHTS. – In Kirkegade, in the old part of the town, stands the *Church of St Martin*, a brick building of the 15th c.; the interior has good carving with a pulpit, font, reredos and organ dating from the 17th and 18th c. Among many old houses near the church special mention should be

Gammel Estrup Manor

made of the *Helligåndshus* (House of the Holy Ghost) dating from about 1435. The building which is the remains of a dissolved monastery was restored between 1894 and 1897 by Hack Kampmann. Passing along Torvegade we reach the *Town Hall* (1778, by Christian Mørup; immediately opposite stands *Påskesønnerns Gård* (Rådhustorvet No. 7), the oldest stone house in the town café).

At Stemannsgade No. 2 can be found the *Culture House*, consisting of an old and a new building (1964–69, by the architect Flemming Lassen); it has two internal courtyards. On the first floor is the *Historical and Cultural Museum* including three burghers' rooms; the Art Museum on the second floor houses works by Danish painters of the 19th c. In the inner courtyard is an Abstract sculpture by Reinhoud. N of the Culture House in Østergade stands the *Amtmannshof* (1928), a house typical of the Biedermeier period.

SURROUNDINGS. – On the Djursland Peninsular, 25 km (16 miles) E of the town, lies the little township of *Auning* (Auning Kro, 17 b.) which has an interesting Romanesque church with wall-painting of 1562. 3 km (2 miles) to the W of Auning stands the old manor-house of ***Gammel Estrup** built about 1500 and rebuilt in Renaissance style in the 17th c. It now houses two museums; in the house itself is the *Jutland Manor-House Museum* with typical furniture, and in the former administrative part of the building is the *Danish Agricultural Musuem* with a first-class collection (open: 1 May–31 Oct. daily 10 a.m.–5 p.m.; 1 Nov.–30 Apr. Sat., Sun. 11 a.m.–3 p.m.; Manor-House Museum closed Mon.).

***Clausholm Manor** (open: 15 May–15 Sept. daily 10 a.m.–noon and 2–5.30 p.m.; park daily 9 a.m.–6 p.m.), 13 km (8 miles) S of Randers, is occasionally used for concerts. The five-winged Baroque building was erected between 1699 and 1723. It contains among other interesting rooms, a garden salon with stucco-work and a chapel which has the oldest organ in the country. 23 km (14 miles) SW of Randers lies *Ulstrup*.

Ribe

Jutland
District: Ribe amt
Population: 18,000
Postal code: DK-6760
Telephone code: 05

Turistbureau
Torvet 3–5
Tel. 42 15 00

HOTELS. – *Dagmar*, Torvet, 78 b.; *Kalvslund Kro*, Koldingvej 105, 10 b.; *Sønderjylland*, Sønderportsgade 22, 23 b.; *Weis Stue*, Torvet 2, 9b. – YOUTH HOSTEL: *Hovedengen*. – CAMP SITES: *Ribe*, *Varupvej* and *Villebøl*.

Clausholm Mansion

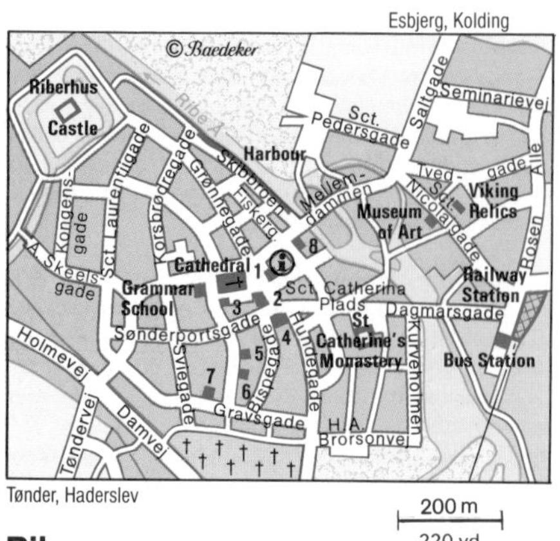

Ribe

1 Torvet
2 Old Town Hall
3 Hans Tausens Hus
4 Maren Spliid Memorial
5 Tarnborg
6 16th c. terrace-houses
7 Puggard
8 Quedens Gard

RESTAURANTS. – *Hvidding Kro*, Ribevej 58; *Weis Stue*, Torvet 2.

EVENTS. – Tulip Festival (May); Rock and Folk Festival (June).

Ribe, one of the oldest towns in the country, lies on the river of the same name (Ribe Å), not far from the place where the river enters the North Sea in the Bay of Fanø.

HISTORY. – Ribe developed near an estuary which formed one of the few harbours on the W coast of Jutland. Ribe at that time lay, as excavations in the 1970s have established, N of the present river (discovery of a Viking settlement of about A.D.700 near Skt. Nicolaj Gade). In the year 860 Ansgar, Archbishop of Hamburg and Bremen, obtained permission to build a church here; and in 948 Ribe was the seat of the Bishop. From the early 12th c. the town was surrounded by a rampart and outside the gates of this arose a castle. The kings resided here about 1200. In the Middle Ages the town traded with England and Germany (export of cattle and fish). However the Reformation led to a decline in the population. Only after the reunification of South Jutland (North Schleswig) with Denmark in 1920 did Ribe begin to thrive again.

SIGHTS. – The twisting streets with their many half-timbered houses of the 16th and 17th c. (storks' nest) give the townscape a particular charm. In the centre at Torvet stands the Romanesque ***Cathedral** (*c.* 1200) which was later rebuilt on several occasions. Today it is the only five-aisled church in Denmark (view from the 50 m (164 ft) high tower; carillon). Inside are epitaphs and tombs and a beautiful wood-carving representing St George fighting the Dragon (viewing possible). Opposite the Cathedral is *Hans Tausens Hus*, an old timbered building. The house is a relic of Denmark's still-existing Bishop's seat (16th c.). Here

Bird's-eye view of part of Ribe old town

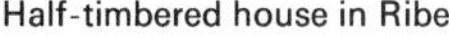
Half-timbered house in Ribe

. . . and a picturesque street

Hans Tausen (1494–1561), a disciple of Luther and first Reformer of Denmark, spent the last 10 years of his life. Today the house is an archaeological museum (open: daily 10 a.m.–noon and 2–4 or 5 p.m.).

SE of the Cathedral stands the **Old Town Hall** (1496; open: 1 May–30 Sept. Mon.–Fri. 2–4 p.m.), which was originally a private residence. Anders Bording (1619–77), who published the first Danish newspaper, was born here. The building served as the Town Hall from 1709 until the administration was moved in 1966. The former debtors' prison is now a museum (weapons, etc.). Farther E lies **St Catherine's Church** (*Skt. Catherinæ Kirke*), part of a Dominican Monastery. The present church dates from the 15th c. but still incorporates relics of the original building of 1228. Passing through the church we come into the medieval monastery court which is surrounded by two cloisters. After the Reformation the monastery served as a hospital until 1864 then as a home for people living on their own (the church and the monastery court are open to visitors). Outside the church stands a fountain with a statue of St Catherine, patron saint of Dominicans.

From Torvet along the street called Overdammen we come to *Quedens Gård* (c. 1580), a merchant's house with four wings. The classical dwelling was built 200 years later. Today Quedens Gård is a *museum* (open: daily 10 a.m.–noon and 2–4 or 5 p.m.) with interiors of 1580, a citizen's home of the 19th c. as well as documents on popular art and customs. Overdammen is bordered on the S by Sortebrødregade, a picturesque street near the river. On the other side of the Ribe Å lies the site by the river where, in recent years, 60,000 artefacts from the Viking settlement have been found. These include objects made by local craftsmen, jewellery and articles of everyday use. Near the excavation site stands the *Museum of Art* (Skt. Nicolaj Gade). It contains sculpture and paintings of Danish artists of the "Golden Age" (first half of the 19th c.) as well as later works up to the present time.

Skibbroen, running along the river, is Ribe's harbour which today merely serves for pleasure and excursion boats. Near by lies the "Johanne Dan", a ship of the shallows, with a museum on board illustrating Ribe as a maritime town. The flat marshland has been subject to flooding by storms for ages. On the harbour a column, the *Stormflodssøjle,* shows the height reached by flood water in various years. In 1634 the water rose more than 6 m (20 ft). NW of the town on a hill are the excavated remains of *Ribehus Castle* (Riberhus Slotsbanke), built in the 12th c. by King Niels and which for several centuries was a favourite residence of the kings. The remains include the ruins of a fortress, the moat and a statue of Queen Dagmar.

SURROUNDINGS. – SW of the town lies *Vester Vetsted* where there is an exhibition illustrating the shallows and the mud-flats of the coast. Offshore lies the little island of *Mandø,* which can be reached at low tide from Vester Vetsted in a bus drawn by a tractor.

Ringkøbing

Jutland
District: Ringkøbing amt
Population: 17,000
Postal code: DK–6950
Telephone code: 07
Turistbureau
Box 27, Ringkøbing
Tel. 32 00 31
Turistbureau
Troldbergvej
DK–6960 Hvide Sande
Tel. (07) 31 14 84

HOTELS. – *Fjordgården,* Vesterkær 28, 111 b.; *Hotel Garni,* Torvet, 53 b.; *Ringkøbing,* Torvet 18, 29 b. – YOUTH HOSTEL. – CAMP SITES.

RESTAURANT. – *Røgind Kro,* Røgind.

The little town of Ringkøbing lies on the northern bank of the large Ringkøbing Fjord on the W coast of Jutland. The lagoon-like fjord is connected by a narrow channel with the sea.

HISTORY. – The oldest known privileges of the place date from 1443. Agriculture, fishing, oyster-catching and shipping formed the principal sources of income for the inhabitants; later came trade in cattle. The 17th c. brought a time of decline caused by the wars with Sweden and the silting up of the channel to the North Sea. In 1793 the district administration was moved to Ringkøbing and in 1904–05 the town received a new harbour. In 1915 the channel to the North Sea was improved.

SIGHTS. – Beautiful old houses, for example the Customs Building in Østergade, are a feature of the townscape. In the Market-Place stands the old *Mayor's House* (1807), a building in the Empire style. The Market Fountain was dedicated as a memorial for the 110th anniversary of the town. The *museum* in the main square has a large collection especially of religious art, coins and, in the Greenland department, a collection of the Polar explorer Ludwig Mylius Erichsen (1872–1907).

SURROUNDINGS. – 14 km (8 miles) NE of the town lies *Ølstrup;* in the church is a reredos by Emil Nolde (1867–1956) who died in Seebüll in northern Friesland. 7 km (4 miles) N of Ringkøbing in *Hee* is a Romanesque church built of granite slabs (12th c.; restored about 1880). The leisure park *"Sommerland West"* offers the opportunity of weaving in a Viking village or cooking according to old recipes. There are sports facilities and a zoo, including camels and zebras (open: 16 May–1 Sept. 10 a.m.–6 or 7 p.m.).

W of Ringkøbing on the North Sea coast lies the tourist centre of *Søndervig* (two camp sites) amid the dunes. To the S stretches the promontory of Holmsland Klit with the *Nørre Lyngvig Lighthouse,* 53 m (174 ft) high, which can be climbed. Near Hvide Sande is the narrow channel through which ships from Ringkøbing Fjord reach the North Sea. The narrow outer strip of the lagoon forms a natural bird sanctuary, and is the constant delight, particularly in the spring and autumn, of ornithologists. Even those who do not claim to know much about birds are fascinated at the sights they see. It is well worth taking a pair of binoculars to do a little bird-spotting.

Ringsted

Zealand
District: Vestsjællands amt
Population: 28,000
Postal code: DK–4100
Telephone code: 03
Turistbureau
Skt. Bendtsgade 10
Tel. 61 34 00
Turistbureau
Rolighed 5 C
DK–4180 Sorø
Tel. 63 02 69
(open only in summer)

HOTELS. – *Børsen,* Torvet 1, 8 b.; *Casino,* Torvet, 23 b. – YOUTH HOSTEL. – CAMP SITE.

RESTAURANT. – *Apotekergården,* Nørregade 12.

The town of Ringsted, situated in Central Zealand, is a traffic junction; road 14 from Næstved to Roskilde intersects the east-west highway A1/E66 from Korsør to Copenhagen.

HISTORY. – Until well into the 4th c. the place was the location of the "Thing" (local assembly), just as Odense was for Funen and Viborg for Jutland. On the occasion of religious festivals peasants from all over

Ringsted: St Benedict's Church and statue of Valdemar I

the island assembled here; justice was also dispensed at the "Thing" site.

In the Middle Ages Ringsted was one of the most important towns in the country. The first church was built about 1080; the body of Duke Knud Lavard, who had been slain by Magnus the Strong a son of King Niels (1104–34), was buried here. In 1169 Knud Lavard, who was revered by the local people, was canonised. From 1160 King Valdemar I had a new and larger church built, and until 1341 the kings were buried here. The town grew round the church and the Benedictine Monastery which had been founded several decades earlier. About 1800 the monastery was destroyed by fire. Industries became established in the town in the 19th c. and the railway arrived.

SIGHTS. – Two towers remain of the town wall which was part of the medieval fortification. In the market square are three stones, the "*Tingstener*", recalling the earliest days of Ringsted. Also in the market square stands **St Benedict's Church** (*Skt. Bendts Kirke*), dating from the 12th c. but restored several times. It is one of the oldest brick churches in the country and contains the tombs of many Danish kings of the 12th and 13th c. the royalty themselves being depicted in the church's wall-paintings. A brass plate in the choir marks the resting-place of King Eric VI (d. 1319) and his wife; in the church museum can be seen a lead tablet preserved from the tomb of Valdemar the Great. On the canopy of the choir-stalls (1430) are scenes from the Old Testament (N side) and the New Testament (S side). In 1920 the land belonging to the former monastery passed into the possession of the town, and on the S and W of St Benedict's Church a park was laid out. Later the E side of the church was also opened up. In 1936–37 on the N side of the open space the *Town Hall* was built; this is a two-storeyed brick building with a copper roof.

SURROUNDINGS. – 8 km (5 miles) W of the town we come to the village of *Fjenneslev*. Of interest is the church with twin towers (restored 1872–74) where can be seen wall-paintings of the second half of the 12th c. 15 km (9 miles) N of Ringsted in a wooded landscape rises *Gyldenløves Høj*, the highest point of Zealand (126 m (414 ft); fine view). Road A1/E66 from Ringsted leads in a westerly direction to Sorø. Just short of Slaglille a country road branches off to the village of *Bjernede*. Here there is a round church, the only one in Zealand, which was built between 1150 and 1175. This two-storeyed church was restored 1890–92 and now has its original form; the square-ribbed vault is borne on pillars. In *Sorø* (hotels: Krebshuset, 10 b.; Postgården, 48 b.; restaurant: Skovperlen; International Organ Festival, June–Sept.), on the lake of the same name, stands a notable ***12th c. church** (completely restored 1861–71) which Bishop Absalon gave to the Cistercian Monastery of Sorø in 1199. Within the church are the tombs of Bishop Absalon (d. 1201), King Christoph II (d. 1332), Valdemar IV (d. 1375) and

Oluf III (d. 1387). Also, in a side aisle, can be seen the tomb of the playwright Ludvig Holberg (d. 1754). In 1586 Frederik II had set up a school in the monastery building and this became an academy for the sons of nobles in 1623. Holberg left his property to the academy, but most of this was destroyed in a fire in the 19th c. In the academy gardens, which extend to the shores of Sorø Lake (Sorø Sø), is a statue of Holberg.

Rømø

District: Sonderjyllands amt
Area: 99 sq. km (38 sq. miles)
Population: 1000
Turistbureau
Havnebyvej 30
DK-6791 Kongsmark
Tel (04) 75 51 30

Rømø, off the W coast of Jutland, is one of the North Frisian islands and is the largest Danish island in the North Sea. A stone causeway, 10 km (6 miles) in length through the mudflats, joins the island with the mainland. Rømø is separated from the German island of Sylt by the Lister Deep (Listerdyb). A car ferry runs to List.

The popular W coast of the island has a broad sandy beach. A road runs diagonally through Rømø to the seaside resort of *Lakolk*, near the W coast. The landscape of the E part of the island is characterised by woodland, heath and marsh. On the E side lie Juvre, Toftum, Tvismark, Kongsmark, Kirkeby, Østerby and Havneby. Mølby and Sønderby are farther inland.

SIGHTS. – In the *Kommandørgård* at **Toftum**, the home of an 18th c. whaling captain, is a local *museum* where examples of architecture and domestic life can be seen. In Kirkeby stands the *"Seamen's Church"*, St Clement's, dating from the 16th c.; inside are models of ships. Concerts take place in the church in summer. From the fishing village of *Havneby* (hotels: Færgegården, 83 b.; Havneby Kro, 18 b., Apr.–Oct.) a ferry serves the island of Sylt. Daring seafarers embarked from here on voyages to Greenland, generally on St Peter's Day (22 February). *"Rømø Ny Sommerland"*, in the S of the island, is worth visiting. Farmhouses in the old style create a village atmosphere. Animals (pony rides) and sports facilities are among the activities, but the main attraction is a water-chute (open: May–Sept.). Day visitors driving along the causeway to the island should take careful note of the tides as it can be covered, and they should not walk or picnic on the island at each side except at very low tides.

Kirkeby: Model ship in the Sailor's Church

Roskilde

Zealand
District: Roskilde amt
Population: 49,000
Postal code: DK–40000
Telephone code: 02
(i) **Turistbureau**
Fonders Bro 3
Tel. 35 27 00
Turistbureau
Jernbaneplads 3
DK–4300 Holbæk
Tel. (03) 43 11 31

HOTELS. – *Roskilde Motorhotel*, Hovedvej A1/E66, 58 b.; *Lindenborg Kro*, Lindenborgvej 90, Gevninge, 30b.; *Prindsen*, Algade 13, 72 b.; *Risø*, Frederiksborgvej, 39 b.

YOUTH HOSTEL. – *Hørgården*, Horhusvej.

CAMP SITE. – *Vigen Strandpark Camping*, 4 km (2 miles) N of Roskilde on A6.

RESTAURANTS. – *Club 42*, Skomagergade 42; *Gastronetten*, Karen Olsdatterstræde 9; *Palæcafeen*, Stændertorvet 8.

EVENTS. – *Rock and Folk Festival* (largest in N; last week-end in June); *flea market* in Stændertorv on Saturdays.

SPORT and RECREATION. – Canoe trips on Roskilde Fjord and Ise Fjord; sailing club – many moorings for yachts in Roskilde Fjord.

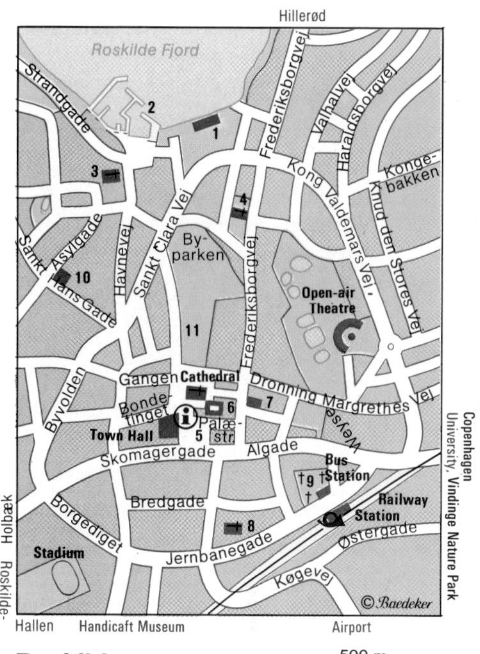

Roskilde

500 m
550 yd

1 Viking Ships
2 Harbour
3 St Jorgensbjerg's Church
4 St Ibs Church
5 Market-place (Stændertorvet)
6 Palace (collections)
7 Roskilde Museum
8 Vor Frue Kirke (Church of Our Lady)
9 Franciscan Cemetery (Gråbrødre Kirkegård)
10 Museum of Games and Playing-cards
11 Foundations of St Hans' Church

Roskilde, which in the Middle Ages was at times a royal residence and the seat of a bishop, is situated in the E of Zealand on Roskilde Fjord which bites deep into the island. Within the town there are several springs; the largest is the "Maglekilde", which delivers 15,000 litres (3,300 gallons) of water in 24 hours. Roskilde can be reached from Copenhagen by train or car in half an hour.

HISTORY. – Roskilde is one of the most ancient towns in Denmark. As early as 960 a wooden church stood on the northern edge of the terrace from which the land slopes to the fjord. Harald Bluetooth, the ruler who converted the Danes to Christianity, is believed to have founded this church. This, at least, is the tradition, but there is no proof. Nevertheless it is a fact that in 1030 a beginning was made to rebuild the church in stone. In the 11th c. Roskilde was a royal and episcopal residence and in the following centuries the town enjoyed its period of greatest prosperity. It was principally an ecclesiastical area, possessing great power and wealth, particularly after King Valdemar brought about the appointment of a young Paris-educated priest as bishop. This was the great Bishop Absalon of the Hvide lineage. In 1168 Valdemar presented to his favourite the town and castle of Havn; Absalon thus became the virtual founder of Copenhagen, then a fishing village of little consequence. Thereafter the focus of power was in Roskilde. The situation changed, however, at the Reformation. Eleven parish churches and all the town's religious houses were closed, and the economic and intellectual life of Roskilde declined. The town later recovered some importance, and in 1658 the peace treaty between Denmark and Sweden was signed in Roskilde Cathedral. By this treaty Denmark lost all its possessions beyond the Kattegat and the Øresund. Much of the old town was destroyed in a series of fires during the 18th c. The economic revivial of Roskilde did not begin until the mid 19th c., after the construction of a railway line from Copenhagen. Roskilde is now one of the major industrial, educational and scientific areas of Denmark, with the Roskilde University Complex (RUC: social sciences) and an atomic research centre at Risø.

SIGHTS. – The Cathedral, one of Denmark's great national monuments, is the central feature of the town which extends N to Roskilde Fjord and S to the motorway (21 or 23).

The imposing **Cathedral of St Luke** (open: 1 Apr.–30 Sept. Mon.–Sat. 9 a.m.–5.45 p.m.; 1 Oct.–31 Mar. Mon.–Sat. 10 a.m.–3.45 p.m.; Sun. 12.30–3.45 or 5.45 p.m.) stands on slightly rising ground

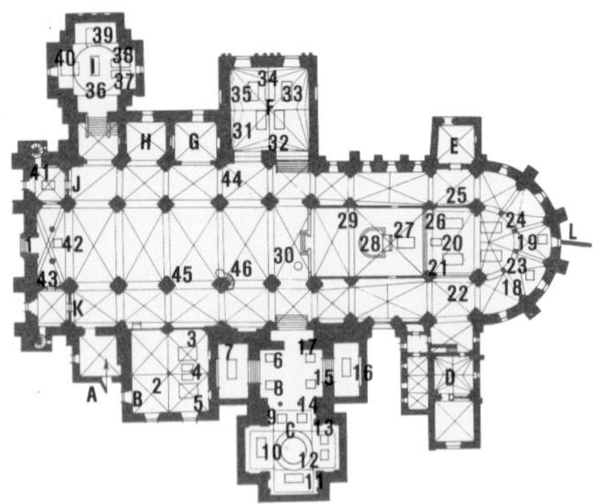

Roskilde Cathedral

A Entrance
B Christian I's Chapel (Chapel of the Three Kings)
C Frederik V's Chapel
D Chapter-house
E Oluf Mortensen's Porch
F Christian IV's Chapel
G St Andrew's Chapel
H St Birgitte's Chapel
I Christian IX's Chapel
J N Tower Chapel
K S Tower Chapel
L Absalon's Arch

1 Main entrance
2 Royal Column
3 Monument of Christian III and Queen Dorothea
4 Tombs of Christian I and Queen Dorothea
5 Monument of Frederik II and Queen Sophie
6 Tomb of Caroline Amalie
7 Tomb of Sophie Magdalene
8 Tomb of Christian VIII
9 Tomb of Marie Sophie Frederike
10 Tomb of Queen Louise
11 Tomb of Frederick V
12 Tomb of Juliane Marie
13 Tomb of Christian VII
14 Tomb of Frekerik VI
15 Tomb of Louise Charlotte
16 Tomb of Christian VI
17 Tomb of Frederik VII
18 Helhestens Sten
19 Gravestone of Bishop Peder Jensen Lodehal
20 Monument of Duke Christopher
21 Tomb of Frederik IV
22 Pillar with remains of Svend Estridsen
23 Tomb of Christian V
24 Tomb of Charlotte Amalie
25 Pillar with remains of Estrid, Knud the Great's sister
26 Tomb of Queen Louise
27 Tomb of Queen Margarethe
28 High Altar
29 Choir-stalls (1420)
30 Font
31 Tomb of Frederik III
32 Tomb of Sophie Amalie
33 Tomb of Anne Catherine
34 Tomb of Christian IV
35 Tomb of Prince Christian
36 Tomb of Frederik IX
37 Tomb of Queen Alexandrine
38 Tomb of Christian X
39 Double tomb of Christian IX and Queen Louise
40 Double tomb of Frederik VIII and Queen Louise
41 Tomb of Anne Sophie Reventlow
42 Kirsten Kimer, Per Døver and St Jørgen
43 Vincentz Hahn's armour
44 Royal Gallery
45 Organ (1554–1654)
46 Pulpit (17th c.)

Roskilde Cathedral: exterior

. . . and a view of the interior

and occupies the site of three earlier churches, including the wooden church built by King Harald Bluetooth. The building of Bishop Absalon's cathedral began about 1170 at the E end and on the plan of a Romanesque basilica with transepts, but this plan was modified about 1200 under the influence of North French Gothic. The church, in red brick, thus shows a mingling of Romanesque and Gothic architecture, and the exterior is further altered by the addition of several funerary chapels. For more than 500 years the Cathedral has been the burial-place of the kings and queens of Denmark. The two W towers were added in the 14th c., and their slender spires, sheathed in copper are dated 1635–36. The "Royal Door" between the towers is opened only for royal funerals. Visitors enter by the S doorway.

The INTERIOR, with lateral aisles flanking the nave, is particularly notable for the magnificent mid-15th c. carved; ***choir-stalls**, above which are reliefs of scenes from the Old Testament (S side) and from the New Testament (N side). An interesting feature of the New Testament series is the representation of the Ascension; the footprints left by Christ can be seen on the ground, and the legs are still visible at the top of the scene. The large carved and gilded *altar-screen* on the High Altar, made in Antwerp in the 16th c., was originally intended for the Chapel of Frederiksborg Castle, but was presented to Roskilde by Christian IV. The altar has been excellently restored after a fire in 1968. Other noteworthy items are the pulpit of sandstone, alabaster, marble and black limestone, and the bronze font of 1602. In the central chapel of the three in the N aisle stands an early 16th c. *figure of St John*. The *royal throne* in the gallery has rich 17th c. wood-carving.

In the **funerary chapels**, built on to the cathedral and entered from the aisles, are the tombs of 38 Danish monarchs, from Margarethe I (d. 1412), who united the Crowns of three northern kingdoms, to Frederick IX, who was buried here in 1972. These royal tombs provide a unique history of funerary monumental art from the early 15th to the 20th c. The finest of the monuments is the recumbent alabaster Gothic figure of Queen Margarethe, behind the High Altar. Christian IV's Chapel on the N side, with a massive vaulted roof, has wall-paintings by William Marstrand and a bronze statue of the King by Thorvaldsen. Also on the N side are the chapels of Christian IX, St Birgitte and St Andrew. In the Chapel of the Three Kings, on the S side a granite column supporting the vaulting is marked with the height of various kings; the tallest is Christian I, in whose reign the chapel was built – a height of 2.1 m (6 ft 9 in), although the King's skeleton measures only 1.88 m (6 ft 2 in). Also on the S side are Frederik V's neo-Classical chapel, modelled on the Pantheon in Rome, with a dome and high windows which let a great deal of light into the chapel, and the chapter-house.

The cathedral is linked by *Absalon's Arch* (*c.* 1200) to the *Palace*, which originally served as the Bishop's seat and later as quarters for royalty who were travelling or who were attending a funeral in the cathedral. In the 18th c. the present palace was built to the designs of the Danish architect Laurids Thura; the building has a handsome courtyard and staircase. Since 1972 five rooms in the palace have housed a *collection* which originated in a gift to Roskilde by the Kornerup family who were merchants of the 18th and 19th c. The exhibits include furniture, paintings (portraits of Peder Kornerup and his wife, and works by the architectural artist Jacob Kornerup). Also on view are champion rifle-shooting targets of the 19th c.; (open: 1 May.–30 Sept. daily 11 a.m.–4 p.m.; 1 Oct.–30 Apr. Sat., Sun. 1–3 p.m.; admission fee).

In the market-place (Stændertorvet), S of the palace, stands the *Town Hall* of 1881. The tower, some 500 years old, once belonged to St Laurence's Church which occupied the site. The *Roskilde Museum* can be found in a town house of 1804 at Skt. Ols Gade 18; exhibits include local costumes, and medieval relics (open: 1 June–31 Aug. daily 11 a.m.–5 p.m.; 1 Sept.–31 May Mon.–Fri. 2–4 p.m., Sun. 2–5 p.m.).

In Fruegade, in the S of the town, stands the *Church of Our Lady* (Vor Frue Kirke), in which remains of the walls of an 11th c. church are to be seen. According to the

Danish historian Saxo (d. 1220) this church was built by Bishop Sven Normand. Restoration work at various dates has severely altered the character of the church. At Ringstedgade 68, a short distance S of the town centre, we come to the *Tool Museum*, a private collection of old woodworking tools (open: Mon.–Fri. 7 a.m.–4.30 p.m., Sat. 8 a.m.–noon).

In the N of the town lies the *Town Park* (Bypparken) with a fine view over Roskilde Fjord. W of the park, at Skt. Hans Gade 20, is the *Games Museum* with the largest collection of games and playing-cards in Scandinavia (open: 3 Jun.–2 Aug. Wed.–Sun. 1–6 p.m.). *St Ibs Church*, to the NE of the Town Park, is a limestone building of about 1100. In the course of centuries parts of the church have been demolished, so that today only the nave remains. Not far away, on a hill near the fjord, in a part of the town which was originally a fishing village, stands the *Church of Skt. Jørgensbjerg* with a choir and nave dating from the end of the 11th c.; the walled-up N doorway is even older and was part of a building which, from coins discovered near by, has been dated to 1040. From the hill there is a good view of the sea.

had been sunk and covered with stones at some time between 1000 and 1050 to block the fjord and to protect the trading town of Roskilde from hostile attack – probably by Norwegian Vikings, who were then prowling the coasts of Denmark. The blockage was drained and the ships brought to the surface. They had disintegrated into thousands of pieces.

There were **five ships**; an ocean-going *freighter* for trading with England, Iceland and Greenland, about 16.5 m (54 ft) long; a *trading vessel* 13.3 m (44 ft) long which was used in the Baltic, the North Sea and on rivers – this was crewed by a maximum of six men and the cargo was stowed amidships under hides; a *warship* some 18 m (59 ft) long for sails or 24 oarsmen; a *ferry-boat*, about 12 m (39 ft) long which was also used for fishing; finally a *longship*, so long – about 28 m (92 ft) – that at first it was believed to be two vessels. The last was the dreaded Viking man-of-war, seaworthy yet easily beached, fast and manœuvrable in battle. Then the task of piecing together and restoring the ships was begun. Although the Viking ships of Roskilde are of little significance to art historians, they are of great interest from a purely historical point of view.

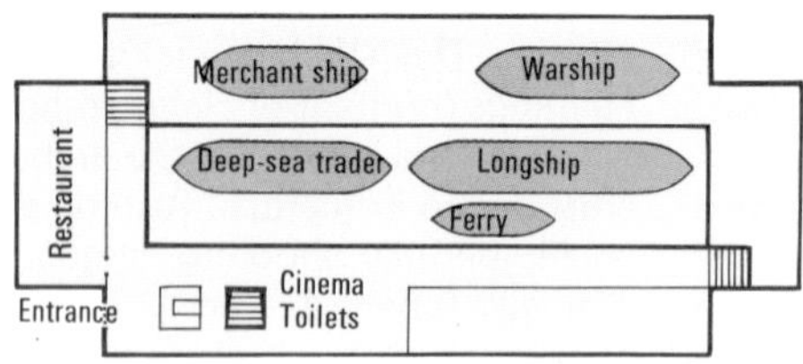

Viking Ship Museum, Roskilde

The ships, found in the Roskilde Fjord in 1957, are still undergoing preservation and restoration

On the bank of the fjord is Roskilde's second main attraction, the ****Viking Ship Museum** which was opened to the public in 1969 (open: 1 Apr.–31 Oct. daily 9 a.m.–5 or 6 p.m.; 1 Nov.–31 Mar. daily 10 a.m.–4 p.m.). The fishermen of Roskilde had known for a long time that there was an underwater stone ridge in the fjord. According to local tradition the accumulation of stones covered a ship which had been sunk by Queen Margarethe (d. 1412). It was only when the Danish National Museum carried out underwater excavations that the barrier was found to date from the Viking Age and to consist of more than one ship. These

There is a cinema where films about the recovery of the ships (commentary also in English) and about the conservation and exhibition of the vessels (commentary in Danish) are shown. A permanent exhibition provides the visitor with information about the Viking Age, the construction of the ships and sub-aqua archaeology.

SURROUNDINGS. – There is a lot to do in the surroundings of Roskilde. At week-ends there are trips on Roskilde Fjord in the coal-fired museum ship "Skjelskør"; departure from the harbour. The ship sails past the Boserup Forest, a popular venue for excursions, where spring flowers are a great attraction, and the nature reserve on the Bognæs Peninsula, where many species of birds are to be seen. SE of the

town at Vindinge we come to **Roskilde Sommerland** (75,000 sq. m (897,000 sq. yd)), a park with extensive open-air enclosures for animals and a games area (open: 18 May–2 Aug. 10 a.m.–6 or 8 p.m.; admission fee). In the Hedehusene recreation area, a short distance N of Vindinge, is the only narrow-gauge museum railway in the country. During the summer months trains run at week-ends. Still farther E in the Vindinge Forest there was found in 1978 the observatory of the celebrated astronomer Ole Rømer (1644–1710). The place is now signposted and in the nearby *museum* at Vridsløsemagle information about Rømer's work as an astronomer can be obtained.

10 km (6 miles) SW of Roskilde near Lejre is **Ledreborg**, a grand 17th and 18th c. Baroque country house with a sumptuously decorated chapel and a large park in the English and French styles (open: July daily 11 a.m.–5 p.m.; June and Aug., Sun., 11 a.m.–5 p.m.; the park is open throughout the year).

The Iron Age begins 4 km (2½ miles) NW of Lejre! In the **Historico-Archaeological *Research Centre of Lejre** the past is brought to life. The theme is the "social and material culture of yesteryear". The principal attraction is the "Iron Age Village" with houses, fields and domestic animals of different kinds.

In the Historico-Archaeological Research Centre on Lejre

Samsø: village pond

. . . and a thatched house

In holiday times "Iron Age families" attempt to exist in the conditions of prehistory and to do without any modern aids; for example they plough with a wooden plough drawn by oxen. In addition there are old workshops (pottery, weaving, smithy) and "Sacrificial Marsh", where visitors can see how the people of the Iron Age worshipped their gods. In the "Valley of Fire" demonstrations are given on such themes as "Fire and Boat", "Iron and Horse", after which visitors can try various activities, such as baking bread on prehistoric hearths or simple iron-forging.

The old village of *Gammel Lejre*, near Lejre, has in the small *Kongsgården Museum* (royal estate) the remains of a ship burial of the Viking Age and, near Øm, a corridor grave of the New Stone Age (*c.* 3000 B.C.). This consists of 15 upright stones and four covering stones. The stone chamber is 7 m (23 ft) long and 1.8 m (6 ft) wide. (A visit is possible; visitors are recommended to carry a torch.)

SW of Lejre, in the wooded region of *Skjoldenæsholm* (Gyldenløves Høj, 125 m (410 ft) – the highest point of Zealand) is Skjoldenæsholm *Tramway Museum*. Here can be seen trams of the period 1863 to 1949; from 1952 trams were replaced by diesel buses. A Museum Tramway is in operation. Texts and pictures provide a survey of the history of public transport in Denmark (open: 5 May–21 Oct. Sat. 1–5 p.m., Sun. 10 a.m.–5 p.m.; 26 June–9 Aug. also Tues.–Thurs. 10 a.m.–5 p.m.; admission fee). The town of *Holbæk* (Hotel Strandparken; Linden Restaurant) lies on Holbæk Fjord, an arm of the extensive Ise Fjord, 30 km (19 miles) NW of Roskilde. The local museum (several old buildings, including a half-timbered house of 1660) can be found at Klosterstræde 1. Sailing and motor boats can be hired at the yacht harbour. 4 km (2½ miles) S of the town we come to *Tveje-Merløse Church* (*c.* 1120; restored 1892–94), one of the oldest village churches in the country. Of special interest is the pulpit of 1571 and wall-paintings of about 1175.

Wall-paintings can also be found in the Romanesque *Tuse Church*, 7 km (4 miles) W of Holbæk.

Samsø

Area: 114 sq. km (44 sq. miles)
Population: 5000

Turistbureau
Langgade 32
DK–8791 Tranebjerg
Tel: (06) 59 14 00

The island of Samsø, popular as a holiday centre, lies in the Kattegat. There is a car ferry from Sælvig on the W coast to Hov in Jutland and another from Kolby Kås (also on the W coast) to Kalundborg on Zealand.

SIGHTS. – The island has fine beaches and a varied landscape. **Tranebjerg** (Sølyst Hotel, 24 b.), the chief place on Samsø, was once the venue of the "Thing" (early Danish assembly). Of interest are a 14th c. church and the fine museum building. On the E coast, near Tranebjerg, lies the fishing village of *Ballen* (Hotel Ballen; Dokken Restaurant), a seaside resort with a yacht harbour. NW of Tranebjerg we reach *Onsbjerg*, where a rare Romanesque Crucifix (*c.* 1200) can be seen in the church. In a park in the S of Samsø stands *Brattingsborg Manor*; the main wing of this country house was built in the English style between 1871 and 1898 (entrance to the park: 1 May–30 Sept. Tues. and Fri. 10 a.m.–4 p.m.; admission fee). The main road passes the park and leads to the coast.

Old half-timbered buildings, a bell-tower and a village pond are features of the picturesque village of *Nordby* (hotels: Nordby Kro, 27 b.; Pension Verona, 25 b., open June–Sept.) in the N of the island. To the NW rises Ballebjerg, 64 m (210 ft).

Silkeborg

Jutland
District: Arhus amt
Population: 47,000
Postal code: DK–8600
Telephone code: 06

(i) **Turistbureau**
Torvet 9
Tel. 82 19 11

HOTELS. – *Ansgar*, Drewsensvej 30, 71 b.; *Dania*, Torvet 5, 80 b.; *Gl. Skovridergård*, Marienlundsvej 36, 109 b.; *Impala*, Vester Ringvej, 104 b.; *Scandinavia*, Christian VIII's vej 7, 62 b.; *Silkeborg Bad*, Gjessøvej 40, 44 b. – YOUTH HOSTEL – Several CAMP SITES.

RESTAURANTS. – *Forsamlingsbygningen*, Vestergade 26; *La Strada*, Torvet 1; *Underhuset*, Torvet 7.

EVENT. – *Riverboat Jazz Festival* (June).

Silkeborg lies on the Langsø ("Long Lake"), in an area of Central Jutland which is characterised by forests and lakes; this is the "Danish Lake Uplands" through which flows the Gudenå.

HISTORY. – In the Middle Ages there was a castle by the Langsø, close to the site of the present Viborg Bridge, but little remains of this building. In 1840 King Christian VIII conceived the plan of founding a town in the vicinity of present-day Silkeborg, in order to open up the interior of Jutland. In 1845 Michael Drewsen set up a paper-factory and other industries followed, many of which made use of water-power from the Gudenå. In 1883 the first spa in Denmark was established here, and in 1900 Silkeborg was raised to the status of a town. Tourism plays an important role in the economy.

SIGHTS. – The town extends along both N and S banks of the Langsø, the centre being in the south. *Hovedgården*, the oldest building in the town, houses the *Historico-Cultural Museum* (open: 15 Apr.–20 Oct. 10 a.m.–5 p.m.; 21 Oct.–14 Apr. Weds., Sat., Sun. noon–4 p.m.; admission fee). The most notable exhibit is the ***head of Tollundmann**, a corpse some 2200 years old, found in a bog in the vicinity. The head which is completely lifelike – it even has a smile on its face – is in a room devoted entirely to the Tollundmann where one can read and follow all the processes from the findings of the body to what it stands for today. It is generally held to be the best-preserved discovery of a prehistoric human. The museum also has documentation on the history of the town and a collection of Danish glass.

The ***Museum of Art** (Gudenåvej 7–9; open: 1 Apr.–31 Oct. Tues.–Fri. 10 a.m.–5 p.m.; Sat., Sun. 10 a.m.–4 p.m.; 1 Nov.–31 Mar. Tues.–Fri. noon–4 p.m., Sat., Sun. 10 a.m.–4 p.m.) has works by modern European artists, including paintings by members of the COBRA group, founded in Amsterdam, and to which Danish, Flemish and Dutch artists belonged. There is also a unique exhibition of works by the well-known Danish painter Asger Jorn (1914–73) which includes oil-paintings, water-colours and ceramic work. During the summer months a colourful display of illuminated fountains can be enjoyed on the lakeside from dusk until about 11 p.m.

SURROUNDINGS. – In summer visitors can take a trip on the paddle-steamer "Hjejlen" through one of the most beautiful parts of Denmark to the *Himmelberg* (147 m (482 ft); see entry). From the summit of the hill (observation tower) there is a splendid view of the surrounding forests and lakes. A 13th c. church in *Grønbæk*, 13 km (8 miles) N of Silkeborg, has interesting wall-paintings; 4 km (2½ miles) away is a very popular typical Jutland inn, the Kongensbro Kro. At Gjern, NE of Silkeborg beyond Voel, is the *Automobile Museum of Jutland*, with over 100 vintage vehicles of 1900 to 1942 (open: 1 May–15 Sept. 10 a.m.–6 p.m. and 16 Sept.–31 Oct. Sat., Sun. 10 a.m.–6 p.m.).

In Skagen Harbour

"Lange Maren" near Skagen

Skagen

Jutland
District: Nordjyllands amt
Population: 14,000
Postal code: DK–9990
Telephone code: 08
Turistbureau
Skt. Laurentiivje 18
Tel. 44 13 77

HOTELS. – *Brøndums Hotel*, Anchersvje 3, 86 b.; *Foldens Hotel*, Skt. Laurentiivej 41, 31 b.; *Norden*, Holstvej 4, 50 b.; *Skagen*, Gammel Landevej 39, 110 b.; *Skagen Strand* (holiday houses), S of Skage; *Pension Strandly*, Østre Strandvej 35, 29 b.

RESTAURANTS. – *Skagen Fish Restaurant*, Fiskehuskajen; *Trekosten*, Hojensvej 4.

EVENT. – *Song Festival*.

Skagen, the most northerly town in Denmark, lies at the northern tip of Jutland. On the far side of the popular seaside resort stretches the Grenen Promontory far into the sea.

HISTORY. – Archaeological finds have established that the site was populated in the Stone and Bronze Ages. In the Middle Ages Old Skagen (Gammel Skagen or Højen) had a settlement on the coast facing the Skagerrak; later the coast of the Kattegat was also populated. The houses were scattered among the dunes. In 1413 the town received its charter, when the principal occupation was fishing. From the beginning of the 17th to the beginning of the 19th c. storms and flooding caused great damage in Skagen. In the second half of the 19th c. an artists' colony, in which Danes predominated, settled in the town. In 1858 a new lighthouse, 46 m (151 ft) high, was brought into use near Grenen. The railway came to the town in 1890.

SIGHTS. – Skagen is characterised by low yellow-painted houses of about 1900. Every morning a fish auction takes place in the auction hall at the harbour. The work of local artists is represented by many paintings in the ***Skagen Museum**, including pictures by P. S. Krøyer (1851–1909), Michael (1849–1909) and Anna (1859–1935) Ancher (open: 1 Apr.–31 Oct. 10 a.m.–5 or 6 p.m.; 1 Nov.–31 Mar. Sat. and Sun. 11 a.m.–3 p.m.). The house of Michael and Anna Ancher (Michael and Anna Anchers Hus, Markvej 2) is furnished as a museum (paintings, drawings).

The *Open-air Museum* "Skagens Fortidsminder" (Svallerbakken) consists of six old buildings, including the houses of a rich and of a poor fisherman; there is also an archaeological collection and exhibits illustrating fishing in the Skagerrak and Kattegat. 3 km (2 miles) W of the town we come to the *"Lange Maren"*, the tower of the former St Laurence's Church, which was enveloped by sand in 1775 and the nave of which was torn away in 1810.

SURROUNDINGS. – 3 km (2 miles) N of Skagen we reach the flat *Grenen* Peninsula, where there is an interesting museum (Grenen Museet). Among the dunes of Grenen lies the grave of the Danish poet and novelist, Holger Drachmann (1846–1908), the "singer of the sea". Beyond Grenen Lighthouse the road ends at a parking place among the dunes and from there visitors can drive in a "sand-worm" (*sandorm* – a tractor drawing a passenger-carrying trailer) or, in dry weather, in their own vehicle, or else they can walk (15 minutes) to the northern tip of Jutland, where the Skagerrak and Kattegat meet. 10 km (6 miles) SW of Skagen is the *"Raberg Mile"*, a 41 m (135 ft) high shifting dune, which moves annually 8–10 m (26–33 ft) to the east.

Visitors to this area should take a raincoat and stout shoes with them, particularly in spring and autumn. For the whole area, though a very attractive and picturesque holiday spot is subject to sudden violent storms.

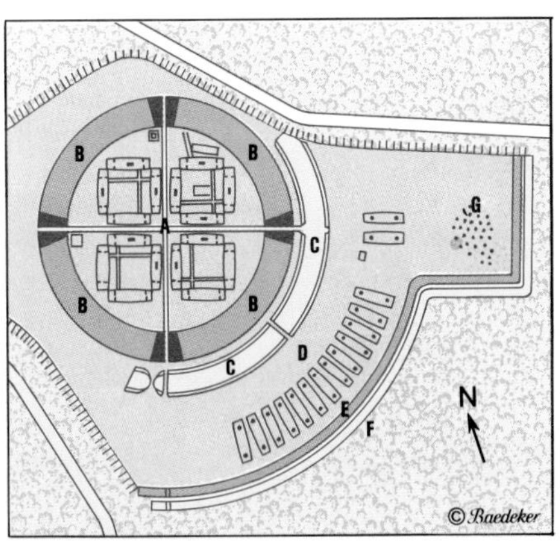

Trelleborg Viking Camp (at A.D. 1000)

A Main Building
B Main Rampart
C Moat
D Outer Ward
E Outer Walls
F Outer Moat
G Burials

Slagelse

Zealand
District: Vestsjællands amt
Population: 33,000
Postal code: DK-4200
Telephone code: 03
Turistbureau
Løvegade 7
Tel. 52 22 06

HOTELS. – *E2*, Idagårdsvej 1, 145 b.; *Slagelse*, Søndre Stationsvej 19, 58 b. – YOUTH HOSTEL – CAMP SITE.

RESTAURANTS. – *Arnehavehus*, Slagelse Lystskov; *Sixpence Pub*, Jernbanegade 10.

Slagelse, a busy port and industrial town, lies on E66 in the W of Zealand.

HISTORY. – As early as the 11th c. Slagelse had a mint, and the first privileges of the town date from 1288. The inhabitants were engaged in agriculture and trade or worked as craftsmen. For several years Hans Christian Andersen attended the Grammar School which had been set up here after the Reformation, but it was closed in 1852. For centuries the town suffered from serious fires and the effects of war. In the 19th c. breweries, distilleries, food-processing factories and engineering works were established here.

SIGHTS. – The central feature of the town is the Gothic *St Michael's Church* (Skt. Mikkels Kirke) which was built about 1330 and restored between 1873 and 1876. Near by stands the former Grammar School. The oldest building in Slagelse is the Romanesque *St Peter's Church* (Skt. Peders Kirke); this was later altered and enlarged. In a chapel can be seen the tomb of St Anders who had been a leading figure in the development of the town. In *Antvorskov Wood* to the SE of the town, off the road to Næstved, are the ruins of a monastery of the Order of St John of Jerusalem, which later became a royal residence. Here the Danish flag, originally the banner of the Order, is flown from the flagpole by the ruins every Sunday.

SURROUNDINGS. – 7 km (5 miles) W of Slagelse lies the reconstruction based on the finds of the excavation of the Viking settlement of ***Trelleborg**, dating from the years 1000–1050. It consists of a circular rampart with four entrances, giving access to two streets intersecting at right angles and dividing the enclosed area into four quarters. Within the ramparts were 16 houses each 29.5 m (97 ft) long with gently rounded walls, four houses being laid out in a square in each quadrant. A moat protected the E side of the ramparts, the other sides being flanked by two small rivers, and between the moat and an outer rampart was a row of houses similar to those inside the main ramparts. Outside the site is a reconstruction of one of the houses, based on evidence recovered by excavation.

Trelleborg: reconstructed Viking house

Svendborg

Funen
District: Fyns amt
Population: 39,000
Postal code: DK–5700
Telephone code: 09
(i) **Turistbureau**
Møllergade 20
Tel. 21 09 80

HOTELS. – *Ærø*, Brogade 1, 18 b.; *HK-Christiansminde*, Christiansmindevej 16, 180 b.; *Kogtvedstrand*, Sundvænget 2, 10 b.; *Royal*, Toldbodvej 5, 45 b.; *Missionshotel Stella Maris*, Kogtvedvænget 3, 38 b.; *Svendborg*, Centrumpladsen, 100 b.; *Tre Roser*, Fåborgvej 90, 140 b.; *Troense*, Strandgade 5–11, 68 b.; *Pension Villa Strandbo*, Børges Allé 13, 10 b. – HOLIDAY HOUSES. – YOUTH HOSTEL. – Several CAMP SITES. RESTAURANTS. – *Spisehus*, Korsgade 1; *Stella Maris*, Kogtvedvænget 3.

The port of Svendborg is situated in the S of Funen, on Svendborg Sound. A ferry links the town with the island of Ærø to the S. Svendborg has shipyards and mills, as well as factories for artificial materials, foodstuffs and packaging.

HISTORY. – The oldest charter dates from 1253. In the Middle Ages Svendborg had trade links with the Hanseatic towns and with the Duchies of Schleswig and Holstein. During the "Counts' Wars" (1534–36) Orkild Castle in the E of the town was burned down. In the 17th c. Svendborg suffered great destruction as a consequence of the wars with Sweden. The 19th c. was a period of prosperity. In 1966 the bridge across Svenborg Sound was completed. Until 1970 Svendborg was a district headquarters; subsequently the two districts of Funen were combined and the administrative offices were henceforth in Odense.

SIGHTS. – There are a number of old houses in the town. In Tinghusgade, S of the market-place, stands *St Nicholas's Church* (Skt. Nicolai Kirke), built in 1220 in Romanesque style and restored in 1892. The *Municipal Museum* is housed in Anne Hvides Gård (Fruestræde 3), the oldest secular building in the town, dating from 1560 (renovated in 1976), and also in the Viebæltegård (Gribbemøllevej 13). The exhibits include documentation concerning the port of Svendborg, natural history and historical collections and works by the painter and sculptor Kai Nielsen (1882–1924) who was born in the town. Sculptures by Nielsen can be found in many places in the town, by St Nicholas's Church, by the swimming-pool and at the library.

The *Zoological Museum* (Dronningemæn 30) is also worth seeing; a feature is the collection of North European birds.

The German poet and dramatist Bertolt Brecht lived from 1933 until 1939 as an emigrant in Svendborg. A memorial tablet was affixed in 1981 to the house where he resided. During his exile in Denmark Brecht wrote, among other things, the play "Mother Courage and her Children" (1939) as well as the "Svendborg Poems" (1939).

SURROUNDINGS. – The *Manor of Hvidkilde* is situated 5 km (3 miles) W of Svendborg. The original white Baroque palace of 1742 was converted into a Renaissance building (no admission to the house, but visitors are admitted to the park on request). About 300 m (330 yd) from the manor an avenue leads to a parking place, from where visitors can walk in the woods along waymarked paths.

From Svendborg a massive bridge (1966: 1200 m (1300 yd) long, clear height 33 m (108 ft)) crosses Svendborg Sound, a popular sailing area, to Vindeby on the island of **Tåsinge** (area 70 sq. km (27 sq. miles)). Vindeby is a much-frequented vacation resort, with huts and a camp site. In 3 km ($1\frac{3}{4}$ miles) we reach the village of *Troense* which has a picturesque main street (Motel Troense, 14 b.). A short distance S stands **Valdemarsslot** (Valdemar's Castle), one of the most beautiful Late Baroque royal houses in Denmark. It was Christian IV who had it built for his son, Count Valdemar Christian. The estate later passed to the maritime hero Niels Juel. Valdemar's Castle is now a museum with exhibits illustrative of the manorial culture of Funen. From the tower of the village church (74 m (243 ft)) in *Bregninge* there are panoramic views. The local museum contains a section devoted to the tragic love-affair of Count Sparre and Elvira Madigan, who are buried in Landet Cemetery, 3 km (2 miles) S.

From the SE side of the island of Tåsinge a causeway and a bridge (1962: 1700 m (1850 yd) long) lead, by way of the little island of Siø to the popular holiday island of Langeland (see entry). Another causeway to the E of the Svendborg bridge crosses to the island of *Thurø* (beautiful church; excellent swimming).

There are also interesting places to the N of Svendborg. 12 km ($7\frac{1}{4}$ miles) along road 163, which leads to Nyborg (see entry), a minor road branches off on the right to the seaside resort of *Lundeborg*, and in another 2 km ($1\frac{1}{4}$ miles) a road bears off to the ***Manor-house of Hesselagergård**, 1.5 km (1 mile) distant. The round gable of the building which dates from 1538 was modelled on a Venetian predecessor and added in 1550. Farther N in a meadow can be seen a boulder some 12 m (39 ft) high with a circumference of 46 m (151 ft). It was deposited here from Norway during the Ice Age and is considered to be Denmark's largest erratic boulder.

6 km (4 miles) along road 163 beyond Hesselagergård, at the village of Langå, a side road on the left of the main road leads in 2 km ($1\frac{1}{4}$ miles) to the 16th c. manor-house of *Rygård*, built on piles. 1 km ($\frac{3}{4}$ mile) N of Langå another road on the left leads to still another manor-house; this is *Glorup* which was rebuilt in Baroque style and which is surrounded by an attractive park. In the park stand several zinc statues and a "Tuscan" Temple of Love (admission to park: Thurs., Sat. and Sun. 9 a.m.–6 p.m.).

Valdemarsslot (Valdemar's Castle) on the Island of Tåsinge

Tønder

Jutland
District: Sonderjyllands amt
Population: 13,000
Postal code: DK–6270
Telephone code: 04
(i) **Turistbureau**
Østergade 2 A
Tel. 72 12 20

HOTELS. – *Abild*, Ribe Landevej 66, in Abild, 22 b.; *Hostrups*, Søndergade 30, 46 b. – YOUTH HOSTEL. – CAMP SITE.

RESTAURANT. – *Hotel Tønderhus*, Jomfrustien 1.

The town of Tønder is situated in the fenland of South Jutland, N of the Danish-German border.

HISTORY. – About 1130 the place is mentioned as "a good harbour". At that time the town had access to the North Sea, thanks to a river with a good depth of water. In 1243 Tønder received a charter from Lübeck. In the following centuries it was alternately under Danish and German jurisdiction. Duke John the Elder (1521–80) had dikes built to protect the town from flooding, but this was a disadvantage for shipping. Tønder traded with the Netherlands and with the ports of North Germany, especially in cattle. At the beginning of the 17th c. the people of Tønder and the neighbourhood began to make lace. After 1813 lace-making declined in importance, but trading in cattle continued to play a role in the town's economy. When the new frontiers were drawn in 1920 Tønder lost its extensive hinterland in the S.

SIGHTS. – In the town there are fine old houses, dating from the time when lace-making was at its height; these include the *Digegrevens Gård* (Dike Administrator's house) in Vestergade and the *Great Pharmacy* in Østergade. The late Gothic **Kristkirke** (Christ Church; 1591) has a richly decorated interior; of particular interest are the carving in the gallery and a tall altar-piece (1696). The 47 m (154 ft) high tower belongs to an earlier church. In the former gatehouse of the castle, which was pulled down in 1750, and in a more recent building are the *Tønder Museum* and the *South Jutland Museum of Art*. In the municipal museum can be seen lace, Dutch tiles and faience, while in the art museum works by contemporary Danish painters are on show (open: 1 May–31 Oct. Tues.–Sun. 10 a.m.–5 p.m.; 1 Nov.–30 Apr. Tues.–Sun. 1–5 p.m.). Look for the storks' nests which may still be seen next to chimneys on some of the roofs in Tønder.

SURROUNDINGS. – *Møgeltønder*, 13 km (8 miles) W of Tønder is probably older than the latter town; here can be found thatched brick houses and cobbled streets. Slotsgade leads N to *Schackenborg Castle*, originally a Baroque building. The park was laid out in the 17th c., but the buildings in their present form are of 19th c. date. SW of Tønder lies the frontier village of *Rudbøl*; since 1920 the Danish–German border has run right through the middle of the village. *Højer*

A lace-maker at work

(sheep market), on the coast NW of Møgeltønder, has an interesting Romanesque church with an altar dating from 1425. Near Højer stands a 30 m (98 ft) high windmill of 1857 which now houses a museum and a restaurant.

The village of *Løgumkloster* (Løgumkloster Hotel, 32 b.; Abbey Market, Aug.), 18 km (11 miles) N of Tønder, grew up round ****Løgum Abbey**, founded in 1144. Of the old Cistercian buildings, only part of the east wing, including the chapter-house, the sacristy, the library and the abbey church remain. The abbey is now used as a religious Folk High School and for other ecclesiastical purposes. The *abbey church* (1230–1330) is impressive, with spacious Early Gothic pointed windows and beautiful pillars. Inside is a winged altar-piece (*c.* 1500), sumptuous choir-stalls and a reliquary with wings and a triumphal cross (*c.* 1300). Opposite the main building stands a 25 m (80 ft) high tower with a carillon (8 and 11 a.m., 3 and 9 p.m.). Some 25 km (16 miles) E of Tønder at Tiglev is the leisure complex of *Sommerland Syd* which is particularly suitable for families with children (open: 17 May–27 Aug. daily 10 a.m.–6 or 7 p.m.).

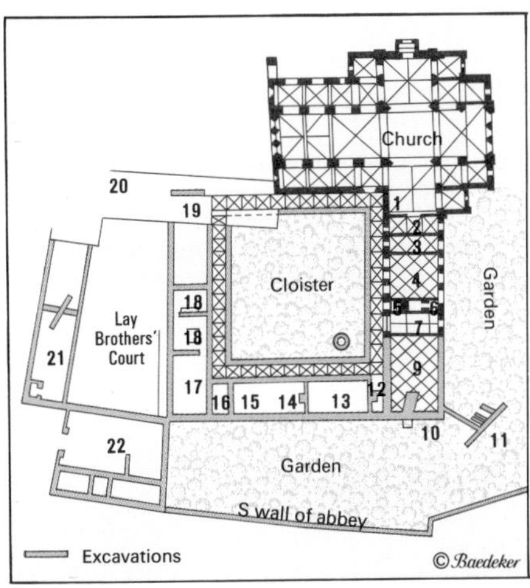

Logum Abbey
Former Cistercian Monastery
Locus Dei

1 Former stair to dormitory
2 Sacristy (Treasury above)
3 Library
4 Chapter-house
5 Stair to Dormitory (Archive Room below)
6 Prison (?)
7 Corridor
8 Well
9 Room for study and work
10 Heating furnace
11 Monks' redorter (toilet)
12 Stair to upper storey
13 Monks' Refectory
14 Kitchen
15 Pantry(?) Warming-room(?)
16 Cellarer's parlour
17 Lay Brothers' Refectory (Dormitory above)
18 Store-rooms
19 Probable site of the cloister door
20 "Palace" former Abbot's Lodging(?) now Court-house
21 Workshops. Stables(?)
22 Infirmary and Lay Brothers' Redorter (toilet) Tithe Barn(?)

Vejle

Jutland
District: Vejle amt
Population: 50,000
Postal code: DK–7100
Telephone code: 05

(i) **Turistbureau**
Rådhustorvet
Tel. 82 19 55
Turistbureau
Gormsgade 19
DK–7300 Jelling
Tel. 87 13 01

HOTELS. – Australia, Dæmningen 6, 133 b.; *Missionshotel Caleb*, Dæmningen 52, 50 b.; *Motel Hedegården*, Valdemar Poulsensvej 4, 74 b.; *Munkebjerg Hotel*, Munkebjergvej 125, 280 b.; *Park Hotel*, Orla Lahmannsgade 5, 80 b.

RESTAURANTS. – *Banketten*, Kirkegade 3; *Paladskroen*, Ved Anlægget 14; *Rådhuskroen*, Radhustorvet.

Vejle, a busy industrial and commercial town, lies on the coast of Central Jutland in a wooded area at the end of the Vejle Fjord.

HISTORY. – Vejle arose round a ford over the Vejle Å and received its charter in the 17th c. For a very long time the town has had trading connections with other countries, especially with the North German towns of Flensburg, Hamburg and Lübeck, as well as with the Netherlands and Norway. From Lübeck came iron and spices, while corn was exported to Norway. At the end of the 18th c. the district administration was removed to Vejle and between 1824 and 1827 a new harbour was constructed. From this time on the production of akvavit (schnapps) played an important part in the economy of the town. During the Schleswig-Holstein Wars of the 19th c. Vejle was occupied at times by German troops and until 1956 was a garrison town.

SIGHTS. – The oldest building in the town is the Gothic **St Nicholas's Church** (13th c.; fine peal of bells), which has been altered on several occasions. Interesting features are a granite font, the reredos (1751) by the sculptor Jens Hiernøe and the Renaissance pulpit (16th c.). Also inside the church can be seen a coffin containing the corpse of a queen which had been buried in a peatbog and which is believed to be from 1500 to 2000 years old. The *Town Hall* was built on the site of a medieval Dominican monastery. The old monastery bell survives and marks the passing of the hours. Two museums are situated in the Flegborg road; at No. 16 is the *Vejle Museum of Art* with pictures by modern Danish artists, while the *Vejle Museum* at No. 18 has collections of archaeological exhibits and of local history.

View of the town of Vejle

SURROUNDINGS. – A 93 m (100 yd) long moving stairway leads across the fjord up to the *Munkebjerg* on the SE of the town, from where there is a fine view of the town. Congresses are held in the hotel on the summit of the hill. 12 km (7 miles) NW of Vejle, best reached on the beautiful road through the Grejsdal (wooded slopes, many viewpoints) is **Jelling** (hotels: Jelling Kro, 16 b.; Tøsby Kro, 12 b.; restaurants: Hos Thyra, Skovdal Kro) which was the political centre of the country about the year 1000. The two 21 and 24 m (70 and 79 ft) high burial mounds by the roadside are the oldest royal graves in Denmark, dating to about 935–50. After excavations in 1941–42 and 1978 it was established that the northern grave held the remains of King Gorm who died about 940 and his wife Thyra. The ****two runic stones** on the site with drawings and inscriptions provide considerable information. The smaller, which Gorm set up for his wife, bears the inscription, "Gorm the King set up these memorials for Thyra his Queen, the pride of Denmark". Harald Bluetooth (940–85), the son of Gorm, embraced Christianity. He had the mound on the S built over a pagan cult site and set up the larger runic stone. On this is written, "Harald the King had these memorials for Gorm, his father, and for Thyra, his mother, the Harald who won Denmark for himself and all Norway and who made the Danes Christian". Harald transferred his seat from Jelling to Zealand, probably to Roskilde. Between the graves and the runic stones there stands a small church, on the site where Harald Bluetooth had previously built a wooden church. This church was probably erected in the 11th c. but was later altered on several occasions. There are remains of Romanesque wall-paintings dating from the early 12th c.; they were restored between 1926 and 1927 and again between 1935 and 1938.

9 km ($5\frac{1}{2}$ miles) NW of Jelling we come to *Givskud* (hotel: Therkeline; restaurant: Harresø Kro) where lions, elephants, buffalo and monkeys can be seen in a *safari park* (open: 1 May–30 Aug. 10 a.m.–4.30 or 6 p.m.). Of the 700 exotic animals on view there are 40 lions.

Viborg

Jutland
District: Viborg amt
Population: 39,000
Postal code: DK-8800
Telephone code: 06

(i) **Turistbureau**
Nytorv 5
Tel. 62 16 17

HOTELS. – *Kongenshus*, Skivevej 142, in Daugbjerg, 19 b. (Apr.–Nov.); *Missionshotel*, Skt. Mathiasgade 5, 80 b.; *Motel Søndersø*, Randersvej 2, 80 b.; *Viborg*, Gravene 20, 23 b. – YOUTH HOSTEL. – CAMP SITES: two at Tjele (16 km (10 miles)) NE and one at Monsted (15 km (10 miles)) W.

RESTAURANTS. – *Palæ*, Skt. Mathiasgade 78; *Salonen*, Randersvej.

EVENTS. – *Hævejsmarchen*, the oldest and the biggest of the "marches" so popular in Denmark, a two-day walk along the old Military Road (30–50 km (20–30 miles) each day).

Runic stones of Jelling

Countryside near Vejle

SPORTS and RECREATION. – Canoe trips on the lakes to Gudenå and Randers (45 km (28 miles)); fishing in many lakes and streams.

Viborg, one of the oldest towns in Denmark, lies in the heart of the country, at the intersection of trade routes from north to south and from east to west. Viborg's attraction is in its beautiful surroundings of forests, lakes and expanses of heathland.

HISTORY. – Archaeological investigation has shown that there was a settlement in the area of the present town about the year 700. The town was originally known as Wibjerg (Wib is an old word for "sacred", hence Wibjerg meant "sacred hill"), and is thought to have been a pagan cult site. This gave rise to trading activity and thus to the rise of the town. After the coming of Christianity Viborg became a religious focal point and in 1065 the see of a bishop. At this period it was the capital of Jutland, and the Danish kings were still elected in Viborg until 1340. For another 300 years it remained the place where the Estates paid homage to the newly elected king. Until 1650 it was the largest town in Jutland and until 1850 the seat of the Landsting (provincial assembly). Between 1525 and 1529 the preacher, Hans Tausen, made Viborg a centre of the Reformation. Most of the town's old buildings were destroyed by great fires in 1567 and 1726, and of its churches only the Cathedral (rebuilt in the 19th c.) and the Dominican church survived. Viborg is now primarily a commercial and industrial town.

SIGHTS. – Many old buildings have survived in Viborg. The ***Cathedral** (*Skt. Mogens Gade*) was built in the 12th c. and rebuilt between 1864 and 1876 as a copy of the original Romanesque building of granite ashlar. Only the three-aisled crypt of the original was preserved. The new church, built of brick and Swedish granite, was modelled on some of the German cathedrals and the churches of Lund and Ribe. Its most distinctive features are the twin towers with their pyramidal roofs, visible from afar. A few Romanesque sculptured stones have been incorporated into the external walls, including the two lions flanking a window in the apse. (Open: Apr., May and Sept. Mon.–Sat. 9 a.m.–4 p.m.; June–Aug. Mon.–Sat. 9 a.m.–5 p.m., Sun. 1–5 p.m.; Oct.–Mar. Mon.–Sat. 10 a.m.–3 p.m., Sun. 1–3 p.m.)

The INTERIOR is dominated by and is famous for the Biblical wall-paintings which Joakim Skovgaard made between 1901 and 1906. In the side aisles are Old Testament scenes, in the transepts scenes from the life of Christ and in the choir the Resurrection and the Ascension. The ceiling-paintings, in oil on mahogany, depict the Nativity, flanked by Moses and

David and the Prophets. English visitors may be interested to know that the artists' grandson, also called Joakim Storgaard, lives in England and is himself an architect, writer and artist. The 19th c. altar is in gilt bronze. The three-aisled Romanesque *crypt* has 12 bays of vaulting borne on 6 columns and 12 semi-columns with granite shafts.

Near the Cathedral stands the *Søndersogn Church* (= Church of the Southern Parish), originally belonging to a Dominican monastery, and dating from 1227; it was destroyed by fire in 1726 and rebuilt two years later. The choir and the nave of the old church survive. The church has a magnificent carved and gilded Gothic Flemish altar of about 1520.

The **Regional Museum** (*Stiftsmuseum*) adjoining the cathedral occupies the Old Town Hall (1728), a Baroque building by Claus Stahlknecht of Altona (Hamburg), who was called to Viborg to help with reconstruction work after the great fire. The prehistoric collection includes Bronze Age material; the modern section displays applied and decorative art of the 16th and 17th c. The *Skovgaard Museum* in Skt. Peder Stræde contains sketches, paintings and sculpture by Joakim Skovgaard (1856–1933), including his preliminary sketches for the frescoes in the cathedral.

On the E side of the town is the *Asmild Church* (*c.* 1100), of which only the walls of the original building survive. Towards the end of the 12th c. it was given to an Augustinian nunnery which was situated to the S of the church but of which nothing now remains. Bishop Eskild of Viborg was murdered in front of the High Altar in 1132. The gallery, with portraits of Danish kings, the carved reredos and the pulpit of 1625 are all noteworthy. In the vestibule can be seen a runic stone.

SURROUNDINGS. – 8 km (5 miles) SW of the town on the **Hald Lake** (*Haldsjø*) is a manor-house, *Hald Hovedgård*; from the Middle Ages several castles were built on this site and later pulled down. The present main building, originally a gateway and carriage-house, dates from 1789. An exhibition illustrating the geology of the area and including models of the previous castles is housed in a restored half-timbered barn. 1.5 km (1 mile) S of the manor-house a marked forest path on a peninsula jutting out into the lake, amid hills, valleys, woodland heath, offers the walker an experience of especial natural beauty. 17 km (10½ miles) N of Viborg we come to the excavation site of *Hvolris* where traces of settlement from the Stone Age to the medieval era have been found (museum).

Vordingborg

Zealand
District: Storstrøms amt
Population: 20,000
Postal code: DK-4760
Telephone code: 03

(i) **Turistbureau**
Glamsbæksvej 3
Box 103
Tel. 77 02 17

HOTELS. – *Kong Valdemar*, Algade 101, 75 b.; *Prins Jørgen*, Algade 1, 33 b.

RESTAURANTS. – *Snekken*, at the harbour; *Pizzeria Roma*, Algade.

Vordingborg has a delightful situation on the S coast of Zealand, not far from the Storstrøm Bridge which links Falster and Zealand.

HISTORY. – In the 12th c. Valdemar the Great built a castle on the plateau which falls steeply away to the S. The castle formed part of the fortifications erected by the Danes on the coasts of the Baltic as protection against the Wends. In addition Vordingborg was important because it was situated at the place where the ferry crossed to Falster. In the Middle Ages Danish kings often resided in the castle and until the end of the 13th c. the Danish Court held its meetings in Vordingborg. The town later lost much of its importance and in 1658 the Swedish King Gustav took Vordingborg after his unopposed landing on Zealand. Since 1886 Vordingborg has had a ferry link with Travermünde in the German Federal Republic and with Warnemünde near Rostock in East Germany. The bridge to Falster (Storstrømsbroen) was completed in 1938.

SIGHTS. – Of the *castle*, one of the most important in the country, only the curtain-walls and the 26 m (85 ft) high ***Goose Tower** (*Gåsetårn*) near the harbour survive. A gilded goose crowns the pointed roof of the tower – hence its name. It is a reminder of the remark of Valdemar IV that the Hanseatic towns were like a flock of chattering geese. There is a good view from the top of the tower (open: 15 May–14 June and 15 Aug.–14 Sept. daily 1–5 p.m.; 15 June–14 Aug. daily 10 a.m.–5 p.m.).

In a little house near the fortress ruins can be found the *South Zealand Museum*, with an historical and cultural collection. Of special interest is an aquamanile (a medieval vessel from which water was poured over the priests's hands during the Mass); the vessel is shaped like a centaur.

Viborg Cathedral

Vordingborg: Castle ruins

. . . and "Goose Tower"

Near the museum lies a herb-garden containing plants which were once used as medicines, and also a compound for stags and birds. In the *Gothic Church of Our Lady* (Vor Frue Kirke) in Kirketovet can be seen wall-paintings dating from about 1400. The reredos is the work of Abel Schrøder.

SURROUNDINGS. – Not far N of Vordingborg we come to *Udby*, where the Danish theologian and popular educationalist Nikolai Frederik Severin Grundtvig (1783–1872) was born (museum).

W of Udby lies *Sværdborg*; in the Romanesque church is a Gothic fresco representing the end of the world.

Zealand/Sjælland

Districts: Københavns amt
Fredriksborg amt
Roskilde amt
Vestsjællands amt
Storstrøms amt
Area: 7026 sq. km (2712 sq. miles)
Population: 1.95 million

Zealand (Danish Sjaelland) is the largest island of Denmark, bounded in the N by the Kattegat and in the S by the Baltic. The coasts are characterised by many fjords, spits and bays. In the N of Zealand the Øresund, which separates the E coast of the island from the W coast of Sweden, is very narrow. A ferry links Helsingør (Denmark) with Helsingborg (Sweden). In the S the Storstrøm and Farø bridges connect Zealand with the island of Falster.

Fertile moraine deposits, with tunnel valleys and "osers" (banks of sand or pebbles formed by meltwater during the Ice Age) are characteristic of the landscape. While in the S agriculture plays a major role, the N of the island is extensively industrialised.

SIGHTS. – Copenhagen (see entry) in the E of the island is particularly attractive with its many palaces (Christiansborg, Amalienborg), museums and places of entertainment (Tivoli). There are also interesting castles in Helsingør (see entry; Kronborg Castle) and in Hillerød (see entry; Frederiksborg Castle). The Danish kings have been buried in the Cathedral of Roskilde (see entry) for more than 500 years; in the Viking Ship Museum can be seen reconstructed vessels which provide a fascinating impression of the importance which ships and shipping once had for the country. Kalundborg and Korsør (see entries) are both ports which are vital links in the internal communications of Denmark.

Practical Information

The car ferry "Danmark" at Rødbyhavn

MA-KH 456

Safety on the Road. Some Reminders for the Vacation Traveller

Always wear your seat-belt, and make sure that your passengers wear theirs.
Note: Compensation for injury may be reduced by up to 50 per cent if seat-belts are not worn.

Change the brake fluid in your car at least every two years.
This vitally important fluid tends to lose its effectiveness in the course of time as a result of condensation of water, dust and chemical decomposition.

Change your tyres when the depth of tread is reduced to 2 mm (0.8 in).
Tyres must have enough depth of tread to get a good grip on the road and hold the car steady even on a wet surface. In the case of wide sports tyres, with their long water channels, a 3 mm (0.12 in) tread is advisable.

You will see better, and be more easily seen, if your car lights are functioning properly.
It is important, therefore, to check your sidelights and headlights regularly. This can be done even without getting out of the car. When you stop at traffic lights in front of a bus or truck you can see whether your rear lights and brake lights are working from the reflection on the front of the other vehicle, and you can check up on your headlights and front directional signals in your own garage or in a shop window.

When driving at night on wet roads you should stop in a parking place every 50 or 100 km (30 or 60 miles) and clear your headlights and rear lights.
Even the thinnest coat of dirt on the glass reduces the strength of your headlights by half, and a heavy coating may reduce their output by as much as 90 per cent.

The best place for fog lights is on the front bumper.
This gives them the maximum range without dazzling oncoming traffic. If they are mounted below the bumper they will have a range of only 5 or 10 m (16 or 32 ft). Fog lights are most effective when used in conjunction with parking lights only: for safe driving, therefore, they must have an adequate range.

It is always advisable to carry a first-aid kit. It is compulsory for all drivers, including visitors, to carry a warning triangle. Remember, however, that if these items are kept on the rear shelf they can become dangerous projectiles in the event of an accident.
The first-aid kit should be kept inside the car, either secured in a holder or under a seat; the warning triangle should be kept ready to hand in the boot (trunk). If there is no more room in the boot any items of equipment or pieces of luggage inside the car should be stowed carefully and securely.

If there is so much luggage in the back of the car that the view through the rear window is obstructed it is a wise precaution, as well as a statutory requirement, to have an outside mirror on the passenger's side. This is useful in any event when driving in heavy traffic on multi-lane highways. It should be of convex type.

Drivers who keep their left foot on the clutch pedal after changing gear may be letting themselves in for a heavy repair bill.
This very rapidly wears down the clutch release bearing, giving rise to whining and grating noises.

As a light bulb grows older its efficiency falls off very markedly. A dark-coloured deposit inside a bulb – wolfram from the filament – is an indication of age.
All bulbs should, therefore, be checked at least once a year. It is advisable to change those which have darkened glass as well as those which are clearly defective.

You can save fuel when driving on highways by keeping the accelerator pedal at least 2 cm (about $\frac{3}{4}$ in) short of the "foot-down" position.
The nearer to its maximum speed a car is travelling the more steeply does fuel consumption increase. A slightly lighter touch on the accelerator will make little difference to your speed but quite a difference to the amount of fuel you use.

If you wear glasses you will increase the safety of night driving by getting special coated lenses; and all drivers should avoid wearing tinted glasses after dusk and at night.
All glass reflects part of the light passing through it, and even through a clear windscreen only about 90 per cent of the light outside reaches the driver's eyes inside the car. If the driver is wearing glasses there is a further light loss of 10 per cent. With a tinted widscreen and tinted glasses only about half the light outside reaches the driver's eyes, and in these conditions driving at night is not possible.

If you have an accident

However carefully you drive, you may nevertheless find yourself involved in an accident. If this does happen do not lose your temper, however great the provocation: remain polite, keep cool and take the following action:

1. Warn other road-users: switch on your hazard warning lights and set out your warning triangle at a sufficient distance from the scene of the accident.

2. Attend to the injured. Expert assistance should be summoned immediately. Unless you have a knowledge of first aid you should be extremely cautious about attending to anyone injured in an accident. Call an ambulance if required.

3. If anyone has been injured, if there has been major damage to the cars involved or if there is disagreement between you and the other party, inform the police.

4. Get the names and addresses of other parties involved; note the registration number and make of the other vehicles and the time and place of the accident. Ask the other parties for the name of their insurers and their insurance number.

5. Note down the names and addresses of witnesses; take photographs and/or make sketches of the scene of the accident.
After a minor accident the police are usually more concerned with getting the road clear for traffic than making a full record of the incident. What you should try to record in your photographs is not the damage to the cars involved – that can be established later – but the general situation at the scene of the accident. It is particularly important to photograph each of the cars in the direction of travel from a sufficient distance.

6. If possible fill in the "European Accident Statement" (which you will have received along with your green card if you own the car) and have it signed by the other party. Do not sign any admission of liability. If the other party asks you to sign an accident form not written in English and you are in doubt of its meaning, add the words "without prejudice to liability" above your signature.

7. Inform your own insurance company by letter, if possible, within 24 hours of the accident. If your car is rented, inform the rental agency by phone immediately.

8. If the accident involves injury to persons (other than yourself and your passengers) or damage to property, inform the bureau named on the back page of your green card.

9. If you own the car follow the instructions of your insurance company – which you will normally have received along with your green card – concerning repair of damage to your car.

In the case of an accident the police can be contacted by dialling 000 anywhere in Denmark (the calls are free). Breakdowns are handled by two organisations – FALCK (*spell out*) and DAHU (*Dansk Autohjælsp Union*). There are 160 offices at the disposal of motorists. Breakdown service must be paid for. The most important offices are:

FALCK	DAHU
Ålborg (08) 13 35 00	Åbenrå (04) 65 94 44
Copenhagen (01) 14 22 22	Ålborg (08) 17 68 01
Haderslev (04) 52 22 22	Copenhagen (01) 49 47 00
Nykøbing S (03) 85 17 44	Frederikshavn (08) 42 46 08
Odense (09) 11 55 28	Hvide Sande (07) 31 20 11
Ringkøbing (07) 32 22 22	Odense (09) 12 42 84

Telephone numbers for other offices can be obtained from the local telephone directories, or the offices of the Danish motoring organisations can be contacted:

Forenede Danske Motorejere (*FDM*: Federation of Danish Motorists)
Blegdamsvej 124
DK–2100 Copenhagen Ø
Tel. (01) 38 21 12

Kongelig Dansk Automobil Klub (*KDAK*: Royal Danish Automobile Club)
Frederisksberg Allé 41
DK–1820 Copenhagen V
Tel. (01) 21 11 01

When to go

Except for the seaside resorts, visits to Denmark can be undertaken with confidence as early in the year as May, and as late as October when the weather is often very pleasant. The favourite months for vacations are July and August, and this is when the Danish schools have their summer break. Because of its maritime situation and the resultant wind conditions Denmark enjoys relatively milder temperatures than the rest of continental Europe. Westerly winds along the North Sea coast of Jutland cause higher rainfall than in the E of the country, where easterly winds more frequently prevail, bringing dry sunny weather.

Daytime temperatures from June to August are between 15 and 17 °C (59 and

63 °F), and can reach 25 °C (77 °F); the water temperature is from 18 to 20 °C (62 to 68 °F).

In spring and early summer the Gulf Stream and the tides cause the temperature of the North Sea to rise more rapidly than it does in the Baltic, but the latter is warmer during the height of the summer. Long light summer nights, which reach their peak in June, are characteristic of the N latitude of the country.

Compared with the other three Scandinavian countries, Denmark offers few facilities for winter sports. With its flat terrain, it has little skiing, but there are artificial ice-rinks in many towns. During the winter months there are a great many cultural events in every town and city of Denmark. From September to April and May the social scene is very busy. Danes are very sociable and extremely welcoming to strangers, particularly to the British, and the difficulty in the months of autumn to spring is not what to do and where to go, but to find some respite from the constant stream of invitations. Those who have the time and would like to get to know the Danes should inquire at the Tourist Board about the programme called "Meet the Danes".

Time

Denmark is on **Central European Time**, one hour ahead of Greenwich Mean Time – six hours ahead of New York. From the end of March/beginning of April until the end of September, **Summer Time** (Greenwich Mean Time plus two hours) is in force.

The Faroes observe **Western European Summer Time** (the same as Greenwich Mean Time). Time in Greenland is three hours ahead of Greenwich Mean Time.

Travel documents

Visitors to Denmark from the United Kingdom, the United States, Canada and many other countries require only a valid passport for a stay of up to three months. A visa is required for a longer stay and also by foreigners proposing to take up employment. There are no passport controls between the five Scandinavian countries of Denmark Iceland, Sweden, Norway and Finland, which have formed a Nordic Customs Union.

Motorists should carry their national *driver's licence*, which is recognised in Denmark, and the vehicle's *registration document*. It is no longer necessary for motorists from EEC countries to carry an *international insurance certificate* ("green card"), but it is very desirable to have the protection which this document gives the motorist. Foreign vehicles must display the *international distinguishing sign*, indicating the country where the vehicle is registered. It must be of the appropriate type and design; failure to display it may result in a fine. A visitor who rents a car needs only a valid driver's licence.

Medical care. – United Kingdom residents are entitled, as citizens of the EEC, to receive free or partly free medical care on the same basis as Danish nationals. Application should be made, at least two months before the date of departure for Denmark, to the Department of Health and Social Security for leaflet SA30, which gives details of reciprocal arrangements for medical treatment, and which contains an application form for a *certificate of entitlement* (E111).

American visitors and others who are not covered by arrangements of this kind should check their health insurance to see if it includes coverage abroad. It it does not, they may wish to take out short-term full-cover medical insurance before leaving home.

Pets. – Domestic animals (dogs or cats) require a *certificate of inoculation* against rabies (carried out at least 1 month and not more than 12 months before arrival in Denmark). This document must always be included in the international inoculation certificate of the animal.

NB. Visitors from the United Kingdom are advised not to bring animals to Denmark, as there is a six months' quarantine requirement for their pets when they return.

Customs regulations

Duty-free allowances
Visitors to Denmark can take in, without payment of duty, articles for their personal use; in addition persons over 15 can take in 1 kilogram of coffee or 400 grams of powdered coffee, and 200 grams of tea or 80 grams of tea extract. Visitors over 17 can import 1.5 litres of spirits above 22° or 3 litres of spirits below 22° or 3 litres of sparkling wine and 5 litres of ordinary wine; also 300 cigarettes or 150 cigarillos or 75 cigars or 400 grams of tobacco.

Persons over 15 can also bring in goods and gifts to a value of 2300 Danish kroner.

For goods bought in a duty-free shop on a ship or aircraft the allowances are reduced by one third (250 grams of tobacco).

Visitors over 18 to the Faroes can take in 200 cigarettes or 50 cigars or 100 cigarillos or 250 grams of tobacco, together with other goods to a maximum value of 300 Faroese kroner. Visitors over 20 years of age may also bring in 1 litre of spirits or 2 litres of wine.

As far as customs duties are concerned Greenland is classed as a foreign country.

Visitors over 15 can take in 200 cigarettes or 250 grams of tobacco and 200 cigarette-papers. Visitors over 20 are also allowed 0.75 litre of spirits and 1 litre of wine.

On leaving Denmark visitors can take out items they have acquired during their visit up to a value of 400 US dollars. In addition 300 cigarettes, 1 kilogram of coffee and 1.5 litres of spirits may be taken out.

Currency

The unit of currency is the **Danish Krone** (Crown) with 100 øre to the Krone (Dkr).
Banknotes: 5, 10, 20, 50, 100, 500 and 1000 kr.
Coins: 5, 10, 25 and 50 øre; 1, 2, 5 and 10 kr.

Importation of foreign currency into Denmark is unrestricted. Sums larger than 40,000 Dkr can only be taken out if a declaration of an equivalent or higher amount had been made on entry.

Eurocheques, travellers' cheques and most international credit cards are accepted by banks, the larger hotels and stores.

The Faroes have their own currency: 1 **Faroese crown**=1 Danish crown. They have their own currency notes but use Danish coins. Danish currency is accepted everywhere.

In Greenland Danish coins and notes are legal tender.

Post

Post offices are generally open from 10 a.m. to 5 p.m.; however in Copenhagen and other large towns they open at 9 a.m.

There is a single postal rate for letters and cards (up to 20 gr) within Denmark, to other Scandinavian countries, to countries within the EEC and to Austria, Switzerland, Liechtenstein, Yugoslavia, Malta, Cyprus and Turkey. Higher charges apply to other countries.

Telephone

Telephone calls from Denmark to other countries can be made from public telephone-boxes and from post offices. Calls via an operator are approximately three times as expensive as self-dialled calls.

Telephone codes: From Denmark

to the United Kingdom	009 44
to the United States and Canada	009 1

To Denmark

from the United Kingdom	010 46
from the United States	011 46

Road bridge over the Svendborgsund between the islands of Funen and Tåsinge

Distances in Denmark

Distances in Denmark (km/miles) (Ferries-hours)	**Ålborg**	**Århus**	**Copenhagen**	**Esbjerg**	**Frederikshavn**	**Gedser**	**Grenå**	**Hanstholm**	**Helsingør**	**Hillerød**	**Hirtshals**	**Kalundborg**	**Kolding**	**Odense**	**Ringkøbing**	**Roskilde**	**Rødby Færge**	**Skagen**	**Tønder**	**Vordingborg**
Ålborg	•	111 (70)	382 (237)	234 (145)	62 (51)	399 (248)	132 (82)	95 (59)	415 (259)	394 (245)	64 (40)	330 (205)	196 (122)	244 (157)	174 (108)	349 (217)	405 (251)	103 (64)	275 (171)	347 (216)
Århus	111 (70)	•	283 (176)	157 (98)	173 (108)	303 (188)	62 (39)	192 (119)	314 (195)	292 (181)	174 (108)	3 hours	99 (62)	147 (91)	128 (80)	253 (157)	309 (192)	214 (133)	180 (119)	251 (156)
Copenhagen	382 (237)	283 (176)	•	276 (172)	445 (277)	147 (91)	345 (214)	404 (251)	46 (29)	36 (22)	445 (278)	100 (62)	206 (128)	136 (85)	320 (199)	32 (20)	152 (94)	486 (302)	383 (238)	92 (57)
Esbjerg	234 (145)	157 (98)	276 (172)	•	294 (183)	293 (182)	215 (134)	204 (127)	307 (191)	285 (177)	298 (185)	226 (140)	71 (44)	137 (85)	80 (50)	242 (150)	299 (186)	337 (209)	77 (48)	251 (150)
Frederikshavn	82 (51)	173 (108)	445 (277)	294 (183)	•	461 (286)	194 (121)	156 (97)	479 (298)	458 (285)	51 (32)	390 (242)	259 (161)	306 (190)	236 (147)	411 (255)	467 (290)	41 (25)	337 (209)	409 (254)
Gedser	399 (248)	303 (188)	147 (91)	293 (182)	461 (286)	•	365 (227)	426 (265)	186 (116)	172 (107)	464 (288)	161 (100)	226 (140)	155 (96)	339 (211)	134 (83)	68 (42)	502 (312)	308 (191)	55 (34)
Grenå	132 (82)	62 (39)	345 (214)	215 (134)	194 (121)	365 (227)	•	213 (132)	375 (233)	354 (220)	197 (122)	293 (182)	160 (99)	209 (130)	188 (117)	312 (194)	374 (232)	235 (146)	241 (149)	315 (196)
Hanstholm	95 (59)	192 (119)	404 (251)	204 (127)	156 (97)	426 (265)	213 (132)	•	439 (273)	415 (257)	134 (83)	351 (218)	222 (138)	270 (167)	144 (89)	371 (231)	432 (268)	176 (109)	273 (170)	373 (232)
Helsingør	415 (259)	314 (195)	46 (29)	307 (191)	479 (298)	186 (116)	375 (233)	439 (273)	•	24 (15)	471 (293)	128 (80)	239 (149)	168 (104)	352 (219)	63 (39)	192 (119)	515 (320)	315 (196)	132 (82)
Hillerød	394 (245)	292 (181)	36 (22)	285 (177)	458 (285)	172 (107)	354 (220)	415 (257)	24 (15)	•	453 (281)	104 (65)	214 (133)	144 (89)	328 (204)	39 (24)	179 (111)	491 (305)	291 (181)	117 (73)
Hirtshals	64 (40)	174 (108)	448 (278)	298 (185)	51 (32)	464 (288)	197 (122)	134 (83)	471 (293)	453 (281)	•	392 (244)	260 (162)	308 (191)	238 (148)	414 (257)	470 (292)	38 (24)	338 (210)	412 (256)
Kalundborg	330 (205)	3 hours	100 (62)	226 (140)	390 (242)	161 (100)	293 (182)	351 (218)	128 (80)	104 (65)	392 (244)	•	156 (97)	78 (48)	262 (163)	67 (42)	159 (99)	425 (264)	225 (140)	101 (63)
Kolding	196 (122)	99 (62)	206 (128)	71 (44)	259 (161)	226 (140)	160 (99)	222 (138)	239 (149)	214 (133)	260 (162)	156 (97)	•	67 (42)	115 (71)	175 (109)	229 (142)	298 (185)	79 (49)	171 (106)
Odense	244 (157)	147 (91)	136 (85)	137 (85)	306 (190)	155 (96)	209 (130)	270 (167)	168 (104)	144 (89)	308 (191)	78 (48)	67 (42)	•	184 (114)	105 (65)	161 (100)	346 (215)	146 (91)	106 (66)
Ringkøbing	174 (108)	128 (80)	320 (199)	80 (50)	236 (147)	339 (211)	188 (117)	144 (89)	352 (219)	328 (204)	238 (148)	262 (163)	115 (71)	184 (114)	•	287 (178)	345 (214)	277 (172)	149 (93)	286 (178)
Roskilde	349 (217)	253 (157)	32 (20)	242 (150)	411 (255)	134 (83)	312 (194)	371 (231)	63 (39)	39 (24)	414 (257)	67 (42)	175 (109)	105 (65)	287 (178)	•	140 (87)	452 (281)	252 (157)	80 (50)
Rødby Færge	405 (251)	309 (192)	152 (94)	299 (186)	467 (290)	68 (42)	374 (232)	432 (268)	192 (119)	179 (111)	470 (292)	159 (99)	229 (142)	161 (106)	345 (214)	140 (87)	•	508 (316)	308 (191)	60 (37)
Skagen	103 (64)	214 (133)	486 (302)	337 (209)	41 (25)	502 (312)	235 (146)	176 (109)	515 (320)	491 (305)	38 (24)	425 (264)	298 (185)	346 (215)	277 (172)	452 (281)	508 (316)	•	377 (234)	450 (280)
Tønder	275 (171)	180 (119)	383 (238)	77 (48)	337 (209)	308 (191)	241 (149)	273 (170)	315 (196)	291 (181)	338 (210)	225 (140)	79 (49)	146 (91)	149 (93)	252 (157)	308 (191)	377 (234)	•	250 (155)
Vordingborg	347 (216)	251 (156)	92 (57)	241 (150)	409 (254)	55 (34)	315 (196)	373 (232)	132 (82)	117 (73)	412 (256)	101 (63)	171 (106)	106 (66)	286 (178)	80 (50)	60 (37)	450 (280)	250 (155)	•

Travel to Denmark

By air

British Airways and *British Caledonian Airways* as well as *SAS* operate international flights between Great Britain and Denmark, and *Pan Am* and *SAS* are the principal companies flying to and from the United States and Canada. **Kastrup International Airport**, some 10 km (6 miles) from the centre of Copenhagen handles almost all international flights as well as domestic services.

By sea

There are car ferries to *Esbjerg* in Jutland from *Harwich* and *Newcastle* (both about 20 hours). A through train that runs from Esbjerg to Copenhagen connects with the ferries from the United Kingdom (about 5 hours). By road the distance is 276 km (172 miles) via Kolding, across the bridge on to the island of Funen, then via Odense to the ferry from Knudshoved.

Travel in Denmark

By road

In Denmark the condition of the motorways/highways (*motorvej*) and main roads (*hovedvej*, which are identified by the letter A and a number) is excellent.

Several international *"Europa Roads"* run through Denmark; they are designated by a sign showing a white E on a green background. The E3 runs from the German–Danish border near Flensburg to Friedrickshavn in North Jutland; its route corresponds closely with the Danish main road A10. The E66 diverges from the E3 W to Esbjerg and E from Kolding over the island of Funen to Zealand (Copenhagen). The Little Belt and/or the Great Belt are crossed by bridges or ferries. The E66 follows almost exactly the route of the A1.

The E4 is particularly important for travel between central and northern Europe; it is the shortest route both for rail and road from central Europe to Scandinavia. Its southern section, from Puttgarden on the German island of Fehmarn to Rødbyhavn on the Danish island of Lolland, is known as the *"Vogelfluglinie"* ("As the crow flies"), because it follows the route taken by migratory birds. The E4 goes from Hamburg to Grossenbrode and from there over the Fehmarn Sound Bridge on to the island of Fehmarn. From Puttgarden ferries cross the Fehmarn Belt to the Danish island of Lolland (Rødbyhavn). A bridge carries the E4 across Guldborg Sound to Falster and over the Farø Bridge to Zealand. From the S of this island it follows the Danish A2 N to Copenhagen. The last section of the road follows the A3 to Helsingør. The E664 diverges from E4 on Falster and goes to Gedser.

In Denmark traffic travels on the right, with passing on the left. Vehicles approaching intersections from the right have priority. Drivers and front-seat passengers must wear seat-belts and motor cyclists must wear helmets. A warning triangle must be carried in the vehicle. At junctions a white triangle on the road means the crossing traffic has priority.
In built-up areas the speed limit is 50 km per hour (31 m.p.h.); on main roads outside towns 80 km (50 m.p.h.) and on motorways (highways) 100 km (62 m.p.h.). Vehicles drawing trailers are restricted to 70 km (44 m.p.h.) and buses 80 km (50 m.p.h.). Exceeding the speed limits even very slightly is punishable in Denmark by a large fine. If a driver is unable to pay, his vehicle is impounded by the police.

By rail and bus

Denmark has a railway network of some 2600 km (1626 miles), of which about 2000 km (1243 miles) are operated by the Danish State Railroad (*DSB*), which is also responsible for ferry routes totalling 210 km (130 miles). The railway network is complemented by buses, run by the DSB or by private operators. Buses mainly serve areas without railway lines.

Inter-city trains linking the larger Danish towns run at regular intervals. Between Copenhagen and the larger towns there are express trains (*lyntog* "lightning train") with few stops. Reservations are compulsory on all inter-city trains across the Great Belt, on express trains and on sleeping-cars and couchettes.

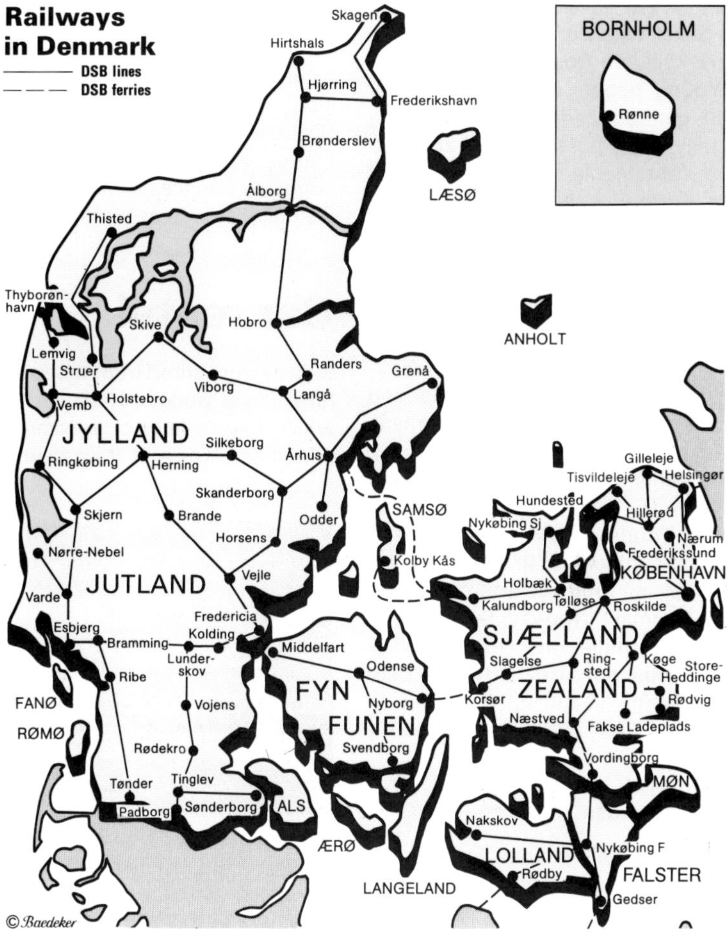

Railways in Denmark
DSB lines
DSB ferries
Skagen
Hirtshals
Hjørring
Frederikshavn
Brønderslev
LÆSØ
BORNHOLM
Rønne
Ålborg
Thisted
Thyborøn-havn
Skive
Hobro
ANHOLT
Lemvig
Struer
Randers
Grenå
Vemb
Holstebro
Viborg
Langå
JYLLAND
Silkeborg
Århus
Ringkøbing
Herning
Gilleleje
Tisvildeleje
Helsingør
Skanderborg
Hundested
Skjern
Brande
Odder
SAMSØ
Nykøbing Sj
Hillerød
Nærum
Nørre-Nebel
Horsens
Frederikssund
Kolby Kås
KØBENHAVN
JUTLAND
Vejle
Holbæk
Varde
Kalundborg
Tølløse
Roskilde
Fredericia
Esbjerg
Kolding
SJÆLLAND
Bramming
Middelfart
Lunder-skov
Odense
Slagelse
Ring-sted
Køge
Store-Heddinge
Ribe
FYN
Nyborg
Korsør
ZEALAND
Rødvig
FANØ
Vojens
FUNEN
Næstved
Fakse Ladeplads
RØMØ
Svendborg
Rødekro
Vordingborg
Tønder
Tinglev
MØN
Padborg
Sønderborg
ALS
Nakskov
ÆRØ
Nykøbing F
LOLLAND
Rødby
FALSTER
LANGELAND
Gedser
© Baedeker

Air Services
DANAIR
Skagen
BORNHOLM
Rønne
Faroes
Thisted
Ålborg
LÆSØ
ANHOLT
Viborg
Karup
JYLLAND
JUTLAND
Århus
Helsingør
SAMSØ
Billund
KØBENHAVN
Kastrup
Roskilde
Esbjerg
Kolding
Odense
SJÆLLAND
ZEALAND
FANØ
FYN
RØMØ
Skrydstrup
FUNEN
Tønder
Sønderborg
ALS
MØN
ÆRØ
Maribo
LOLLAND
FALSTER
Rødby
LANGELAND
Gedser
© Baedeker

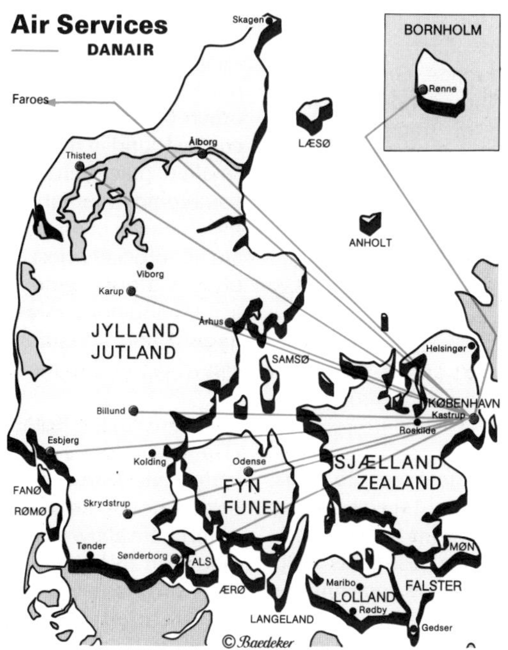

Children under 4 years of age do not need a ticket when travelling by train in Denmark; children from 4 to 12 pay half price. Young people under 26 years of age can get reduced rate tickets, providing they are in possession of an interrail card (obtainable in all countries of western Europe and also in Hungary, Romania and Morocco), which is valid for one month. Senior citizens over 65 can also obtain a reduced fare (no pass is necessary).

There is also a national ticket (*landsrejsekort*) valid for one month in Second Class on all trains and ferries in Denmark, and excursion tickets of the DSB for journeys to interesting places in Denmark.

The Nordic Tourist Card (valid for 21 days; 50 per cent supplement in First Class) is available for rail journeys and on certain ferries in Denmark, Norway, Sweden and Finland. For families the Nordic Family Card, with reductions of 25 to 45 per cent is good value.

Eurail Youth Pass

This pass is on sale outside Europe and may be bought by passengers under 26 who are permanently resident outside Europe. The holder is entitled to unlimited 2nd class travel – free of charge – on the rail systems of the 16 participating countries. These are Austria, Belgium, Denmark, Finland, France, Greece, Italy, Luxembourg, the Netherlands, Norway, Portugal, Republic of Ireland, Spain, Sweden, Switzerland and West Germany. The pass is available for periods of 1 or 2 months. A number of bonuses are open to pass-holders including travel on certain buses and ferries run by the rail companies. The pass costs $310 for 1 month and $400 for 2 months.

Eurail Pass

This pass is for passengers over 26 years old. The holder must travel 1st class and is entitled to the same benefits as the Youth Pass holder (above). The pass costs $280 for 15 days, $350 for 21 days and $440 for 1 month.

By air

Air services within Denmark are operated by Scandinavian Airlines System which also provides services with the other Scandinavian countries and with the Faroes and Greenland. The DANAIR company also flies to most major towns in Denmark as well as to the Faroes.

Car rental

Cars can be rented from the four principal firms (Avis, Budget, Hertz and InterRent) which have offices or agencies in all the principal towns and at Kastrup Airport.

Ferry

Accommodation

Hotels in Denmark, noted for their cleanliness, offer comfort and service of international standards in the various price ranges that correspond to hotels in other Western countries. Luxury hotels can be found in the larger towns, but even smaller places have excellent hotels, combining international standards with the character of the country. Danish hotels are not officially classified into categories; price is a good guide to the standard of accommodation offered. Prices in Copenhagen are considerably higher than elsewhere in Denmark.

There are several hotel chains in Denmark (Dantop Hotels, Hvide Hus Kæden Hotels, etc.). During the summer months the 24 hotels belonging to the Inter DK hotel chain allow a free fifth-night accommodation to holders of the Holiday Pass issued by the chain (details from the Danish Tourist Board).

Ferries

Within Denmark

Århus-Årø
Assens-Bågø
Ballebro-Hardeshøj
Bandholm-Askø
Bøjden-Fynshav
Branden-Fur
Copenhagen-Rønne (Bornholm)
Esbjerg-Fanø
Fåborg-Avernakø-Lyø-Fåborg
Fåborg-Søby (Ærø)
Frederikshavn-Læsø
Grenå-Anholt
Hals-Egense
Halsskov-Sejerø
Holbæk-Orø
Hov-Samsø
Hundested-Grenå
Hundested-Rørvig
Hvalpsund-Sundsøre
Kalundborg-Århus
Kalundborg-Juelsminde
Kalundborg-Samsø
Kleppen-Venø
Korsør-Lohals (Langeland)
Kragenæs-Fejø
Kragenæs-Femø
Mommark-Søby (Ærø)
Mors-Thy (Feggesund)
Mors-Thy (Næssund)
Rudkøbing-Marstal (Ærø)
Rudkøbing-Strynø
Sjællands Odde-Ebeltoft
Snaptun-Hjarnø
Stigsnæs-Agersø
Stigsnæs-Omø
Stubbekøbing-Bogø
Svendborg-Ærøskøbing
Svendborg-Skarø-Drejø
Tårs-Spodsbjerg (Langeland)
Thyborøn-Agger

All the above ferries run daily

Denmark-Norway

Copenhagen-Oslo	daily
Frederikshavn-Larvik	daily
Frederikshavn-Oslo	daily
Frederikshavn-Fredrikstad	daily
Frederikshavn-Moss	several times a week
Hanstholm-Egersund	several times a week (only operates between 20 June and 26 Aug.)
Hanstholm-Kristiansand	several times a week (only operates between 20 June and 18 Aug.)
Hirtshals-Stavanger	twice a week (operates between 16 Jan. and 10 June; and 28 Aug. and 31 Dec.)
Hirtshals-Bergen	twice a week (operates between 16 Jan. and 10 June; and 28 Aug. and 31 Dec.)
Hirtshals-Egersund	once a week
Hirtshals-Kristiansand	daily
Hirtshals-Oslo	several times a week

Denmark-Sweden

Dragør-Limhamn	daily
Frederikshavn-Göteborg	daily
Grenå-Helsingborg	daily
Grenå-Varberg	daily
Helsingør-Helsingborg	daily
Tuborg Havn (Copenhagen)-Landskrona	daily
Rønne (Bornholn)-Ystad	daily
Rønne (Bornholm)-Borgholm (Øland)	six times a week (1 June-1 Sept.)

Hovercraft operate between Copenhagen and Malmö (Sweden); the 28 km (16 miles) crossing takes 36 minutes.

The following ferry services run between Denmark and the Faroes in the North Atlantic:

Esbjerg-Tórshavn	once a week (10 June-15 Aug.)
Hanstholm-Tórshavn	once a week (25 May-6 Sept.)

The Danish Tourist Office publishes a brochure "Car Ferries" which gives the addresses and telephone numbers of all the ferry companies and full details of departure times and fares.

Visitors with trailers, motor homes, or campers should ask the ferry company, or a travel agent, for information about the maximum dimensions for vehicles carried on the various ferries.

In addition to hotel chains, the *Mission Hotels*, which can be found in most towns, play a leading role in Denmark. These hotels offer comfortable, clean rooms for a modest outlay. Some, although not religiously orientated, do not allow alcohol on the premises.

Holiday hotels and centres, situated mostly near the beaches, provide a combination of hotel and apartment amenities and are becoming more and more popular with families. A typical holiday centre has an indoor swimming-pool, sauna, television room and restaurant.

Discriminating visitors may choose to stay in a Danish stately home, now a hotel or pension that accommodates guests.

Comfortable accommodation with a family atmosphere is available in a *kro* (plural *kroer*), which is a typical Danish inn. Vouchers, called "Kro-checks", entitling the holder to one night's accommodation with breakfast, must be obtained in advance from a travel agent or from:

Danske Kroferie
Kongensgade 25
DK–8700 Horsens
Tel. (06) 62 38 22

Farm holidays – Visitors who wish to stay on a farm have two options. They can take a room in the farmhouse and share the everyday life of the family, including meals. Or visitors may rent a holiday apartment belonging to a farm. In the latter case visitors must either prepare their own meals or eat out. Bed linen, towels and table linen are not provided. These holidays are becoming exceedingly popular and application for the holiday months should be made in good time. The Danish Tourist Board will give details of farmhouse holidays and itineraries.

Holiday homes offer an inexpensive way to spend a vacation in Denmark. Most are situated by the sea, but they can also be found inland, on lakes or near woodland. The majority of these houses are equipped with modern facilities (shower, refrigerator, etc.); crockery and cutlery are supplied, but the renter must provide bed linen and towels.

Holiday homes are let by the week. The cost depends on the value of the property and can vary in different parts of the country. A house on the North Sea coast will be dearer than one on the Baltic. Outside the high season rentals are often considerably reduced. Holiday homes can be booked in advance at certain travel bureaux; the Danish Tourist Office will supply the necessary information.

Camping and Caravanning

There are about 500 official **camp sites** in Denmark designated with one, two or three stars, according to the standard of amenities provided. Sites with three stars are supervised 24 hours a day. During the high season chalets and static caravans can be hired, mainly on a weekly basis. In general it is preferable to reserve a site in advance (return postage in the form of an *international reply coupon*, obtainable at any post office, should be enclosed).

Visitors from abroad need an international camping certificate. Alternatively, foreign visitors can obtain, at the first site used, a *visitor's permit* valid for one year for the holder, together with a spouse and their children.

In Denmark camping is permitted only on official camp sites. This is strictly enforced, especially at beaches and nature reserves.

A free list of one-, two-, and three-star camp sites can be obtained from the Danish Tourist Office. A complete list of approved camp sites is published annually by the camping authority:

Campingrådet
Skjoldsgade 10
DK–2100 Copenhagen Ø

Danish **youth hostels** accept both young people and adults; they often provide family rooms. Bed linen or the normal youth-hostel linen sleeping-bag must either be brought or can be hired; quilted sleeping-bags are not permitted.

In order to use a Danish youth hostel the visitor must normally have an international youth hostel card issued in the visitor's home country, but a card can be obtained in Denmark.

The Danish Tourist Office publishes a free leaflet on youth hostels. An even more detailed brochure is obtainable from:

Danmarks Vandrerhjem
Vesterbrogade 39
DK–1620 Copenhagen V
Tel. (01) 31 36 12.

Facilities for disabled travellers

The Danes are mindful of their disabled visitors from abroad. On arrival at Kastrup Airport in Copenhagen and also on domestic flights disabled people are given every assistance by the SAS and the other airlines. This is equally true of the Danish State Railways.

There are a number of Danish hotels which have special facilities for access. Information from:

Bolig-, Motor-og Hjælpemiddelvalget
Hans Knudsens Plads 1 A
DK–2100 Copenhagen Ø.

Further information for disabled persons (entrance to museums, participation in events and amusements) is available from the Danish Tourist Board.

Electricity

Electric current in Denmark is 220 volt AC at a frequency of 50 cycles.

Language

English is widely spoken in Denmark, so that visitors are unlikely to have any difficulty getting about, even if they know no Danish. It is worth while, however, to learn a few words and phrases and to carry a small dictionary or phrase book.

Useful words and Phrases

English	Danish
Do you speak?	taler De?
Danish	dansk
English	engelsk
I do not understand	jeg forstår ikke
yes	ja, jo
no	nej
please	værsågod
excuse me	unskyld
thank you	tak
thank you very much	mange tak
good morning	god morgen
good day	god dag
good evening	god aften
good night	god nat
goodbye	farvel
man	herre
woman	dame, kvinde
girl	frøken
to the right	til højre
to the left	til venstre
straight ahead	lige ud
up, down	oppe, ovenpå
down, below	nede
old	gammel
new	ny
what does it cost?	hvad koster?
dear	dyr

English	Danish
Where is?	hvor er?
. . . street	. . . gaden
. . . square	. . . pladsen
the road to	vejen til
the church	kirke(n)
the museum	museet
the Town Hall	rådhuset
the post office	posthuset
a bank	bank
the station	banegården, stationen
the airport	lufthaun
when?	hvornår?
open	åbnet
a hotel	hotel
I should like	jeg vil gerne
a room	et værelse
single	enkelt værelse
double	dobbelt værelse
with bath	met bad
without bath	uden bad
the key	nøglen
the lavatory (bathroom)	toilettet
a doctor	læge
dentist	tandlæge
pharmacist	apoteker
aspirin	aspirin

Food and drink: see page 179

Months of the Year

English	Danish
January	januar
February	februar
March	marts
April	april
May	maj
June	juni
July	juli
August	august
September	september
October	oktober
November	november
December	december

Days of the Week

English	Danish
Sunday	søndag
Monday	mandag
Tuesday	tirsdag
Wednesday	onsdag
Thursday	torsdag
Friday	fredag
Saturday	lørdag

Road Signs and Warnings

English	Danish
Stop	Stop
Customs	Told
Caution	Pas på
Slow	Langsom
One-way street	Ensrettet
No entry	Ingen indkørsel
Road works	Vejarbejde

Motoring Terms

English	Danish
air	luft
battery	batteri
brake	bremse
breakdown	motorskade
car	bil
carburetor	karburator
cylinder	cylinder
driving licence	kørekort
fuse	sikring
garage	autoværksted
(for repairs)	bilværksted
headlight	lygte
horn	tudehorn
ignition	tænding
indicator	blinklys
motor cycle	motorcykel
oil	olie
oil change	skifte olie
parking place	parkeringsplads
petrol (gas)	benzin
petrol (gas) station	benzintank
puncture	punktering
radiator	køler
spare part	reservedel
spark-plug	tæmdrør
starter	selvstarter
tow away	tag på slæb
tyre	dæk
valve	ventil
wash	vaske
wheel	hjul
windscreen (windshield)-wiper	vinduesvisker

Cardinal Numbers

0	nul
1	en, et
2	to
3	tre
4	fire
5	fem
6	seks
7	syv
8	otte
9	ni
10	ti
11	elleve
12	tolv
13	tretten
14	fjorten
15	femten
16	seksten
17	sytten
18	atten
19	nitten
20	tyve
21	en og tyve
22	to og tyve
30	tredive
40	fyrre
50	halvtreds
60	tres
70	halvfjerds
80	firs
90	halvfems
100	hundrede
101	hundrede og en
200	to hundrede
300	tre hundrede
1000	tusind

Ordinal Numbers

1st	første
2nd	anden
3rd	tredje

Fractions

$\frac{1}{2}$	en halv
$\frac{1}{3}$	en tredjedel

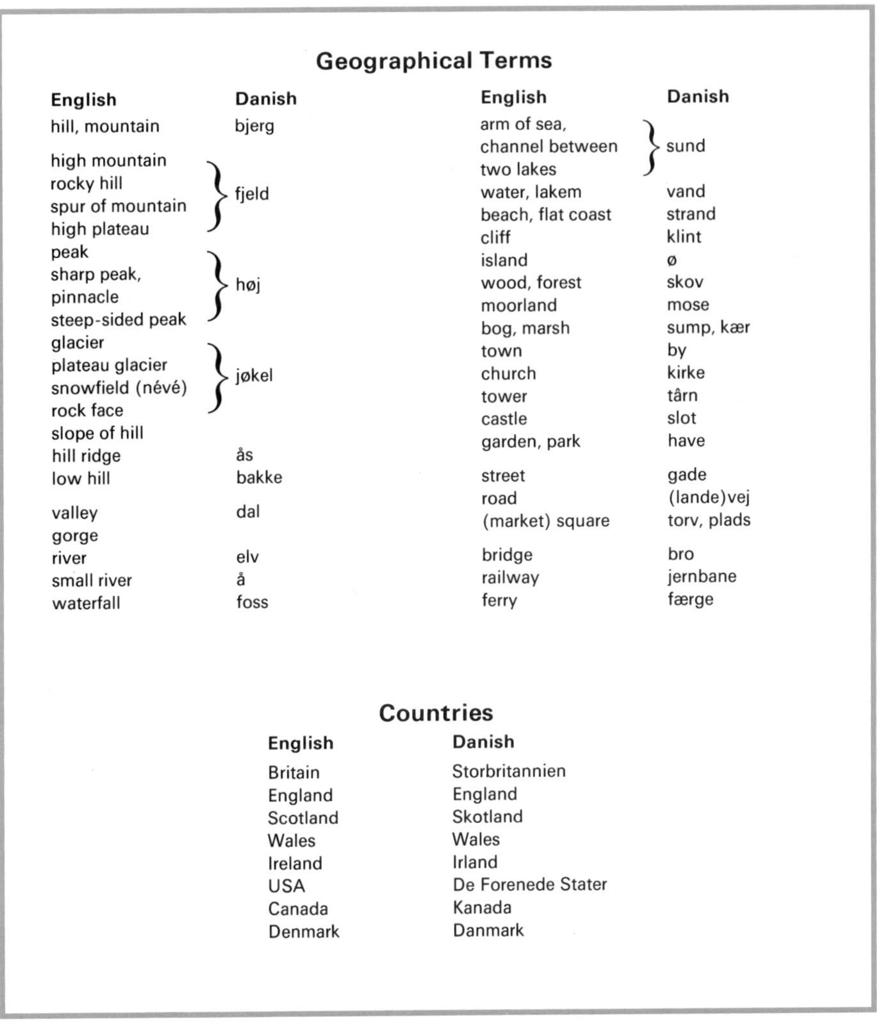

Geographical Terms

English	Danish
hill, mountain	bjerg
high mountain, rocky hill, spur of mountain, high plateau	fjeld
peak, sharp peak, pinnacle, steep-sided peak	høj
glacier, plateau glacier, snowfield (névé), rock face	jøkel
slope of hill	
hill ridge	ås
low hill	bakke
valley	dal
gorge	
river	elv
small river	å
waterfall	foss

English	Danish
arm of sea, channel between two lakes	sund
water, lakem	vand
beach, flat coast	strand
cliff	klint
island	ø
wood, forest	skov
moorland	mose
bog, marsh	sump, kær
town	by
church	kirke
tower	târn
castle	slot
garden, park	have
street	gade
road	(lande)vej
(market) square	torv, plads
bridge	bro
railway	jernbane
ferry	færge

Countries

English	Danish
Britain	Storbritannien
England	England
Scotland	Skotland
Wales	Wales
Ireland	Irland
USA	De Forenede Stater
Canada	Kanada
Denmark	Danmark

Danish is a Germanic language and is not difficult to read if you have some knowledge of German or Dutch; spoken Danish, however, is not easy to master, principally because of the frequent use of a glottal stop and the tendency (shared with English) to "swallow" part of a word.

The pronunciation of some letters differs from English: *d* after a vowel is softened to the sound of th in "the", or may be mute; *g* is hard as in "go" at the beginning of a syllable, but at other times is like the ch in "loch" or mute; *j* is like y in "yes"; *r* is a soft sound, not trilled; *v* before a consonant or at the end of a word becomes a vowel like the French *u* in "lune"; *ej* is like the vowel sound in "high"; *æ* is like a in "take"; *ø* is like eu in French "deux"; *å* has the vowel sound of "awe".

Although *æ*, *ø* and *å* come at the end of the Danish alphabet, words beginning with these letters in this guide have been placed with a and o for the convenience of our readers.

Food and drink

A continental breakfast (*morgenmad*) is served in hotels and restaurants until about 11 a.m. It usually consists of rolls, cheese, eggs and jam, and may include sliced cold meats. Lunch (either the same word or *middagsmad*), served between noon and 2 p.m. is not the main meal, which is dinner, served between 6 and 8 p.m.

Visitors will want to sample the famous open sandwiches called *smørrebrød* in all their tempting variety. From the *smørrebrødsseddel*, which the waiter hands the guest, a choice is made, by marking the list, from the large selection of open sandwiches (*franskbrød* is white bread; *rugbrød*, rye bread; *surbrød*, a kind of "grey" bread also made from rye flour.

Smørrebrød can also be bought in the many *smørrebrødforetninger*, shops that specialise in smørrebrød. Another typically Danish speciality, *det kolde bord* is a substantial buffet meal of hot and cold dishes, including a "starter", sweet, cheese and coffee.

Traditional dishes in a Danish restaurant include *frikadeller*, meatballs made of pork; *hakkebøf*, beef meatballs; *Flæskesteg med røkål*, roast pork with crackling and red cabbage; *medisterpølse*, a kind of grilled sausage; *Gule ærter*, pea soup with pieces of sausage and pork; and *dyreryg*, venison with cranberries.

Fish dishes mainly consist of trout, flounder or grilled plaice.

Of the sweets, often served with cream, *rødgrød met fløde* (red fruit jelly and cream) should be mentioned.

As appetisers at dinner or as a second breakfast, portions of eel, salmon, ham, vegetable salads, etc. are available in small bowls. A meal often finishes with cheese (Danish *ost*).

The usual drink is light beer (*øl*) generally served in small glasses. The Carlsberg and Tuborg breweries in Copenhagen are well known outside Denmark. Wine is expensive, since it must be imported. A typical Danish drink, popular after dinner, is *akvavit* (Latin "*aqua vitaë* or water of life), an aromatic brandy (minimum alcohol content 38 per cent) prepared with caraway and other spices.

Smørrebrød: assorted open sandwiches

Restaurants

In addition to the restaurants in hotels there are many others in the larger towns which provide fare ranging from modest home style to gourmet. They are often called "kro", which actually means "jug". Some of these are essentially Danish inns furnished in traditional style (candles on the tables, etc.) and almost all serve excellent food. A visitor who wants a quick or an inexpensive meal should eat at one of the milk bars or cafés (bars, cafeterias), or visit one of the pub-like establishments where sandwiches are usually served. Prices include a 15 per cent service charge and 22 per cent Value Added Tax.

More than 700 restaurants offer a Dan-menu, a tourist table d'hôte meal which is good value for money.

The Danish Menu

English	Danish
restaurant	restaurant
snack bar	cafeteria
breakfast	morgenmad
lunch	middagsmad
dinner	aftensmad
eat	spise
drink	drikke
a lot, many	meget, mange
a little	lidt
the bill	regning
pay	betale
at once	straks
menu	spisekort
soup	suppe
meat	kød
grilled	stegt på grill
roast	steg
mutton	bede
roast lamb	fåresteg
calf (veal)	kalv
lamb	lam
reindeer	ren
ox, bullock	okse
ham	skinke
pig	svin
roast pork	flæskesteg
sausage	pølse
fish	fisk
fried	stegt
boiled	kogt
fish balls	fiskeboller
cod	torsk
crayfish	krebs
herring	sild
lobster	hummer
salmon	laks
smoked salmon	røget laks
shrimp	reje
trout	ørred

English	Danish
vegetables	grøn(t)sager
beans	bønner
cabbage	kål
cauliflower	blomkål
cucumber	agurk
green salad	grøn salat
peas	ærter
potatoes	kartoffel
red cabbage	rødkål
spinach	spinat
tomato	tomat
ice	is
stewed fruit	kompot
fruit jelly	rødgrød
pudding	budding
whipped cream	flødeskum
cake	kage
fruit	frugt
apple	æble
bilberry	blåbær
cherry	kirsebær
cranberry	tyttebær
lemon	citron
orange	appelsin
pear	pære
plum	blomme
raspberry	hindbær
strawberry	jordbær
drinks	drik
beer	øl
coffee	kaffe
cream	fløde
milk	mælk
mineral water	mineralvand
tea	te
water	vand
wine	vin
white	hvidvin
red	rødvin
bread	brød
white bread	franskbrød
rolls	rundstykke

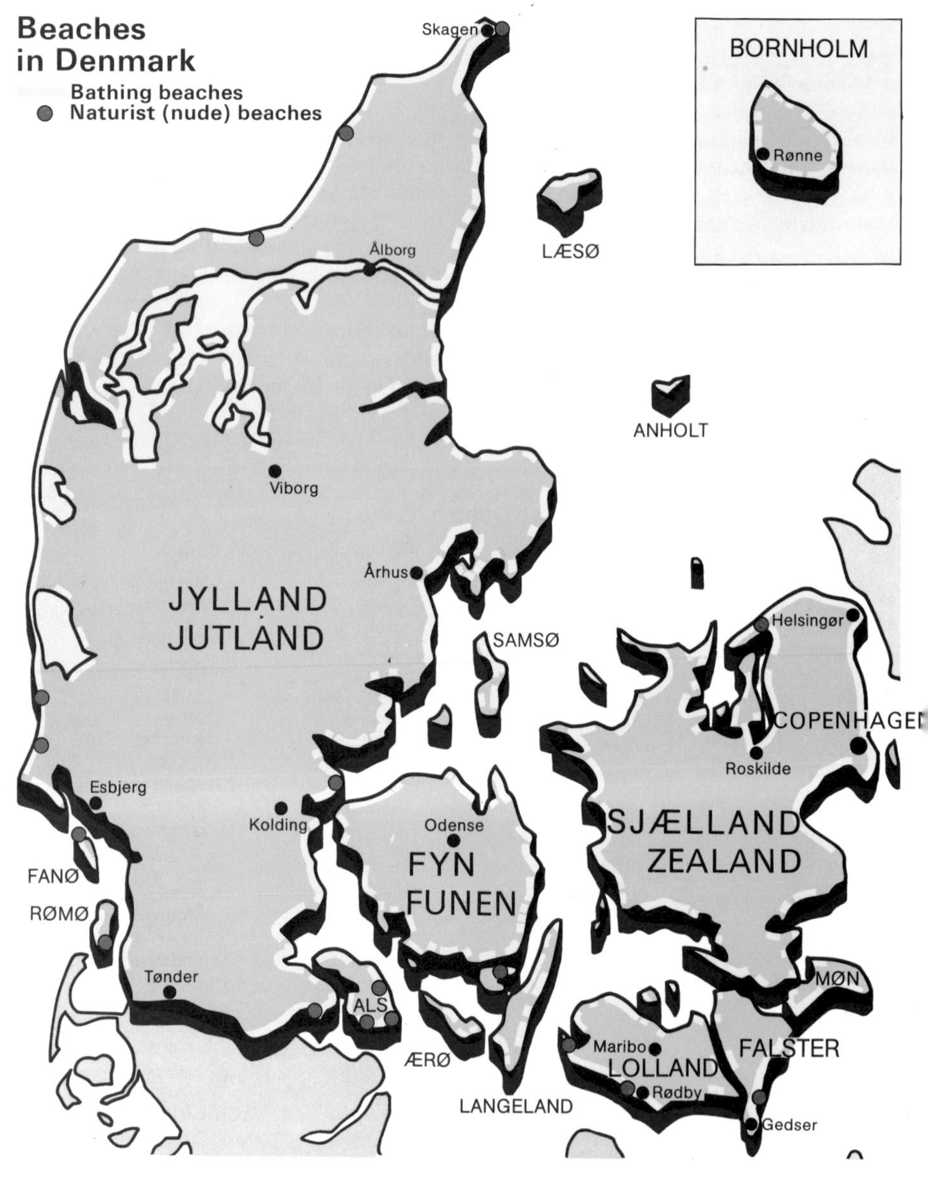

Sports and Pastimes

Beaches and seaside resorts

The coastline of Denmark is over 7400 km (4598 miles) long. The most extensive bathing **beaches**, often fringed with dunes that provide protection from the wind, stretch in an almost unbroken line along the W coast of Jutland, from the islands of Rømø and Fanø in the S to Denmark's northernmost point at Skagen. Most Danish beaches preserve their natural landscape, and deck-chairs, beach umbrellas and windbreaks are only rarely encountered.

The best-known **seaside resorts** lie on the N coast of Zealand, on the E coast of Falster and in the S of Bornholm. Bornholm is the only area of Denmark with fairly long rocky coasts, but it also has excellent sandy beaches. On the Mols Peninsula and along the E coast of Jutland, woodland often borders the shore. Funen and the neighbouring islands also have fine beaches.

Experienced divers can rent equipment in Denmark; information can be obtained from the Tourist Bureau in Middelfart. Strib, a village on the Little Belt, has facilities for diving.

There are several beaches in Denmark that permit nude bathing. Many of these naturist beaches are open to both nude and more conventional bathers.

There are no resort taxes payable in Denmark, but there is correspondingly less provision of facilities than in countries where such taxes are levied.

Parking places can generally be found near the beaches; parking fees are rarely charged but there is, of course, no supervision of vehicles.

Fishing

No point in Denmark is more than 55 km (34 miles) from the sea, so deep-sea fishing enthusiasts do not lack facilities. In addition there are many well-stocked rivers and lakes.

For sea fishing no special permit is required. Many fishing-boats will willingly take sports fishermen out for a modest fee. Deep-sea fishing for cod, mackerel, and ray is available throughout the year from Copenhagen, Helsingør and Frederikshavn.

A permit is not required for coastal fishing.

Most sea-coasts are accessible, but fishermen must take public paths to reach the water. Fishing within 50 m (55 yd) of a cultivated plot of land is allowed only with permission, but this is normally granted.

Visitor should inquire locally about any prohibitions or protective measures that must be observed. The following species of fish are commonly found in Danish coastal waters: *sea salmon, sea trout, codling, mackerel, turbot, plaice, flounder* and *eel*.

A permit, issued on a daily or weekly basis, is required for freshwater fishing; it can be obtained from tourist offices or local sports clubs. Fishing rights for inland waters are nearly always privately owned.

In Jutland there is good *trout* fishing and in places *salmon* are also found. The principal fish found in lakes include *perch, pike, eel, flounder, carp* and *roach*.

Information about freshwater angling can be obtained from:

Danmarks Sportfiskerforbund
Worsæsgade 1
DK–7100 Vejle

Golf

The gently undulating landscape so characteristic of Denmark is ideal for golf, and the country has some 50 golf-courses. Visitors are welcome, providing they have a valid membership card from a recognised golf-club.

Details of opening times, tournaments, etc. can be obtained from:

Dansk Golf Union
Bredgade 56
DK 1250 Copenhagen K
Tel. (01) 13 12 21

Golf-courses in Jutland

1 Hvide Klit Golf Club (18)
Bunken, DK–9982 Ålbæk

2 Brønderslev Golf Club (9)
Golfvejen, DK–9700 Brønderslev

3 Nordvestjysk Golf Club (9)
Nystrupvej 19, DK–7700 Thisted

4 Ålborg Golf Club (18)
Jægerspris, Frejlev, DK–9000 Ålborg

5 Himmerlands Golf Club (18)
Centervej, Gatten, DK–9670 Løgstor

6 Nykøbing Mors Golf Club (6)
DK–7900 Nykøbing Mors

7 Skive Golf Club (9)
Resen, DK–7800 Skive

8 Holstebro Golf Club (18)
Råsted, DK–7570 Vemb

9 Viborg Golf Club (9)
Møllevej, Overlund, DK–8800 Viborg

10 Randers Golf Club (9)
Himmelbovej 22, DK–8900 Randers

11 Vestjysk Golf Club (9)
Letagervej 1, Dejbjerg, DK–6900 Skjern

12 Herning Golf Club (18)
Golfvej 2, DK–7400 Herning

13 Silkeborg Golf Club (18)
Resenbro, DK–8600 Silkeborg

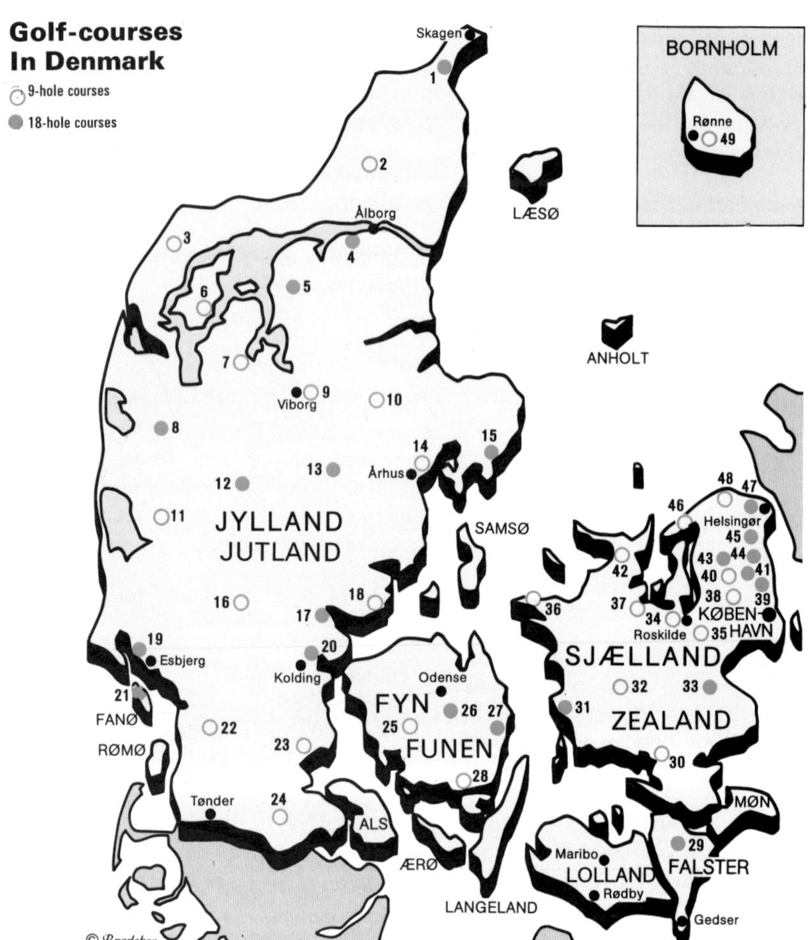

14 Århus Golf Club (9)
Mollerupvej, DK–8240 Risskov

15 Djursland Golf Club (18)
Strandgårdshøj, DK–8400 Ebeltoft

16 Sydjydsk Golf Club (9)
Gyttegård, DK–7200 Grindsted

17 Vejle Golf Club (18)
Fællesletgård, Ibækvej, DK–7100 Vejle

18 Horsens Golf Club (9)
Bolbroholtvej 9, DK–7130 Juelsminde

19 Esbjerg Golf Club (18)
Sønderhedevej, Marbæk, DK–6800 Varde

20 Kolding Golf Club (18)
Emerholtsvej, DK–6000 Kolding

21 Fanø Vesterhavsbads Golf Club (18)
DK–6720 Nordby, Fanø

22 Ribe Golf Club (9)
Rønnehave, Snepsgårdsvej 14, Skallebæk, DK–6760 Ribe

23 Haderslev Golf Club (9)
Egevej, DK–6100 Haderslev

24 Sønderjyllands Golf Club (14)
Uge Hedegård, DK–6360 Tinglev

Funen

25 Vestfyns Golf Club (9)
Krengerupvej 27, DK–5620 Glamsbjerg

26 Odense Golf Club (27)
Hollufgård, Hestehaven 201, DK–5000 Odense

27 Skt. Knuds Golf Club (18)
Sliphavnsvej 16, DK–5800 Nyborg

28 Svendborg Golf Club (9)
Tordensgårdevej, Sørup, DK–5700 Svendborg

Falster

29 Golf Club Storstrømmen (18)
Køllegården, DK–4863 Eskilstrup

Zealand

30 Sydsjællands Golf Club (9)
Borupgården, Mogenstrup, DK–4700 Næstved

31 Korsør Golf Club (18)
Tårnborgparken, DK–4220 Korsør

32 Sorø Golf Club (9)
DK–4180 Sorø

33 Køge Golf Club (18)
Golfgården, Gammel Hastrup, DK–4600 Køge

34 Roskilde Golf Club (9)
Gedevad, Kongemarken, Boserup, DK–4000 Roskilde

35 Hedeland Golf Club (9)
Stærkendevej 232 A, DK–2640 Hedeland/Tastrup

36 Kalundborg Golf Club (9)
Kildekærdegård, Røsnæsvejen 225, Kongstrup, DK–4400 Kalundborg

37 Holbæk Golf Club (9)
Kirsebærholmen, DK–4300 Holbæk

38 Mølleåens Golf Club (9)
Stenbækgård, Rosenlundvej 3, Bastrup, DK–3540 Lynge

39 Copenhagen Golf Club (18)
Dyrehaven 2, DK–2800 Lyngby

40 Furesø Golf Club (9)
Hestkøbvænge 4, DK–3460 Birkerød

41 Søllerød Golf Club (18)
Gammel Holtegård, Attemosevej 170, DK–2840 Holte

42 Odsherred Golf Club (12)
DK–4573 Højby, Sjælland

43 Hillerød Golf Club (18)
Nysøgård, Ny Hammersholt, DK–3400 Hillerød

44 Rungsted Golf Club (18)
Vestre Stationsvej 16, DK–2960 Rungsted Kyst

45 Kokkedal Golf Club (18)
Kokkedal Allé, DK–2980 Kokkedal

46 Asserbo Golf Club (9)
Bødkergårdsvej, DK–3300 Frederiksværk

47 Helsingør/Elsinore Golf Club (18)
Gammel Hellebækvej, DK–3000 Helsingør

48 Gilleleje Golf Club (9)
Passebækgård, Bregnerødvej 35, DK–3250 Gilleleje

Bornholm

49 Bornholms Golf Club (9)
Plantagevej, Robbedale, DK–3700 Rønne

Nature Trails

The Danish Tourist Council publishes a leaflet "Activities for Naturalists" (*Naturvejleder-aktiviteter*) that contains details of organised tours – mostly on foot, but also by bicycle and bus – in the Danish countryside.

The routes for two- or three-day tours cover areas throughout Denmark, and feature local experts who comment on the flora and fauna and cultural monuments encountered on the way. The groups are generally limited to about 30 persons. Many tours are free; others cost from 1 to 95 Dkr. In some cases the commentary is only in Danish, but in others it's also in English (or German). The leaflet, which the Danish Tourist Office will forward on request, lists the names and telephone numbers of the tour organisers, so further information can be obtained directly.

Riding

Denmark offers good facilities for riding, and there are many riding-schools where horses can be hired. A visitor who wishes to ride across open country should obtain information in advance, as riding is not permitted everywhere. Riding holidays are available in Jutland and Zealand. For children special arrangements at camps and farms are made.

Boating

There are many opportunities for boating in Danish inland waters and some 600 harbours, both small and large, provide a mooring for small vessels. The sportsman can choose between short or longer trips, either in open water on the Kattegat and the Baltic, or in the sheltered waters of the South Funen Sea between Zealand and Lolland/Falster, or the Limfjord in North Jutland. Sailing-boats and motor boats

Sailing regatta "Around Zealand"

can be hired in many places; they are provided with all the necessary safety equipment, navigational aids, crockery, cutlery, etc. Outside the high season prices are considerably reduced. Visitors can also choose to hire a motor boat with a skipper.

In accordance with Danish law, boats which are hired must be approved by the maritime authorities; before signing a hiring agreement the hirer should make certain that this approval has been given.

Windsurfing

The coastal waters of Denmark offer good surfing, and there are a number of windsurfing schools. The ability to swim well is essential for participating in a course. Anyone wishing to hire a surfboard will, under certain conditions, be required to produce a certificate from the International Windsurfing School (IWS).

Information about courses and the hire of equipment can be obtained from local tourist bureaux and from the Danish Tourist Office.

Illums Bolighus

Danish porcelain

Shopping

The Danes, famed for their avant-garde interior design and arts and crafts, offer some of Europe's finest buys in silver, porcelain, china, glassware, stainless steel, furniture, toys and textiles. In Copenhagen a showcase for quality arts and crafts items, chosen for their merit by a special committee, is Den Permanente (The Permanent Exhibition). Every item shown is also for sale. Illums Bolighus (Illum's Department Store) in Copenhagen is a sophisticated centre of modern design that exhibits (and sells) furniture, household accessories, men's and women's fashions, jewellery, and kitchen ware. Visitors can tour the factory where Royal Copenhagen Porcelain, identified by its traditional three wavy blue lines, is manufactured; purchases may not be made at the factory.

There is a Value Added Tax (in Danish "*MOMS*") of 22 per cent added to almost every item sold and service rendered in Denmark. Visitors can avoid paying this tax if purchases are dispatched direct to an address abroad.

Opening times

The opening times of **shops** and **offices** vary. Shops are usually open from Monday to Friday between 9 a.m. and 5.30 p.m.; some remain open on Friday until 7 or 8 p.m. and many are open on Saturday until noon or 2 p.m. In small towns shops often close for lunch.

Banks in Copenhagen are open for business at the following times: Monday to Wednesday and Friday 9.30 a.m.–4 p.m.; Thursday 9.30 a.m.–6 p.m. Many **bureaux de change** particularly at the main stations are open until 10 p.m. or even later. Opening times in the provinces vary from place to place and some banks close between noon and 2 p.m.

For opening times of post offices see Post Office.

Information

Danish Tourist Board
(*Danmarks Turistråd*)
Head office:
Banegårdspladsen 2,
DK–1570 **Copenhagen** V;
tel. (01) 11 14 15

Danish Tourist Board,
Sceptre House,
169–173 Regent Street,
London W1R 8PY;
tel. (01) 734 2637–8.

Danish National Tourist Office,
655 Third Avenue,
New York, NY 10019;
tel. (212) 949–2333

Danish National Tourist Office,
151 Bloor Street West, 8th floor,
Toronto M5S 1S4, Ontario;
tel. (416) 960 3305

In the larger towns and resorts of Denmark, there are branch offices of the Danish Tourist Board. In writing to one of these offices, it is sufficient to address the letter to *Turistbureauet*, followed by the postal code and name of the town.

Radio messages for tourists

In cases of serious emergency, the Scandinavian radio stations will broadcast messages for tourists. Information from motoring organisations and the police.

Motoring organisations

Forenede Danske Motorejere (*FDM*: Federation of Danish Motorists),
Blegdamsvej 124,
DK–2100 **Copenhagen** Ø;
tel. (01) 38 21 12

Kongelig Dansk Automobil Klub
(*KDAK*: Royal Danish Automobile Club),
Frederiksberg Allé 41,
DK–1820 **Copenhagen** V;
tel. (01) 21 11 01.

Embassies

British Embassy,
Kastelsvej 36–40,
DK–2100 **Copenhagen** Ø;
tel. (01) 26 46 00.

United States Embassy,
Dag Hammarksjölds Allé 24,
DK–2100 **Copenhagen** Ø;
tel. (01) 42 31 44.

Canadian Embassy,
Kr. Bernikowsgade 1,
DK–1105 **Copenhagen** K;
tel. (01) 12 22 99.

Airlines

Scandinavian Airlines System
(*SAS*), SAS Building, Hammerichsgade,
DK–1611 **Copenhagen** V;
tel. (01) 59 66 22.

British Airways,
Vesterbrogade 2,
DK–1620 **Copenhagen** V;
tel. (01) 14 60 00.

Danish State Railways

Representatives in the United Kingdom
DFDS (UK) Ltd,
Mariner House, Pepys Street,
London EC3N 4BX.

Statutory Public Holidays

1 January
Maundy Thursday
(day before Good Friday)
Good Friday
Easter Monday
Day of Repentance
(beginning of May)
Ascension
Whit Monday
(seventh after Easter)
5 June
(Constitution Day)
Christmas
(25 and 26 December)

Emergency Calls

On the Danish motorways there are *emergency telephones* at intervals of 2 km ($1\frac{3}{4}$ miles).

Emergency calls (police, ambulance): throughout the country dial 000 (no coin required in public telephone boxes).

(The letters æ, å and ø are placed with a and o)